helen

PORTRAIT OF A PRIME MINISTER

brian **edwards**

EXISLE
PUBLISHING

ISBN 0908988-20-6

Published November 2001
Exisle Publishing Limited
PO Box 8077, Symonds St, Auckland 1035, New Zealand.
Ph: 64-9-520 1162; Fax 64-9-520 1146.
email: mail@exisle.co.nz
www.exisle.co.nz

Design by Craig Humberstone.
Typeset in Adobe Garamond and Gothic.
Artwork by Streamline Creative Ltd, Auckland.
Printed by Tien Wah Press (Pte) Ltd, Singapore.

CONTENTS

ACKNOWLEDGEMENTS

A large number of people were interviewed for this book either by me or my wife, Judy Callingham. All gave their time willingly and were open and honest in responding to our questions. I thank each of them very much.

Special mention must be made of some:

The Prime Minister submitted to more than 20 hours of interviews on weekends when she should have been enjoying her very limited free time with her husband. I thank her for her hospitality and patience, and her husband, Peter Davis, for many excellent cups of refreshing tea, made in the pot.

Helen's parents, George and Margaret Clark, welcomed us to their home at Waihi Beach, where they fed and watered us, put up with hours of impertinent questioning and hunted out seemingly endless boxes of photographs and other memorabilia. Thank you. You were wonderful.

So too were Helen's sisters, Suzanne, Jenefer and Sandra, none of whom really wanted to be dragged into the spotlight, but who, out of affection for their big sister, agreed to put up with it.

Helen's Aunt Fay, a delightful woman with a wicked sense of humour, was a tireless source of information and anecdote and is responsible for some of the pithiest observations in this book.

The irrepressible and ever-young Dame Catherine Tizard was equalled only by her daughter Judith in the wealth of story and insight which she had to offer about their close friend Helen Clark.

The Speaker of the House, Jonathan Hunt, probably the repository of more knowledge on the inner workings of Parliament than any other living person, had so many wonderful tales to tell that this book could accommodate only a fraction. Perhaps another day.

Two former Prime Ministers, Sir Geoffrey Palmer and David Lange, provided fascinating insights into the sometimes bizarre world of party politics.

My appalling ignorance of both history and politics led me to seek the help of several erudite and kindly academics:

My old friend Bob Chapman, Emeritus Professor of Political Studies at Auckland University, not only submitted, with his wife Noeline, to a four-hour interview, but answered endless phone enquiries about New Zealand elections since 1975. Without his expertise, it's doubtful that this book would ever have been finished.

Professor Barry Gustafson and Dr Raymond Miller of the Political Studies Department at Auckland University provided long-suffering advice and, where they could not answer a question, referred me to sources where I could find out for myself.

A number of journalists and political commentators were interviewed. All expressed their opinions of prominent politicians without apparent fear of recrimination or the loss of their bread and butter. I am particularly indebted to Colin James for joining the lengthy queue of unpaid advisors.

I am also grateful to Penguin Books who gave permission for me to quote at length from the historically significant interview with Helen Clark in Virginia Myers' *Head and Shoulders*, and to Janet McCallum who allowed me to cite passages from her book *Women in the House*, published by Cape Catley.

Stephen Mills of UMR Insight and Steve Kirk of NFO CM Research both supplied invaluable information on public opinion polling on the political parties and their leaders.

Throughout this project I have had unstinting co-operation from staff in the Prime Minister's office, but especially from Mike Munro, Helen's Chief Press Secretary, and Dot Kettle, keeper of the Prime Ministerial diary.

Helen: Portrait of a Prime Minister was edited by Tim Chamberlain, who has burnt so much midnight oil that supplies must be running out. I thank him for the professional care and attention to detail which he has shown throughout this project.

One significant name is missing from the list of those interviewed for this book. Jim Anderton declined my invitation, on the grounds that it was important for the Coalition Government that the close personal and political working relationship between Prime Minister and Deputy Prime Minister remained private. While respecting his decision, I regret his absence from these pages.

Less surprising, perhaps, is the absence of Sir Roger Douglas, who initially agreed to be interviewed, then changed his mind, stating that the issues surrounding the fourth Labour Government had already been fully canvassed.

There is a tradition in showbiz that the big, big credits come right at the beginning or right at the end. In that spirit I want to end by thanking two very special people.

Joan Caulfield has been Helen Clark's Electorate Secretary since 1996 and her close friend for more than 25 years. I first met her when Judy and I were producing Helen's television opening for the 1999 election and I now regard her as a friend as well. Joan is a remarkable person, perhaps the warmest and kindest I have met. Her contribution to this book as researcher, advisor, informant, facilitator, conduit to the Prime Minister and, occasionally, smoother of the author's ruffled feathers, has been immense. I cannot thank her enough.

Of my wife, Judy Callingham's contribution it can only be said that she had nothing to offer but blood, toil, tears and sweat. She was interviewer, researcher, typist, collator, proof-reader, photo-editor, finder of lost references, pages, articles, books, telephone numbers, email addresses, glasses, pens, bulldog clips and highlighters, maker of tea, coffee, meals and beds, driver, courier, returner of overdue library books, inspiration and critic. Without Judy, the book simply would not have happened.

B.E.

FOREWORD

You have to be mad to take on an assignment like this – writing a book about a Prime Minister in office. It's no-win. If the book is negative, the Prime Minister will not be pleased. If the book is positive, the author will be dismissed as a fawning apologist.

The trouble is that I genuinely admire Helen Clark. I think she's an exceptional person and I agree with those who say that, given the chance, she may come to be regarded as one of New Zealand's great Prime Ministers, perhaps the greatest. So it may seem that there is a fine line for an author to tread here – avoiding an overly glowing depiction while at the same time taking care not to invite the wrath of his subject.

But I have made no attempt to tread any line at all. The reader will discover in these pages a largely positive picture of Helen Clark, not because I have set out to paint my subject in a flattering light, but because that, in my view, is the true picture. And I am consoled by the fact that, in general terms, it is also the picture painted by those merciless practitioners of the negative – journalists.

Not that everything in this book is going to please Helen Clark. As Cath Tizard reports having told her, "You've got to have a wart somewhere. If Oliver Cromwell can have a wart, you can have a wart too." So there are trenchant criticisms of both the person and the politician here, some from unexpected quarters.

Readers looking for scandal will, however, be disappointed. There are two reasons for this. The first is that Helen laid down one condition for her co-operation in the writing of this book, that it not deal with matters of personal morality. I willingly agreed to that condition, since I considered such matters irrelevant to her political career. And the second reason is that there appeared to be no scandal to find.

In a sense, *Helen: Portrait of a Prime Minister* was not written by me at all. The book is based on over one hundred hours of interviews with Helen herself, with her family, friends and colleagues and with political scientists, commentators and journalists. Their observations and opinions make up perhaps 90 percent of the text, so that it would probably not be far off the mark to categorise the result as oral history.

There is weakness and strength in such an approach. The weakness is that the material is of necessity highly subjective. The strength is that much of it is first hand, the story often told by the players themselves. It could not have been otherwise. I am neither historian, nor political scientist, nor biographer.

And anyway this is not a biography. It is, as the title suggests, a portrait, an attempt to convey a true likeness. If it succeeds, it will be arguably the first such likeness. For Helen is no different to the rest of us – she has a good side and a side that is not so good. And until very recently we have been allowed to see only the not-so-good side. Allowed, that is, by the media, by her political opponents and, sometimes perhaps, by Helen herself.

What is most remarkable about Helen Clark is her endurance. This is the story of a journey that has taken more than 30 years. A journey towards a goal that at almost every step seemed to recede further into the distance. A journey punctuated by disappointment, defeat and occasional despair. A journey from which even the strongest of us might have turned back, without dishonour.

In those 30 years she overcame contempt for her gender, rejection for her beliefs, vilification for her looks and personality, slander about her sexuality, the treachery of enemies and some friends, and the relentless hostility of journalists unable or unwilling to see the person behind the mask. She endured. But to endure against such odds you have to be tough or to develop toughness. And that too, if you are a woman, is evidence against you. So for years she was portrayed as a cold, hard, unattractive woman whose chances of succeeding in politics were below the margin of error. Clearly the picture was wrong or, at best, hopelessly incomplete.

The purpose of this book is therefore to say, "Take another look. Maybe you missed something. Maybe there were people obscuring your view. Or maybe you just weren't able to get close enough. Here, borrow my glasses. With sharper focus you may get to see Helen's good side – attractive, generous, warm, caring, funny… Of course, the imperfections may become clearer too."

To praise any politician invites derision. But I find myself believing that Helen really is in this business for the greater good, that she is largely without ego or personal ambition and that she genuinely aspires to be that rarest of political animals, 'the servant leader'.

Read on and judge for yourself.

Brian Edwards
October 2001

HELEN CLARK'S FAMILY TREE – THE NEW ZEALANDERS

John Marsh
m.
Emma Gibbins

Archibald Hutchinson
m.
Elizabeth Lambert

Ronald McMillan

Mary Ann Marsh
m.
Leslie Arthur

Thomas Clark
m.
Elizabeth Evans

Catherine Hutchinson
m.
William McMillan

Henry McMurray
m.
Margaret Rusk

Elizabeth Grace Arthur m. Fred Clark

Sarah McMillan m. David McMurray

George Clark m. Margaret Helen McMurray

Helen Elizabeth Clark

chapter one

PIONEER FAMILIES

THE MARSHES

Helen Clark is a fourth generation New Zealander on both sides of her family. John Marsh, her great-great-grandfather on her father's side, came from a long line of boat people, plying cargo on the Thames between Oxfordshire and London. He was born at Thame in Oxfordshire in 1830 and married 24-year-old Emma Gibbins in 1852 at Chertsey in Surrey. Emma was a seamstress, reputed because of her smooth, sweat-free hands, to have sewn for the daughters of Queen Victoria. The couple prospered and John and his father-in-law, Joseph Gibbins, were granted the freedom of the City of London in recognition of their services in transporting steel for the construction of the London Underground.

But John was ambitious for a better life and he and Emma set sail for Australia in the mid-1850s to seek their fortune prospecting for gold. They landed in Victoria and set up house at Sandhurst where John scraped a living from a variety of jobs, then mined for several years at Bendigo. Four children, one of whom died in infancy, were born in Australia before news of the Dunstan gold rush in central Otago persuaded John and Emma to cross the Tasman.

They disembarked at Dunedin in 1862, Emma pregnant with twins. William Marsh, John and Emma's fourth child, takes up the story:

"My parents arrived in Dunedin in 1862, my father going immediately to the Dunstan and straight on to Fox's. In the following year, my mother, my two sisters

Left **From Thames bargeman to Mayor of Cromwell: Helen's great-great grandfather, John Marsh.** *Right* **Emma Marsh managed the Bridge Hotel while her husband explored his other business interests.** *(Opposite)* **The Bridge Hotel was renowned for its fresh vegetables.**

and I were taken in a dray to the goldfields, to a place opposite Cromwell called Cornish Point, where Father built a store and where the twins were born, April 18, 1863. Father was the only one present when the event took place, no doctor or nurse being available. At first it was proposed to call them Kawarau and Clutha, but an old Frenchman in the place protested and so, when Archdeacon Edwards performed the christening ceremony, Jeannette and Mary Ann were the names chosen. They were said to be the first white children born in that region. At that time the nearest registrar was at Waikouaiti, 150 miles off, and for registering later than the two months allowed Father had to pay the late fee, 10s.6d. for each."

Emma, with William and her daughters, six-year-old Elizabeth Jane and seven-year-old Emma, had walked the last part of the Dunstan trail, the girls carrying the family clock and a sulphur-crested cockatoo which they had brought from Australia. The twins were born prematurely under canvas on the banks of the Clutha, but despite the primitive conditions both survived.

John and Emma were soon to establish themselves as prominent citizens of Cromwell. Having built and run the store at Cornish Point, John bought the Bridge Hotel on the banks of the Clutha at Cromwell. Three more children, John Thomas, Rose and George "Goldie", were born between 1866 and 1870. While Emma looked after the children and managed the hotel, her husband ran a carrying business, mined for gold and interested himself in the affairs of the district. He became Mayor of Cromwell in 1883. The Bridge Hotel soon became famous for its fresh vegetables at a time when the miners' teeth were said to be falling out from lack of greens. Some of them may have thought that a crisp apple would solve the problem, as this notice in the *Cromwell Argus* might suggest:

NOTICE

If the unprincipled Thief who stole all my unripe apples feels unwell, I shall be happy to supply him with medicine, gratis: application externally. At home between the hours of 8 a.m. and 8 p.m.

JOHN MARSH Bridge Hotel, Cromwell 21/12/75

John clearly understood the power of advertising. In December 1877 he placed this notice in the *Argus*:

MARSH'S PROCLAMATION. 1ST DECEMBER 1877

In consideration of our having a Liberal Government allowing the people to settle on the soil and thereby produce food for local consumption, thus preventing our mineral wealth going to benefit other districts and foreign capitalists, John Marsh, Cromwell intends to supply a long-felt want, which will also be found to answer the projector's well-known motto – 'Value for Money.' After 1st December, 1877, a DINING ROOM – unconnected with the sale of alcohol – will be opened adjoining the Bridge Hotel, at which ample and substantial MEALS will be dispensed at the usual hours. Breakfast – 1s. Dinner – 1s.6d. Tea – 1s. VALUE FOR MONEY!

Two days before this notice appeared, John and Emma had celebrated their 25th wedding anniversary. The *Argus* reported:

On Thursday evening last (November 29, 1877) a number of friends and acquaintances of Mr John Marsh met together by invitation to celebrate a rather important epoch in that gentleman's history, namely the 25th anniversary of his

marriage or 'silver wedding'. Some forty guests sat down to a most sumptuous dinner, with which the most fastidious epicure must have been satisfied, embracing, as it did, flesh and fowl of almost every variety, and the first vegetables and fruits of the season. The company having lingered long enough over the dainties to evince their appreciation, the chair was assumed by the Mayor, Mr S.N. Brown, who, in proposing the toast of the evening, 'Long life and prosperity to Mr and Mrs Marsh', offered some remarks suitable to the occasion, expressing a hope that their host and hostess might live to enjoy their 'golden wedding' of fifty years matrimonial felicity.

Mr and Mrs Marsh would not live to see their Golden Wedding. Emma died in 1890, two years before her husband.

THE ARTHURS

It was probably at her parents' hotel that Mary Ann Marsh, more commonly known as Dolly, met Leslie Arthur, a local stonemason and bridge-builder. Or it may have been at church, where Dolly, who was also a Sunday School teacher, sometimes played the organ, hopefully more willingly than her great-granddaughter, Helen Clark, three-quarters of a century later.

The Arthurs, whose family tree, according to Helen, can be traced back to the 17th century, were crofters in the Shetlands. Leslie was born in 1853 at Kuckron,

Left **Leslie and Mary Ann Arthur with nine of their eleven children. Elizabeth Grace standing on the far left.** *Opposite Page, Left* **Leslie Arthur's reference.** *Opposite Right* **Helen's great-grandparents, Mary Ann Marsh and Leslie Arthur, on their wedding day in 1883.**

Weisdale, in the Shetlands. He arrived in New Zealand in 1874, bearing a reference from his former employer, Joseph Irwin:

> Tingwall, 4 March 1874. I hereby certify that I have been personally acquainted with the bearer Leslie Arthur since a boy, and have ever found him to be sober, honest and industrious and possess a good moral character. Also during this last three years have had him employed as a mason and he has rendered satisfaction in work. Joseph Irwin. Builder. Tingwall.

Mary Ann Marsh and Leslie Arthur were married in Cromwell in 1883. The couple were to have 11 children.

Elizabeth Grace Arthur, their middle child and Helen's paternal grandmother, was born in 1896. She was beautiful and fair and her father at once dubbed her "my little Lily". This endearment was soon contracted to "Lil", much to Elizabeth Grace's displeasure. She preferred her given name.

Elizabeth was a bright, intelligent girl and received a good education in Cromwell where she attended school with her cousin Fred Gair, whose father William had married Elizabeth Jane Marsh, older sister of the twins, in 1888. The Gairs were Tories. Fred's son, George Gair, would rise to prominence in the National Party, serving as a Cabinet Minister in the Holyoake and Muldoon administrations and as New Zealand's High Commissioner to the United Kingdom and Ambassador to Ireland.

Right **Mary Ann Arthur and daughter Elizabeth Grace Clark with the cockatoo the family brought with them from Australia in 1862.** *Opposite Page* **The McMillan family at Southburn, 1921. Helen's great-grandparents, Willam and Catherine, are seated. Her grandmother, Sarah, is second from right at back.**

Elizabeth was clearly strong-willed. Having finished Standard 6 at Cromwell School, she refused to go out and learn tailoring, as her sisters had done, in order to work as a seamstress in a more affluent home. Instead she stayed at home and helped with the younger children, including her sister Maude, 11 years her junior.

"I should imagine my grandmother kept her fairly busy," says Helen's aunt, Fay Burndred, "because my grandmother was a perfectionist, a great cook and a great housekeeper."

Leslie Arthur became a prominent and respected citizen of Cromwell, and he prospered in business. In partnership with his wife's brother-in-law, fellow Shetland Island émigré William Gair, he won masonry contracts to work on the Cromwell bridge and on the swingbridge over the Clutha at Deadman's Point. But with the advent of the First World War, Leslie had trouble finding workers to build his bridges. Two of his sons had already gone up to the little Waikato settlement of Te Pahu to farm, so in 1915 he shifted the rest of the family to the Waikato and left Cromwell behind. The move was something of a culture shock to Elizabeth, who had lived all her life in town, but she quickly adapted to country life and found new friends.

But the war years were to deprive her of two of her family. Her father Leslie, who had built a house for the family which still stands at Te Pahu, developed heart

disease and died on 14 July 1918. Three months later, on 5 October, shortly before Armistice Day, her closest brother George, who was serving with the 4th Battalion of the 3rd New Zealand Rifle Brigade in France, was killed in action.

Elizabeth's mother, Mary Ann Arthur, died in 1950, having lived to the age of 87.

THE HUTCHINSONS AND THE McMILLANS

Catherine Helen Hutchinson, Helen's great-grandmother on her mother's side, was the daughter of Archibald Hutchinson, who farmed at Awamoka near Oamaru. Archie and his wife Elizabeth Lambert are buried in the Georgetown cemetery on the road from Oamaru to Kurow.

In 1883 Catherine married William McMillan whose father Ronald, a Scottish shepherd, had arrived with his family on the *Invercargill* at Port Chalmers in 1874. William was 11 when they landed.

Catherine and William were to strike good fortune. Seddon's Liberal Government had decided they wanted a country where people of limited means would have a chance to get onto the land. So in the 1890s the large rural estates began to be broken up into much smaller farms. To have a chance of getting one of these farms, you had to go into a ballot. Applicants were screened for good character, had to provide evidence that that they had been savers and were required to put down a deposit. Catherine and William both put their names in the ballot. Catherine's button came up. The McMillans were now the owners of Willowtree Farm, part of the huge Pareora Estate, on the Pareora River Road near Timaru, which later became known as the Lyalldale settlement. A century later, Helen Clark would return to Lyalldale as Prime Minister of New Zealand:

"I went and launched a book on the centenary of the Lyalldale settlement, because someone had worked out that the Prime Minister's great-grandmother was one of the original ballot winners."

The local children put on a pageant about the first ballot. Helen's mother Margaret recalls that the little girl who played Catherine McMillan, her long hair plaited around her thin face, looked very much like the photographs of her granny.

Catherine and William, in the manner of the times, were prolific breeders. They had ten children – six boys and four girls. Their eighth child, Sarah, Helen's maternal grandmother, was born in 1900. Little seems to be known of her early life, other than that she grew up on the family farm and went to Southburn Primary School near Timaru, where she won lots of prizes. She was a bright girl.

THE McMURRAYS

At the age of 23, Sarah married David McMurray. Like his wife, David was one of a family of ten, six boys and four girls. The family came from Lurgan in Northern Ireland. David's elder brother was the first to come to New Zealand. David himself, aged 20, arrived in 1910, followed by other brothers. Over a period of time these young men saved enough money to bring all of the family but one out to New Zealand, including their elderly parents – Helen's great-grandparents, Henry McMurray and Margaret Ann (Rusk) – their three youngest sisters and brother. They settled in Dunedin and South Canterbury.

In 1917 David and his brothers went off to the First World War. Five of the six returned. David was perhaps lucky. He was gassed in October 1918, a month before the war ended. Helen believes that by removing him from the field of battle, the gassing may have saved her grandfather's life:

"I never knew until I got his defence records last year that he had been a gas victim in World War One, which would have been very interesting for us to know as kids. I asked for them at one point with the thought of fitting in with an official visit to France last year. I was interested to know where my grandfather and great-

Left **Helen's mother Margaret on her wedding day, with father of the bride David McMurray, Helen's grandfather.** *Opposite* **Helen's grandmother, Sarah McMurray, with her first-born, Margaret Helen. Southburn, 1925.**

uncles had actually fought. My grandfather and ten great-uncles went to World War One, and that cast a very long shadow over the family. All these four families, except the McMillans, lost people. So it was always a shadow. My Dad's father lost both his brothers and there were only the three of them in the family. So whenever I went to my grandmother's house from the time I was a baby until when she died in 1983, there were these two photos of the dead great-uncles in military uniform taken before they went. And then my grandmother herself lost a brother in the war just before Armistice Day and Mum's father lost a brother. So that was always quite a big shadow."

When he returned from the war, David McMurray was allocated a rehab farm in Waitahuna, near Lawrence. Like many of the farms allocated to returned servicemen, the Waitahuna property was not economically viable. David was allocated another farm, but this also proved unsuccessful. Now married to Sarah, he moved to Dunedin, where Helen's mother Margaret was born in 1924. But Sarah was unhappy in Dunedin and missed her family, who lived near Timaru. So they shifted up there. David worked as a wood merchant. He had his own truck, but when petrol became scarce during World War Two he began to work for other wood merchants. By 1940 the family had grown to eight – four boys and four girls.

By all accounts David was a hard worker, a good father, very interested in and proud of his family. None of his family's generation had had a secondary education and he was determined that his children would enjoy all the opportunities that he and his siblings had been denied. His son Malcolm was the first of the family to go to university. David was over the moon: "Malcolm's made it to university. He's made it there. I don't care if he even walks in the front door and out the back, at least he's got there."

David was an Ulsterman and had brought his sectarian prejudices with him. He was a dyed-in-the-wool Orangeman.

"To Dad's family," Margaret says, "anything green was like a red rag to a bull. It was almost a disease with those people. When Dad built a house when we were older children, there was nothing green about the house. It had an orange roof. And we weren't even allowed to have green ribbons in our hair – which was a shame because green happens to be my favourite colour. They had a bad dose of it, I can tell you. One brother who married a Catholic was ostracised. And we used to give cheek to the Catholic kids who used to bike past on their way to the Catholic school. And they used to give cheek to us."

Helen, who met her grandfather on relatively few occasions and remembers him as a rather old man, discussed the matter with the President of Ireland:

"Mary MacAleese told me a few years ago that McMurrays were on both sides of the sectarian divide in Northern Ireland. I remember that my grandfather's brother had his living room decorated with relics of the Orange Order – the Battle of the Boyne, tapestries, that kind of thing."

Having given birth to eight children, including twins who were now five, Sarah McMurray moved out of the family home in 1945. According to Helen, her grandmother's departure was never spoken about in the family:

"By the time I was born she had been separated from him for about five years. All we knew as kids was that, when we went to Timaru, Grandma and Granddad lived in a different place, which was quite unusual in those days, a broken marriage. But no one ever talked about it; it was unspoken. My grandmother went out, which was very unusual, and went back to work. And really quite close until the time she died, which was around 1983, she was still working. She was a night sister at Bidwell, a hospital in Timaru, for years and years and years. So my grandfather brought up the kids. He died in 1971."

THE CLARKS

Thomas Clark, Helen's great-grandfather, was born in 1857 in Giggleswick, Yorkshire. The family were working class people and Thomas found employment in the woollen or pottery mills in Settle, but left England in 1900 to make a better life for himself and his family in New Zealand. Arriving at Raglan, he found his way over the hills and settled on a patch of bush near Te Pahu, at Kaniwhaniwha. Thomas was married and had three living children, but had left the family at home in Yorkshire while he set about getting a stake and building a house. However, his wife Elizabeth (Evans), who was of Welsh descent, perhaps anxious to be reunited with her husband, turned up with the children before the house was finished. What she found was a structure built out of pit-sawn timber and split planks, the walls lined with copies of the *Auckland Weekly*. There was no grass, only native bush which Thomas set about clearing.

"This was the part of the Waikato where the land had been confiscated," Helen adds. "This was the Raupata land that Tainui got its big compensation for in 1995. Their land was sold right over their heads. The land was sold to my great-grandfather off the plans in London."

By 1912 Thomas had built the house that Helen's parents, George and Margaret Clark, would live in together for 22 years. Thomas neither drank nor swore. Fay remembers her grandfather as a man whom she respected:

"My grandfather had quite a hard life. He came out to New Zealand to make a better life for his children. He'd lost two sons in England before he emigrated and then he lost two sons in the First World War, so that left just my father. And

PIONEER FAMILIES

21

my father only lived to the age of 59, so they were rather an unfortunate family.

"But he was a very hard man. And when Mum and Dad got married he wouldn't allow them to build a house because he held the purse-strings. My mother and father bought a farm several miles down the road and they would have liked to have lived on that farm, but grandfather held the purse-strings. He had his wife Elizabeth ill in the house, and my mother, a nice, frisky, strong young daughter-in-law who had to live with her in-laws, a situation which she detested and hated.

"He lived with us until his death in 1942. When I was about seven, he got a radio and he used to listen to Parliament on it all the time. We would sit in front of the fire and grandfather would be saying, 'Ssh, be quiet.' He never swore. 'Ssh, be quiet.' We must have nearly driven him crazy.

"He was a red-hot Labourite and was delighted when the first Labour Government was elected. I well remember that day and so does my sister Marian. Below our farm in Te Pahu there was a large Public Works camp, where many of the men were living in tents. That evening all of these men came up to our house to listen to the election results on our radio. We'll always remember their cheers as the seats went to Labour."

Fred Clark, Helen's paternal grandfather, was seven when he arrived early with his mother and older brothers, Frank and Herbert, at their new home in Kaniwhaniwha. Life in New Zealand was to prove far from easy. Each school-day Fred had to walk two miles down the road to a more established farmer who had enough

grass to graze a horse. He then rode another three or four miles to Karamu Primary School.

Frank went off to the war in 1914. Herbert enlisted in February 1917. Their younger brother was keen to join them and began training in camp, but was sent back to the farm because his brothers were already overseas. He would never see either of them again. Frank was killed on Hill 60 at Gallipoli on 28 August 1915. Herbert died of influenza at an army camp in Wiltshire on 10 September 1917, just before he was due to go to France.

Both men had written home regularly, and their letters and a mass of other historic family information were discovered by George and Margaret in the rafters of the woolshed in an old tin trunk, which Thomas had presumably brought out from England. Helen takes up the story:

"When Mum and Dad left the farm they took everything that had been stored there for the best part of 90 years. There'd always been trunks of my grandfather's and great-grandfather's possessions stored up in the ceiling of the shearing shed. And in the trunks were all the letters from Frank in Gallipoli and from Herbert who died of the 'flu in Wiltshire. Tons of letters from my great-uncles. My father started reading them and said they were very interesting and then I got interested in it enough to go to Gallipoli in 1995.

"I read a lot about that campaign before I went. And then I started to take an interest in where others had been, like my grandparents' brothers who died in

Left **Helen's great-grand-father Thomas Clark, stepping out in Garden Place, Hamilton.** *Opposite* **Elizabeth Clark (née Evans), Helen's great-grandmother, outside the original hut on the Clark farm at Te Pahu, Waikato. Note bush being burnt off on the hills behind.**

Gallipoli Peninsular, August 21/1915

Dear Herbert,

Here I am at last in the trenches — it has taken just 8 calendar months to get here to a day, we landed on the 15th Aug. We landed at night without any mishap, although there were a few bullets hissing about the ship. We stayed on the beach that night & early in the morning we had a bit of breakfast & moved off to join the remnants of our Reg. the 4th Waikatos. Our first job in the trenches was to dig ourselves dugouts to sleep in. These are just little caves dug under the side of the trenches, ours is about 6 by 5 ft & about 3 ft high, for two of us. I sent you a post card telling you that Charlie & Bert Godfrey were not coming over this time with me, but I suppose they will be here shortly. I was very sorry to have to part from them, but I have some pretty good camp mates with me. There were only 8 fourth Rein., Waikato men came over this time. We got a bit of a fright coming over, another transport which left Alexandria a few hours after us & caught us up was torpedoed by a submarine before our eyes. We saw her go down & I think it was the most awe inspiring sight I ever saw. Her stern went down & she almost stood on end, & then as a plank slides over a bar, she slipped back and was gone for ever. She had ▓▓▓ men aboard & of these only some ▓▓▓▓▓▓ were saved, by a passing "Red Cross" ship. Our boat of course put on full steam at once & we were fortunate enough to escape. All hands got on their lifebelts for we did not know but that at any moment we might suffer a like fate, but thank God we were spared. We felt terribly helpless—we were like rats in a trap & could not help ourselves whatever happened, for we had not a single gun on board. I can tell you I would sooner have my chance here than the chance of being torpedoed again. Now I have some worse news for you although you probably know all about it by now even, but still I will tell you again. While we were having breakfast on the beach, I espied old Gib Johnson strolling about & I went down to see him & get the news from him. Poor old Gib he is not looking to get on well.

Above **Frank Clark fought at Gallipoli in 1915. He wrote this letter to his brother Herbert shortly before he died in battle.**

24

France. I've seen the cemetery at Hill 60 at Gallipoli where Frank's name is and I've read a lot about the battle for Hill 60. It was quite hopeless. And when you go there – I mean, Hill 60 wasn't even really a hill, it was a gentle slope and anyone running up it was cannon-fodder. The enormous waste. Looking at it from a 21st century perspective of course, it's ridiculous, and it's hard to comprehend why anyone would have got on a boat and sailed the best part of 11,000 miles away to go to Turkey to fight. But when you read the letters in the context of the time, they saw themselves as foot soldiers for the Empire and they went in that spirit and they were happy to go. I still feel angry when I think about how people's lives were thrown away like chess pieces on a board. But we re-interpret history from here. They were foot soldiers for the Empire and proud to be. The attitude 'where Britain goes, we go' has now long gone."

George and Margaret also visited Hill 60 in 1995.

George: "We walked up this road and came to the monument with Frank's name on it. It was really quite moving after all this time."

Margaret: "We were with a 'British Battle Tours' group, led by Colonel David Storey, a real English gentleman. And George took this letter that his uncle had written from Hill 60 and this Englishman read it out in his best English voice, and there wasn't a sound from this whole group while he read this letter out beside the monument with Frank Clark's name on it."

George: "But when you stood on this hill and looked at the scrub and stuff where they fought their way out, and we walked in trenches behind, and there's broken rum bottles and barbed wire and bones... I even remember that when we were walking up the Sidi Bar range one day there was a big leg bone lying on the ground, and I said to our tour leader, 'There's a big leg bone.' 'Oh,' he says, 'probably only a Turk's.' I always take little curios to give to people, little New Zealand kiwis and things, and I went up to one of these fellows who looked like a Turkish general or something like that. I gave one to him and I said, 'Yours were brave soldiers too.' And he thanked me profusely in English. And when we were outside the Blue Mosque a chap came up to us and he said, 'You know, Kiwi, we shouldn't have been fighting each other. We should have shot Churchill.'"

Fred Clark continued to farm at Te Pahu after the war and to live in his parents' house. He was a hard worker and, according to George, a farmer ahead of his time, clearing native bush, applying superphosphate to his paddocks and always keen to improve his stock.

Although his father was a staunch Labour supporter and his mother a woman of strong religious faith, Fred himself showed little interest in either politics or religion. George remembers listening to Parliament on the radio with his father and

Right **Helen's grandparents Fred and Elizabeth Grace Clark (née Arthur). Fred died in 1952, aged 59.**

grandfather when he was quite a young boy, but Fred rarely expressed any strong political views. "So we skipped a generation!"

Fred first set eyes on Elizabeth Arthur when he came to the Arthur farm looking for a dog he had lost. Despite the four mile distance between the farms, his visits became more frequent and the couple were married in 1920. Fred was 27, one year older than his bride. The newlyweds were keen to buy a farm of their own but, as we have seen, their lack of financial independence from Fred's parents made this impossible. Elizabeth moved in with her in-laws. The babies followed quickly, one each year for four years – Tom, George, Fay and Lois who died after one or two days. Marian followed four years later, Bryan three years after Marian, and that, as Fay puts it, "was the end of that tribe". According to Fay, Elizabeth's life was not easy:

"Her life was just having babies and caring for her children, wasn't it? But she always gardened, she loved the garden and always kept a nice garden as best she could. But in the house she had a mother-in-law who'd had several strokes and was bed-ridden and a hard taskmaster of a father-in-law who kept continually saying to her, 'The women in England would get up early in the morning and blacken the stove. The women in England would have done this...' And she found that quite trying.

"But as well as all of us children, there were men working for us, and she cooked, sewed, cleaned for perhaps nine people. She worked very hard on the farm. She also went out and helped my father on the farm to get away from her father-in-law. And when my grandmother died, which was when I was about four, he began to suffer from hardening of the arteries and couldn't get around so well. So he would sit on the couch chipping her all the time. Her life was not a happy one."

But life was not entirely bleak. Fred was full of fun. He loved having parties and would regularly invite the neighbours to a hooley at the farm. Elizabeth would play the piano as the revellers sang and danced around the house – *Lily Of Laguna*, *Look For The Silver Lining*, *Pack Up Your Troubles In Your Old Kit Bag*. By the time the fun was over, the pianist would be exhausted. Fay remembers her father with affection:

"He just wanted to enjoy life, loved sport, gave my brothers a wonderful, wonderful life. We didn't have electric power, only one lamp and candles. In the evenings Dad would take the lamp and they would play fantastic games of marbles all through the house. They would play table tennis. And my poor mother would be trying to sit and sew with a candle. Dad really was full of fun. And even when he was up having radiotherapy and my son was just a little fellow, he could still play with kids. I had a neighbour living next door and she had a couple of little girls and she looked out one day and she saw my father there trying to catch these kids with a rope, having fun with them. And she said, 'It nearly made me cry to see your father playing with those children.'"

Fred's determination to have fun may well have been a reaction to the strict, religious upbringing he had had from his father. For much of his early life he was not allowed to drink, though he was always a heavy smoker. He liked a trip to the races, but rarely if ever gambled. But he was an outgoing man who loved nothing more than being with friends and enjoying life.

His wife Elizabeth appears to have had as little interest in politics as her husband.

"My mother," Fay says, "didn't really want to get involved in politics because her mother, my Arthur grandmother, was very politically minded, as were all that side of the family. My mother's side of the family were all Tories. It was the Clarks who were Labour people. Mum didn't really discuss politics particularly, but my grandmother, Mary Ann Arthur, was a very outspoken domineering woman and she would come around to my mother's home and argue for hours with my grandfather, who took great pleasure in political argument. (I wonder where George got it from!) And grandfather wouldn't be happy until he had my grandmother on the other side hopping mad, and he would sit on the couch and laugh and laugh and laugh till the couch shook."

Elizabeth was active in the Presbyterian Women's Guild and the Country Women's Institute. She would ride from her home to meetings of the Country Women's Institute at the Te Pahu Hall with one of her young children in front of her astride the horse.

But despite her apparent lack of interest in politics, she had a strong social conscience. According to Helen, her grandmother took great pride in the fact that she had voted Labour in 1935:

"This did not go down at all well with her siblings. But she told me that when she was a young housewife on the farm, she used to look out of the kitchen window and she could see the Depression workers who had been brought out to live in tent camps down on the river flat, down below where we lived. The men had brought their families out to live in these Depression camps. And she could see the conditions that the men and their families were in. She was quite shaken by the Depression."

Her mother, according to Fay, was dignified, intelligent and caring: "She cared terribly for people and always went an extra mile to help others. If people were handicapped or a bit down on their luck, she would always do something nice for them. We had a storekeeper down at the local store, down where the Women's Institute meetings were held, and she would always take her a bunch of flowers or some other present. And there was a strange elderly lady who lived in a little cottage not far from our home. She was almost like a hermit and she walked everywhere. And when we were kids Mum would always stop to pick up this bedraggled old lady and we used to hate her getting in the car. But Mum was a very kind, caring woman with a well-balanced view of things, a real family woman, intelligent, well-liked, up with things and could hold her own with dignity in any situation."

Fred Clark died of cancer in 1952, just two years after Helen was born. Elizabeth lived to the age of 89 and was to have a considerable influence on the life of the future Prime Minister. Helen loved her and her grandmother loved Helen. She was, after all, her first granddaughter. But Helen had a special significance for Elizabeth, as Fay explains:

"When Helen was born, my mother had both my father and her mother with terminal cancer in the house. And she used to tell me that when Margaret came in with Helen it was like a little bit of sunshine coming into a house that was full of misery. And she was able to forget her troubles. And so Margaret would call in to see how the invalids were and bring Helen with her. It was a symbol of life starting in an atmosphere where life was ending. And my mother absolutely adored Helen throughout her life. She thought she was wonderful. She was so intelligent and did everything right. In Mum's eyes, Helen could do no wrong."

The feeling was clearly mutual. There is perhaps no one of whom Helen speaks with greater affection than her grandmother Elizabeth:

"I was the eldest granddaughter, so we were very close, very, very close. I remember that when my mother had the younger children we used to go and stay with my grandmother. She taught us to tie our shoelaces and things which my mother had always done for us and she would not. And if my mother had to go into Hamilton shopping for the day, we would get off the bus at my grandmother's house on the way home and she would give us the Anzac biscuits she had baked and a cup of orange juice and we would wait until Mum picked us up. She always had a photo up on her wall of Cromwell where she was born and brought up, and she'd often talk about Cromwell and her cousins there. She used to like to listen to *The Archers*, which came on at four o'clock every day. [Helen sings the theme of the BBC radio programme.] So we always went quiet during *The Archers* and by then probably mother had got home from town to pick us up. We were very, very close. We were in and out of there all the time. And I used to play the piano for her. She loved hearing me play the piano."

Helen inherited the piano from her grandmother and it still has pride of place in the sitting room of her Mount Eden home.

"My mother," Fay comments, "says that the way she chose Helen to give the piano to was as follows: she put all her grandchildren's names in a hat, closed her eyes and drew out one name. It was Helen's name. We in the family always say that she had Helen's name stuck to her finger. But no one really minded."

Tom Clark, Fred and Elizabeth's first child, was born in 1921; George, Helen's father, in 1922, and Fay in 1923.

George was born in Frankton. His earliest memories are of going out with his mother, lighting fires and burning logs, where the bush had been felled. And sometimes, at night, they would go out onto a hill and watch the fires burning below.

Educational facilities in the district were primitive and Elizabeth taught her two sons by correspondence until 1930, when she and others were instrumental in getting Kaniwhaniwha School built for the local children. It had one room and held 13 pupils. Tom, George and Fay would set off to walk the two miles to school together.

Country children were expected to pull their weight on the farm and the Clark kids grew up milking cows. Later, when George and Tom were in Standard Five and Six, their job was to catch the horses in the morning, take the cream cans down the road on a sledge to the school for collection by the cream lorry, then catch the horses again after school and bring the empty cans back.

These were the Depression years and often the cans would be filled with bread to bring to the relief camp below the house, to families who had no transport of their own. George remembers one of the cans falling over and the bread spilling onto the ground one night as they arrived home. The kids stuffed the bread back in the can and took it to the men, women and children in the camp. No one complained.

George was 14 and Tom 15 when the brothers left Te Pahu and went to board at Mount Albert Grammar School in Auckland. This would have involved considerable financial sacrifice by their parents, but Fred was a strong believer in the value of education. George can remember being told off by his mother for reading at the table and his father replying: "If he's reading, he's learning."

The move from a small country primary school to a large city boarding school with 650 boys was a major culture shock for the Clark boys. But George was determined not to let his feelings show: "When we left our little 13-pupil school to go to Mount Albert, there was never a tear that got out of my eye. Nothing. I kept it all bottled up."

Despite the one-year difference in their ages, George and Tom remained in the same class throughout their three years at Mount Albert Grammar, where they were known as "Clark Minor" and "Clark Major". Those three years were sheer torture for George:

"We used to get tripe sometimes. And you chew it and chew it and chew it and then just swallow it whole, because we were always hungry. And then we were given seaweed soup and coleslaw. And I used to put my hanky under the table, tip it into that and empty it onto somebody's garden as I went back to school. And we had to go to church on Sunday. We were given threepence to put in the plate. So on the way to church we bought a penny ice cream, a penny drink and a halfpenny worth of chewing gum. We put the remaining halfpenny in the plate. That's business, isn't it?"

After three years of misery, 16-year-old George, to his great joy, returned to the farm. The year was 1938. Aside from the family's annual holiday at Waihi Beach, the three years George spent at Mount Albert Grammar were the only time in his life he left Te Pahu, until he sold the farm and retired to Waihi Beach in 1987.

War broke out in 1939 and in 1940 both Tom and George were called up. Tom went away to the Solomon Islands where he served for two years, but George, who at this time had his father, elderly grandfather and 10-year-old brother at home, remained behind to run the farms. In his will, Thomas Clark had left the farm to his grandsons Tom and George, rather than to his son Fred, a common strategy in those days to avoid the payment of death duties. When the war ended, Tom was allocated a rehab farm and George bought his brother's share in the family farm. He was now a man of property.

THE McMURRAYS MEET THE CLARKS

Margaret McMurray, the oldest of David and Sarah McMurray's eight children, was born in Dunedin in 1924. Three years later, as we have seen, the family moved to Timaru. Margaret remembers living at Makikihi, a little country district, where her father had a job on a farm:

"And I can remember as tiny children – I suppose my brother must have been in a push-chair – I had to walk about a mile down the Main South Road and we caught a bus which took us to the Pareora turn-off and our grannie, Catherine McMillan, met us there in a horse and gig. I can vaguely remember sitting back and being driven to the farm, and we probably stayed there for a few days and then did the same in reverse to get back again."

Margaret went to Waimataitai Primary and then to Timaru Girls High School. She remembers her childhood as having been a happy one in a large and close family:

"Children in those days had something going for them. We amused ourselves and played our own games and didn't always plague our parents to take us to this, that and all over, like children today do. We made our own amusements. And I must have been always very education-oriented. I can remember in the long sunroom in the old house where I lived we used to play 'schools', with atlases and dictionaries. You wouldn't believe it, but we knew the capitals of all the countries in the then world, and all the rivers and mountains, for what it's worth. And I was always the teacher, because I was the eldest. And I know we had lots of jigsaws. And another thing we did plenty of was walking. We used to walk for miles out into the country, which kids probably couldn't do now anyway. We didn't have a car in those days. Dad had a truck of course for his work and in the summertime we used to go out to our grandparents' farm and we'd ride on the back of the truck."

Margaret finished her education at Timaru Girls High and at 17 went to Christ-church Teachers Training College. She was paid £7.19s.9d a month, out of which she outlaid 25 shillings a week for board. Her financial situation improved slightly when she turned 18 and her pay was increased to £9.3s.9d. With her teaching diploma in her pocket, she taught in Timaru and went relief teaching in Waimate, Ashburton and Blackball.

There was heavy competition for jobs. Servicemen who had returned from the War and gone to Training College were given the first option on teaching positions as they came up. Margaret found it difficult to find a job anywhere near home and she and her friends applied for positions "in the most unlikely places":

"And one of the ones for which I applied was Te Pahu which was advertised as 22 miles from Hamilton. It didn't tell you there was no earthly way of getting to Hamilton in those days. So I applied for that to do my country service. You were supposed to do two years country service before you went up to a higher pay bracket. And I got the job. And the Chairman of the School Committee wrote me a letter saying, there's a bus leaves Hamilton at half-past one on a Saturday which takes you to Te Pahu. It was called the Old Pirongia bus.

"So I got there on the early morning train from Wellington which arrived at Frankton at half-past 4 or some ungodly hour of the morning, and hung around and hung around and hung around half-asleep, and eventually another man who also wanted a ride to Hamilton shared a taxi with me and we got in there. And I can remember standing outside in Garden Place, where the bus left from at 1:30, with my earthly possessions in a huge suitcase and a little case. And I just hung around there for hours and hours and hours till half-past 1 and then went out on this bus. And some other people on the bus told me where Mrs Follett lived, the lady with whom I was to board. She lived away back off the road in an old, old house up a hill. She had boarded the schoolteachers since Adam was a boy. She was 70 and very deaf. And I lugged these cases up to the house. And I was so tired I went to bed and slept right through till the next day."

On the following Monday, her 22nd birthday, Margaret walked the mile from her lodgings to school and began her teaching. Te Pahu was a two-teacher school with about 60 children. Margaret was the Infant Mistress. She taught the Primers and Standards One and Two. The headmaster, a Mr Gillies, was extremely strict and took a rather dim view of farmers. His objection may have been based on the anomaly that farmers who came back from the war were entitled to rehab loans, and teachers weren't. He was a highly educated man and may also have felt somewhat intellectually superior to his charges' parents.

Margaret had only been in Te Pahu three weeks when she met George Clark: "I had met a friend of Fay's who had gone to school with Fay in Hamilton, and when I told her I had got the Te Pahu position, she wrote and said, 'Oh, I know a family there called the Clarks. I went to school with Fay and I'll write and tell them you've arrived.' Which she did. And George's mother rang and asked me if I'd like to come

Above **Helen's parents George and Margaret Clark were married at St Paul's Presbyterian Church in Timaru, May 1949.** *Left* **George and Margaret on honeymoon at Crabbe's farm in Cromwell.**

round on Sunday. I was to catch the cream lorry, and this was quite something for a city person.

"I stood way down the hill from Mrs Follett's house and waited till this rattling old cream lorry came along. I thought I was going to the end of the world, down this winding metal road. And Mrs Clark was waiting down at the cream stand to meet me and we walked up to the house. The Clarks were having their breakfast and there was my future husband, sitting at the end of a long table, making the toast for breakfast. And it didn't take me too long to learn that his cooking skills were confined to making toast."

George was impressed. Margaret was not merely attractive, she was intelligent and educated as well: "The farm girls didn't interest me, because education meant so much and to meet someone who was a schoolteacher was quite an experience."

And there was another, perhaps less serious reason. George's grandfather had always advised him to marry a town girl: "You got seven years work out of them before they woke up!"

So George plucked up his courage and after one of the old-style country dances at the Te Pahu Hall, asked Margaret whether he could drive her home. Margaret taught for almost three years at Te Pahu, then went relief-teaching in Timaru for a term. The couple were married there on 14 May 1949. Margaret stopped working:

Margaret: "Stopped working *at teaching!* I kept on working forever. I just stopped working at teaching."

George: "And then she started working!"

Margaret: "And then I did my 'country service' for many, many years."

Margaret moved in to the farm at Te Pahu: "I had experience of farms because I had aunts and uncles on farms where we used to spend holidays. And when we were children we spent holidays at my grandparents' farm. So I did have some inkling of country life. I think I settled in fairly well, did what I had to do. I don't know that it was too much of a shock."

There was a plan for George's parents to build a house for themselves on the farm down below. But the house hadn't been finished and for the first year of her married life, Margaret lived with her in-laws. She never lacked for company. There were boys who worked on the farm, shearers, dockers, haymakers, topdressers and eventually four daughters. George and Margaret did not spend a single night alone until Sandra, their youngest, went off to secondary school 23 years later.

Their first daughter, Helen Elizabeth Clark, was born in the Campbell-John-stone Maternity Annexe of Waikato Hospital in Hamilton on 26 February 1950, the Year of the Tiger. The future Prime Minister of New Zealand was, according to her mother, "a determined little devil of a child".

chapter two

A COUNTRY
CHILDHOOD

"IN those days, at the Campbell-Johnstone, babies didn't sleep with their mothers. I walked around looking for 'Clark', and you see all sorts of babies, and I thought, 'Oh god, I'm glad that one's not mine, and I don't like that one,' and so it goes on. And then I came to this one with 'Clark', and there looking at me was this child with these blue eyes staring at me. And I always thought from then on I might have a certain amount of trouble. She looked bright. She was awake, with those blue eyes sparkling."

If there was trouble in store for the father of the future Prime Minister, it was not to be seen for some time. Even taking into account the rose-coloured spectacles through which adoring parents see their first-born, Helen Elizabeth Clark appears to have been the perfect baby. Margaret's labour was not difficult, the baby arrived at the right time, was the right weight, produced teeth in due order, was a good sleeper, had a healthy appetite, grew beautiful blond curls on her originally bald head, was bright and alert, smiled when talked to, took her first tottering steps at the tender age of 13 months and was, in her mother's words, "beautiful and marvellous and wonderful".

"She was a very good baby and she had a perfect Plunket record. I had great faith in Plunket. George's joke was that I used to go round with baby under one arm, and *Modern Motherhood*, the Plunket book, in the other, reading to see if she was doing all the things she ought to do at the right time."

At 15½ months Helen was presented with a sister, Suzanne. According to her mother, the new arrival was more placid than her older sibling, more even. She had a nicer nature and would never argue. Helen got cross more easily.

Suzanne describes her own personality as more passive than Helen's, and it is perhaps not surprising that Helen should become her younger sister's protector, not merely in childhood but into her adult life. This was the first indication of the caring and mentoring role which has characterised Helen's relationships with her extended family throughout her life.

Helen's childhood was spent on the family farm in the Kaniwhaniwha Valley at Te Pahu. She and her sisters grew up in the house her great-grandfather, Thomas Clark, had built in 1912.

Helen and Suzanne got on well together. They had a large garden to run around and play games in, pet lambs in season, calves, chickens, a guinea pig called Gin, pet goats Silk and Satin, and various cats. Helen recalls that her mother would not allow the cats in the house, but her earliest memories are of life on the farm:

"I remember things like haymaking in the days long before there were tedders and balers. I remember them making haystacks. It's a great thing for kids on a farm, making sandwiches and tea for the haymakers or the shearers or dockers or whatever, and going with Mum to take them out. I remember we used to have old draught-horses and they used to pull some kind of mechanical appliance which actually lifted the hay up. This was before the days when they had engines for haymaking."

Not all her early memories are as pleasant:

"I remember having a row with my mother when I was a very small child and going into hiding, and she couldn't find me and she searched the house and called my father to the farm and found me virtually suffocating between mattresses. That was when I was about three."

Margaret remembers the occasion vividly too, but the "row" is missing from her account:

"George used to play these games with the kids, 'run away and hide from Daddy' and the rest of it, and he'd make this great show of finding them. Anyway, one day he wasn't there but she must have decided she was going to hide from me. I'd looked through all the four bedrooms and wardrobes and under beds and in cupboards and everywhere and I really was in a panic. So I grabbed Suzanne, who was no lightweight at two, and rushed out to the farm and said, 'Helen's lost'. And George rushed home and we went through the whole performance all through the house again, and we were at our wits' end. We didn't know what to do. In those days you had old kapok mattresses. And I was looking in despair in a bedroom off

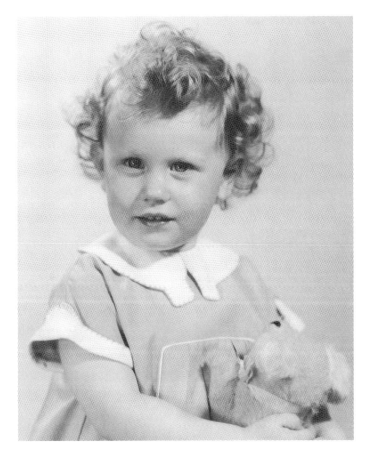

Left **Blonde curls and a favourite toy: Helen, aged 22 months.** *Below* **Suzanne and Helen with their adoring granny, Elizabeth Grace Clark.**

the kitchen, and I just saw this little movement and there she was, stuffed in between these two mattresses. And her face was all red and flushed, and her hair all damp. We didn't ask her what she was doing. We were so relieved to see the dashed kid, weren't we? We got her out and told her never to do that again. She must have been about three and she nearly got smothered. I assume she put her head out and got her breath or she'd have been dead."

Three was clearly a dangerous age. In 1953 Helen and Suzanne were both given tricycles for Christmas. On Christmas morning they went along to the milking shed with their father to practise. Suzanne immediately toppled over and hit her head on the concrete. Helen lost control, careered down a slope, crashed into a lemon tree and was removed scratched and screaming from her new trike. They must have made toys sturdy in those days. George and Margaret still have the trike.

Helen was apparently possessive about her belongings. Her mother remembers her hiding her toys when her young cousins arrived from Auckland in the school holidays. Fay recalls that the trikes in particular were inviolate:

"She was possessive of her belongings. She and Suzanne had two large tricycles. When we visited, Helen often sat on her bike and held the other to prevent Neil, my son, from riding it. We always found this amusing. Suzanne didn't care who rode the bike. My son only had a small tricycle and so of course he really wanted a ride on this precious tricycle."

If this was a character flaw, it was one of very few. The pre-school Helen was by all accounts rarely mischievous or naughty, and her infringements were minor:

"Below our house," Margaret recalls, "was the Kaniwhaniwha Stream. It was a trout-fishing stream and every 1st of October Helen's father went off to try his luck. On one such morning he had his equipment ready, fishing line upright against a doorway. Helen decided to try flicking the line, got it caught in a crack in the wall and broke off the end. Not a popular move!"

George remembers that when he went to put his boots on in the morning all the laces had been pulled out and rethreaded, but these two episodes seem to represent the full extent of his first-born's criminal activity. Indeed, in her eyes, it may have been her parents who were naughty.

George: "Helen had read this story about these parents being bad to their children. And when they got into bed that night there was a hedgehog in the bed. That was how they punished their parents. Well, one night I went to bed and settled myself down and there was something prickly down the bed. It was one of those spiky wire hairbrushes. She'd got the idea out of the story and put the brush in our bed. So I'm just wondering whether perhaps we'd done something wrong."

Helen and Suzanne slept in the same room, which was sparsely furnished – two

Left **The farmhouse at Te Pahu, built in 1912, housed four generations of Clarks.** *Below* **Suzanne and Helen on their precious tricycles.** *Overleaf* **Helen (4) and Suzanne (3) on a family picnic at Raglan, swimming with their father George and Uncle Bryan.**

beds, an old-fashioned wardrobe, a bookcase and a shared dressing table:

"There were two little drawers on top and two bigger drawers underneath," Suzanne remembers. "I had the right side and Helen had the left. She had the top drawer and I had the bottom. And boxes under the bed with all our stuff in it. We didn't really have much stuff, only a few clothes, I guess."

Nonetheless, Fay remembers her nieces as being extremely well-dressed:

"They used to come down to my mother's quite often. Helen was a shy little girl who would be watching everything that went on. She was always well-dressed, over-clothed perhaps. Margaret was very concerned about the children being warm and healthy. And she was well before her time. The girls had these beautiful little dresses and jackets and they wore little long trousers under the dresses, which was very unusual in those days."

Helen and Suzanne were joined in 1955 by another sister, Jenefer, and four years later by Sandra. "And that was the end of that tribe."

The family was comfortable but not well-off. The house had four bedrooms – George and Margaret in one, Helen and Suzanne in the next, Jenefer and Sandra in the third and a spare bedroom for guests. There was a large dining room area with a coal range which Margaret often used to cook on as well as the electric stove, and a formal dining room in which a large antique radio took pride of place.

'Mod cons' consisted of the stove, a washing machine, vacuum cleaner, electric toaster and jug and a lino polisher. "My mother," says Helen, "liked her lino well-polished. This was very common in those days before particleboard had been invented. Lino was the standard kitchen floor. There was no dryer and no television of course. Television didn't come until 1960. I think we got a television in 1966, but I was long away at school by then."

The Clark children got a penny pocket-money for each year of their age and a shilling when they made it to Standard Six. Threepence of that had to be put in the mission box.

Helen: "To be honest, money really played no part in our lives at all. But when you live 20 miles from town – I know it sounds strange to talk about going to town – the only time we left Te Pahu was to go into Frankton for the school dental nurse or later the orthodontist. Once a year, but that was it. Before I went to High School, I don't think I had even been to the movies. So it was a very rural existence. We were not really in the cash economy at all. I mean, when you see kids now, they have to have the right brands on things. We were completely out of that and we lived in a community where every other kid was like us. And then in the summer, in the school holidays, cousins would come down from the city and they were a lot more worldly-wise than we were. We lived in a very sheltered cocoon. We weren't poor, but money wasn't really a factor, because you were living in an economy where Dad grew all the vegetables, and the meat you ate had been killed on the farm. You really didn't need money."

For those farmers like Helen's father, who had converted from dairying to sheep farming, these were times of considerable prosperity. The Korean War, which had created a demand for woollen clothing for the troops, was partly responsible, and prices for wool were to remain high until the collapse of the market in 1967.

But Helen and her sisters had few, if any, of the expensive toys that present-day kids take for granted. There were tractors and trucks and FunHo toys and each of the girls was given a doll. But Helen would not get a bicycle until her final year at Epsom Girls Grammar. The children made their own amusement. They did jigsaws, collected Weetbix cards, books and magazines. And there were endless games. According to Suzanne, marbles was a big thing:

"I've still got all the marbles. Marbles was huge. People used to go out under the trees and make marble circles. And we used to play cards. And board games – Ludo and Snakes and Ladders. We never had Monopoly in the house. My cousins used to play it. I was never any good at it because I'd always lend people money. Helen would probably have done all right, even though she didn't agree with the principles. Dad was a great card player. He still loves playing cards with all the kids. He tried to teach us Crib, but we couldn't get the hang of it. Cooncan, Strip-Jack-

Naked, all those sort of games. Dad was a lot of fun. He'd have horsey games in the front room. And we had a tennis court at home. It was a grass court and every spring Helen and I used to have to go and mark it out. Dad would put little wooden pegs where all the lines were. We'd get the creosote, burn off the grass, put the net up, and away we'd go. We played a lot of tennis."

There were more serious pursuits. As the children got slightly older, they learned to knit. Helen was apparently a good knitter. But her reputation as someone willing to help around the house is less impressive. Ask Margaret whether Helen was a helpful little girl and you get an instant reply: "No, she always had her nose in a book. She'd do what she had to do."

What she had to do included helping make those sandwiches for the farm workers, and Margaret was very particular. The butter had to be spread right round to the crust and done properly. Helen helped with this "sometimes". She also occasionally helped with rounding up sheep, moving them from paddock to paddock, and docking lambs, jobs which farm kids generally enjoyed. But after an initial and unsuccessful attempt, she gave up on milking the cow.

She was not to be found in the kitchen either. She didn't cook.

Margaret: "Once a fortnight, Te Pahu School Form One and Two pupils went by school bus to Te Awamutu College – the girls for cooking lessons, the boys for manual training. So that gave Helen her first experience of a large school. The highlight of this fortnightly visit was spending pocket money at the dairy across the road from the school. Helen's first attempt at making a Fielder's sponge cake was not successful. But she was never interested in cooking as a child. Reading was her first preference."

Helen has never made a Fielder's sponge since, but says that her mother really didn't want the kids in the kitchen anyway:

"My mother's never really liked people fussing round her kitchen. So she'd have tasks like peeling the potatoes or going to get firewood or something, but otherwise stay out of her hair."

Clockwise from Top Left **From the family album: cousins at the swimming hole; wearing pixie hats, which would later be pulled off by the boys on the school bus; Helen dressed up to go visiting; with cousins on the farm; family celebration, with Elizabeth and Fred Clark on the right.**

Suzanne: "We weren't allowed in the kitchen to do any baking or anything. Mum couldn't stand the mess. If you dropped a grain of sugar on the floor, you'd have to wipe it up."

Unlike her older sister, Suzanne had plenty to do:

"My jobs were feeding the hens, collecting the eggs, milking the cow if it had to be done that night, locking the calf up if it had to be milked in the morning, feeding the dogs if they needed feeding, and getting all the wood. I had to get all the wood in for the fire, chop all the kindling and stack it all on the old verandah. I was an outside girl. I loved feeding the chooks, milking the cow and shifting a mob of sheep. I didn't so much like getting the wood in, and chopping kindling's a rather boring job. So I probably didn't like the wood much. Mum had a routine and we stuck to that routine. Rooms had to be tidy, beds made in the morning, the dressing table had to be dusted and so on. I think she did the major floor work and all the washing, though we had to hang it. That was probably the worst job.

"When we started to have music lessons a bit later on, we had to get up early to practise our music. We'd have our half-hour practices. I had to get up quite early, which in winter was very cold. I had to have the early shift because I was hardier. I had to get up and light this old kerosene heater and get the room warm, and Helen came in half an hour later when the room was warm. I still remember lighting that stupid old heater. I primed it and got a match and lit the wick, got it going."

The story is told without a hint of resentment. In general, Helen's three sisters enjoyed the farm work they were expected to do. They preferred it to being inside doing housework or reading like their older sister. Jenefer had a pony and "lived for the outdoors". Sandra says she's glad she didn't have a brother, because a brother might have deprived her of the pleasure of working on the farm: "Who wants to be inside when you can be outside? I'd rather ride a horse at that age and shift a mob of cows than stay inside and vacuum the floor, or do some sewing or iron clothes."

But there was a more substantial reason why Helen was not more heavily involved in the farm work or household chores. From around 1955 when she went to Te Pahu Primary School, she began to suffer from debilitating allergies. She became asthmatic. The problem was so acute that Margaret withdrew her from school in 1956 and began teaching her at home by correspondence. Since she was teaching one of her daughters, Margaret thought it sensible to teach two. So she held Suzanne back from school for a year and taught her to read. Her older daughter enjoyed staying home and learning by correspondence, but it was hard work for her mother who by then had a six-year-old, a five-year-old and a small baby in the house.

In Virginia Myers' *Head and Shoulders*, a collection of interviews with prominent women of the day published in 1986, Helen attributes her illness to the culture shock of going to school:

"I was terribly shy because of the lack of contact with other children. There were no others in the area and when I went to primary school, I developed a lot

Opposite from Top Left **Every summer the Clark family holidayed at Waihi Beach; Helen and Suzanne as bridesmaids for their aunt Diana; There was never a shortage of cousins at Christmas time. Helen is third from right at back.**

Above **Edna "Buddy" Arthur with her Standard One class at Te Pahu Primary School, 1957. Helen is front row, second from right**

of psychosomatic illnesses from having to mix with other kids. I became a terrible asthmatic, and had bronchitis, pneumonia and a collapsed lung during my primary school years. I was the weak one who stayed at home and read while the others rode horses."

George has his own theory on this: "I say a lot had to do with that first teacher. I used to get dogs sent up from a fellow at New Plymouth, and I got this little dog and it was cowed. I found out this dog used to like to nip people, and somebody on the train had belted the dog. He never recovered. And I think something similar happened at that stage in Helen's life."

Margaret also traces Helen's illness back to Te Pahu Primary: "She'd never, never had anything. I suppose because they were isolated and didn't have contact with other children. Then she went to school. I think she got every cold going and brought it home to us. And then the next year, when she was six, she developed asthma. And after Jenefer arrived, that seemed to upset her. That was when she really started getting asthma. With a baby who needed all the attention, perhaps my attention wasn't on her and Suzanne all the time."

But whatever its source, Helen's asthma was real enough:

"I can remember the day I was admitted to Waikato Public Hospital in 1956. I had been suffering from very bad asthma and allergies. There was no medication whatsoever for these things in the 1950s. You used to wheeze yourself into a total state, and I remember that my parents got the doctor out to the house. God knows what it cost. We were 20 miles from Hamilton and I remember the doctor said, 'Your child must go to hospital'. So I went to Waikato Hospital. I can't remember how long I was there, but I was admitted with a collapsed lung and pneumonia and went home with the German measles. There was obviously very poor cross-infection control at Waikato Hospital."

Helen still suffers from allergies and hayfever. And she still doesn't do house-work. But the childhood illnesses that spared her many of the family chores and often kept her indoors, had one significant advantage – they gave her time to read. And reading was to become a lifelong pleasure and obsession:

"I read everything. If you were in a country school in those days, every so often the school Country Library Service would come round to your school and would deposit a fresh lot of books and take away the books it had left the time before. My objective was to read every book appropriate to my age prior to the books being taken away again. So I used to read like crazy. And when I went to stay with other children, their mothers would complain to my mother that Helen wouldn't go out to the farm because she was too busy reading Patricia's books, or whoever's books. Then, at the end of every year at the Presbyterian Sunday School, we each got a book donated by my Aunt Emily, grandmother's elder sister. So I had a sort of row of books presented to me every year from there."

Helen's early reading was the staple children's diet of the times: the Janet and John books and Enid Blyton – Noddy, The Famous Five, The Secret Seven. According-ing to Margaret, she could read some of the Janet and John books before she started school and even showed a passing interest in the newspaper headlines. On the rare occasions when her parents went to town they had strict instructions to bring home the latest Noddy books. Margaret recalls that Helen got up to book 38.

Helen and Suzanne would read in bed at night – *The Bobsy Twins*, *The Riddle of the Blue Moon*, *The Case of the Speckled Dragon*. The reading would continue until Margaret came in to tell the girls to turn out the light. She probably suspected (correctly) that the light would be turned on again when the coast was clear. But it's unlikely that she would have made much of a fuss. Margaret, after all, was a teacher by training and inclination, and reading was encouraged in the Clark household. There were books everywhere.

Both parents read bedtime stories to the children every night. This was perhaps unusual for parents of the time and certainly for fathers. But George was a strong believer in education and was given to quoting the old adage, "If you educate a woman, you educate a family." And, he says, "it's true today."

Helen's love of reading has contributed to her encyclopaedic knowledge on a bewildering variety of topics. She has always been keen to inspire others with her enthusiasm for the written word, as her younger sisters can testify.

Sandra: "I remember her reading us Patricia Wrightson's *The Rocks of Honey*, an Australian children's classic, one summer holiday. She and Suzanne had a bedroom together and we used to go in and they'd both read us stories. So in that way they were quite kind older sisters, because a lot of older sisters wouldn't bother reading a long, chunky sort of book like that. Later, when I was at primary school and high school, Helen used to give me books to read that were a little advanced for my reading age at the time. She used to give me classics to improve me, like Thomas Mann and D.H. Lawrence and Patrick White and other books. Books played quite a big part in our lives, with both our parents and Dad's mother and Helen reading us stories and giving us books as birthday presents. We still buy each other books."

Jenefer also remembers getting books as presents that were beyond her reading or intellectual ability at the time:

"For example, Helen would give me Simone de Beauvoir's *The Second Sex* when I was in my early teens. I may have been 14 or 16. Radical feminist works like Germaine Greer's *The Female Eunuch*. That was the type of literature she was giving her younger sisters."

The aim was to educate rather than to shock and is a further indication of what one might call Helen's "mentoring instinct", her determination to do everything in her power to ensure that all the members of her extended family have the best possible education and make the most of their opportunities in life.

Helen's formal education began in February 1955 at Te Pahu Primary School, the school where her mother had taught before she married George and "stopped working". The Clark home was about four miles from the school. Margaret was the unpaid taxi driver:

"We lived on a narrow, winding metal road. Below our house was a one-lane swingbridge which really did sway when vehicles drove over it. The school committee of the day considered it unsafe for a bus-load of children. So for five years I drove Helen, and later Suzanne, two miles to catch the bus and then went to collect them again in the afternoon. It was a real performance. Jenefer was a baby then and I used to have to put the bassinet in the back seat of the car and put Jenefer in it, then do the same in the afternoon. And sometimes the cream lorry used to come past at about the time I'd be taking them to the school bus, and the cream lorry driver would give them a ride down to the bus, a novel means of transport."

Te Pahu at the time was a three-teacher school which had been formed by the aggregation of four small schools in the district. Later there would be four

teachers at the school, caring for the education of between 100 and 120 children. Helen would come to love Te Pahu but, although there were no tears, according to her mother her first day was not entirely propitious:

Above **Jenefer, Suzanne, Sandra and Helen, 1960.**

"She wasn't very happy at school. There was a very strict little woman there who was the teacher and I think she and Helen clashed from day one."

"Sometimes a teacher can put down a bright child who sticks up for herself," adds George. "I think they might have clashed even at that age."

But these problems were short-lived. Helen remembers Te Pahu Primary with considerable affection. It was, she says, "a lovely little school".

Helen's teacher in Standard One was her father's first cousin, Edna Arthur. Edna, more commonly known as "Buddy", describes Te Pahu as a well-equipped school with lots going on:

"It was friendly. In those days they were all family schools. More a farming community. The children were really good, well-behaved, more outdoor sort of children, different from the kids you see at primary school today. They were mostly European, with probably two Maori families who had always lived in the area."

Buddy remembers Helen as a quiet, shy girl: "I think she probably was a bit within herself. You know, some children take in everything, but they don't say much. She was perhaps a little withdrawn, probably did live in her own world quite a bit, probably in the world of books. She was never a problem. She always did what she was asked and completed all her work. Work wasn't a problem to her. But if it came to where she had some free choice, she always read. I remember her mother saying to me, 'Get her to do something else besides read. Have a go at doing some art things or something like that.' Yes, she was always quiet and she always read."

Helen attributes her early shyness to lack of social contact:

"When you look at kids today, from the time they're quite little, they're mixing with other kids. Even in rural areas kids get the opportunity of early childhood education through playcentres and playgroups and so on. And the kids who go to kindies and early childhood centres, they're confidently interacting with other children. Now we didn't have that. The only time we interacted with other kids was when our cousins came from the city in the holidays. And so you didn't have a lot of experience of other kids before you went to school, and that probably has a marked effect on you. The early years are important in how you see the world. We had a very narrow social experience."

Helen was undoubtedly bright. Ask her whether she was the smartest kid in her class at primary school and she answers "Yes" without missing a beat. But, as her mother points out, she had a head start. Most of the other children didn't have teachers for parents. Or Helen's thirst for books:

"I was a great reader. I read everything – social studies, everything to do with history or geography. I was never the least bit interested in science of any sort. But that didn't matter at primary school. The most you would ever have done was an insect collection. History was always my favourite subject – what forces shaped our world. As simple as that."

But life wasn't all reading and study. Helen was keen on sport, swam in the school's War Memorial Pool in summer, played netball, took part in athletics and was, according to Suzanne, a more than competent tennis player:

"Our little primary school was really fixated on tennis. It was a lot more popular in schools than it is now. We had two courts which were very well maintained. And every spring the tennis tournament used to go up and at every interval and lunchtime we would be out on those courts playing tennis. We had ladders and challenges and booking systems and it was a really big thing. Helen was a good player."

And then there was Calf Club Day, a major event not only in the life of the school, but the life of the entire farming community. Calf Club Day was usually held in October. Though Te Pahu was predominantly a dairying area, the sheep farmers' children entered their pet lambs in the competition, lambs on which they had lavished all their care and attention for the previous three months. The Clark kids were no exception, as Helen recalls:

"Come springtime, when all the lambs and calves were born, your attention turned to school Calf Club Day. There used to be three grades in the competition

for the lambs. One was leading. You had to teach your lamb to sort of trot along beside you on a lead. Another one was for most obedient pet. You had to put your lamb in the far corner

of the pen and call 'lambie, lambie, lambie'. I did well at that actually. And then you had rearing. Rearing was the condition of the lamb and that really depended on how much your mother was prepared to feed it at home. If you were really good and emerged from your school Calf Club with lots of prizes, you then went on to the regional competition, the Lower Waipa School Association Calf Club. And if you did very well at that, you graduated all the way to the Waikato Agricultural and Pastoral Show, to the showgrounds at Claudelands where you displayed your lamb. I had a couple of sisters who did quite well with this and used to go all the way to the Waikato Show. Our prizes were pinned to the bedroom wall."

Later in her primary school career the formerly shy young pupil would venture into more traditional forms of show business, featuring in the end-of-year school concert at the Te Pahu Community Hall. According to Suzanne, there were no auditions; the children were simply given their parts. 'Important historical figures' was the theme of one concert and Helen was cast as Queen Elizabeth I. She always remembered her lines, gave a creditable performance and apparently quite enjoyed it. Fay also recalls that when her daughter Gillian, Helen's cousin, stayed at the farm during the holidays, Helen would organise little concerts and plays: "Someone would play the piano and they would act little plays and put them on for us when we came to collect them. Helen was a good organiser. She was a leader."

It may have been Helen herself who played the piano. There were no Guides or Brownies in the district when her daughter was small, so Margaret decided to take her to music lessons instead: "That was her sole sort of cultural thing."

Helen began learning the piano when she was seven. The lessons were held at the school with other children from the district. It wouldn't have been worthwhile for the music teacher to come out to Te Pahu for just one pupil. So Margaret was on a parent roster and would go into Te Awamutu to pick her up.

Helen proved an able student and was soon playing requests for her father and grandmother: war songs and popular favourites of the day – *"The Old Tin Cup, Roamin' in the Gloamin'*, that sort of thing". By 1962, teenagers around the world were already screaming for The Beatles, but if Helen had heard of them at all, their music would not have been to her taste. The love of music which was engendered in her in those early days was for "serious stuff" – classical music and later, opera. Pop music held no appeal for her and never would.

Life at home, meanwhile, was stable and uneventful. Helen describes a typical day:

"Get ready, have breakfast, make your lunch, go down to the bottom of the road to the school bus, and go to school for the day. Get dropped back by the school bus at about half-past 4, I suppose. Depending on the season, you'd either feed your pet lambs or go and see what Dad was up to on the farm, then come back for dinner, go to bed and read a book, then put the light out. No TV. There was no luxury. Luxury was ham at the weekend, meat that you'd bought and not raised on the farm yourself. No frills, no luxuries. Good home cooking. My mother always served good, hot, nutritious meals, but she never used spices."

Those good, hot, nutritious meals were to leave Helen with a taste for more exotic fare:

"I loathe plain food. The stew, potatoes and other vegetables, the meat and three veg that I was brought up on. I love food. I love Indian food. I love Asian food generally. From the blandest, Korea and Japan, through to the highly spicy South-East Asia, Southern China, India. I basically love food. Very occasionally in New Zealand you get to eat African food – fantastic. You eat Caribbean food sometimes – very tasty. A great French meal, Italian meal. I don't particularly like North European cooking, I find it quite stodgy. German cooking – dumplings, wiener schnitzel – I don't like that. It's too plain for me. On the other hand, if you go to Scandinavia you'll get served cold meats and fish for breakfast, which is rather nice. I really don't like plain food, I like highly flavoured food."

Dinner in the Clark household was a reasonably formal affair, eaten at the table.

According to Suzanne, the three younger girls sat on a long wooden stool or bench. She draws a mental map of the seating arrangements:

"Dad sat there, Mum sat here, Helen sat there. I sat over there, because Mum could always see me doing things wrong. But she couldn't see Helen, because Helen was there. Jenefer and Sandra sat next to Dad. We would sit around the table and Dad would usually talk. We were brought up with good manners. We weren't allowed elbows on the table. We didn't have serviettes, but we had to use a knife and fork correctly. 'Please' and 'thank you' for salt and pepper.

"Then we would do the dishes. Helen would usually wash and I would dry. Then we'd stack away and do our homework. Not that I remember a lot of homework."

Helen remembers the dinner-table conversations as having centred around how things were going at school and what was happening on the farm:

"We took a great interest in what Dad was doing on the farm. Where he had shifted the sheep from that day, where he was putting the cattle. When were the shearers coming, when were the haymakers coming? When were we going to dock the lambs? It was all really around the life on the farm. The outside world had really no impact on us. Nowadays politics are in your house, on the TV screen, you can't get away from it. We were completely isolated."

After dinner the family would read, play games, talk, listen to the radio in the front room. The Australian comedy *Life with Dexter* was a favourite. When she came to visit, Helen's grandmother liked to listen to the BBC serial *The Archers*, "an everyday story of country folk". George and Margaret couldn't stand it. George was more interested in listening to Parliament.

Then early to bed, reading, lights out and ready for the next 'stable and uneventful' day.

The values which Helen learnt from her parents were honesty, hard work, thrift, respect for others, good manners, kindness and a sense of community. Margaret and George were both community-minded. Margaret was a member of the Parent Teachers Association, the Presbyterian Women's Guild and the Country Women's Institute. George was on the school committee. They conveyed to their children their own strong sense of obligation and responsibility to their neighbours.

On the subject of religion, however, the parents were divided. George never went to church at all and professes to have no religious belief. Margaret, though not devout, felt it her duty to give the children a Christian education. So they went to Sunday school. Helen remembers it with amusement:

"It was really weird because, before the community at Te Pahu raised the money to build a church in the late 1960s, there was an old Settlers Hall in Te Pahu which had a sort of hall area, a supper room, ladies' and men's rest room and so on. Most of the community were Presbyterian and the minister would come out to Te Pahu at about two in the afternoon to conduct the hour's service.

"After the first hymn or so, the children would be excused to go to Sunday School, and I can remember sitting with the Sunday School teacher, who must have been a local lady, literally in the vestibule of the ladies' rest room. That was where the Sunday School took place. I can't remember a single thing we were taught or told, but I do remember sitting in the vestibule of the ladies' rest room for the Sunday School class."

No one smoked or gambled in the Clark family and drinking was restricted to a beer on a hot day after the shearing. According to Helen, there was a strong work ethic in the home:

"My father worked a seven-day job, as did my mother. But it also has to be remembered that we grew up at a time when nobody was unemployed. So it was expected that you would be self-reliant, get on with it. Though my parents never discouraged us from lying around reading. Making a pest of yourself, yes. On a farm there are always things for kids to do, if you're not inclined to be reading all day."

Helen's cousin Gillian remembers Margaret offering rewards and prizes to the children to get them to do little tasks. She set goals, was always well organised and never growled. Fay believes that this goal-setting was to stand Helen in good stead in her later life.

Honesty was at a premium in the Clark family.

George: "I always tell people, 'At least you've got a Prime Minister who's honest', because when they were young, if they'd sworn at me, it wouldn't have worried me, because I swore at the dogs. But if they'd ever cheated or lied, I'd have been down on them like a ton of hot bricks. So at least she's a hundred percent honest."

Margaret: "Ask Suzanne. Once George reckoned he caught her cheating at cards. He just picked her up by the scruff of her little neck and dumped her in her bedroom. And she said it was most unfair because she wasn't cheating."

George: "They were playing that game called Cheat and I would never let them play it in my presence."

Margaret: "If they were cheating, lying or thieving, they'd get a hiding."

It's unlikely that Helen ever got a hiding. Discipline in the Clark home was firm nonetheless and largely administered by Margaret. George got to play "fun daddy":

Suzanne: "Then I guess he hadn't been round kids all day and he could come in fresh. He liked children and he was a good dad. Well, they were both good parents. Dad wasn't strict at all. We never pushed it though. We always knew that he had authority if he needed it, so we would never have pushed it. That was left to Mum to be the disciplinarian, which perhaps wasn't fair, but I guess one person does it."

There are perhaps echoes here of the relationship between Fred Clark, George's father, and his wife Elizabeth – he full of energy and looking for fun at the end of the working day, she tired and perhaps a little frustrated after a day spent keeping the household running, caring for her children, helping out on the farm, often feeding not only her family but an army of seasonal farm workers as well.

Certainly, the picture which emerges of Helen's mother from conversations with her children is of a strong, no-nonsense, enormously practical, hugely efficient woman who managed her extraordinarily busy life on the farm, at home and in the community by adhering to a strict and necessary routine. Like so many farmers' wives, her life was extremely hard. But the interests of her children remained ever paramount. They could not have been cared for better, or had a better teacher.

All in all, Helen's childhood in Te Pahu was probably a happy one. In a note which she composed specially for this book, her mother wrote:

"Early in 1987 Te Pahu School celebrated its 75th Jubilee. Helen was MP for Mount Albert at that time. As a past pupil she was invited to make the opening speech. I remember her recounting her time at the school and her childhood in this very community-oriented district. Among other things she mentioned that she wished many more children at that time could have the sort of childhood that she and her family and most other Te Pahu children had – a stable home, loving parents, well fed, well clothed, in a wonderful, picturesque environment."

And so it was. But those happy days were soon to end.

chapter three

INCARCERATION

GEORGE and Margaret's decision to send Helen to Epsom Girls Grammar School in Auckland, rather than to a school in Hamilton, was based partly on family tradition. George and his older brother Tom had gone to Mount Albert Grammar and Epsom was its sister school. It was also a school with an outstanding academic reputation.

But there were more pressing practical reasons. The Hamilton school bus didn't go past the Clark farm and Margaret would have had to drive Helen four miles over a narrow metal road in the early hours of the morning to the nearest school bus stop, then pick her up again at around 4:30. The whole arrangement would have been inconvenient and onerous for both mother and daughter.

Helen could have boarded at Hamilton Girls High, but the school's hostel was on the banks of the Waikato, damp and cold in winter, and unsuitable for a young girl prone to asthmatic attacks. George's sisters, Fay and Marian, had boarded there and brought back horror stories of the Dickensian conditions. Fay recalls the chilling mists of the Waikato coming in through the dormitory windows which had to be kept open six inches, summer or winter, and the girls being admonished by the headmistress to take a cold shower every morning: "She told us that she took a cold shower herself every morning and that if we didn't believe her, we could come and see for ourselves. None of us did."

So Helen's parents decided that she would become a boarder at Epsom Girls

Above **Holidays at home provided relief from the loneliness of boarding school. Back row: Jenefer, George, Helen. Front row: Suzanne, Sandra, Margaret.**

Grammar. Her long "incarceration" was about to begin.

But first there was a uniform to buy. George drove mother and daughter into Hamilton and from there the trio caught the bus to the big smoke of Auckland. John Courts were the official stockists of the Epsom Girls Grammar school uniform.

It would not have been cheap. Nor would the fees to board a girl at one of New Zealand's most prestigious schools. But the cost of their daughter's education was not an issue for the Clarks:

George: "It never entered our heads. Helen and Suzanne had to have a certain amount of orthodontic treatment for their teeth and it cost us hundreds and hundreds of pounds. It didn't matter to us. That was money spent on your children. And you made the money available."

Helen was a month away from her 13th birthday when she left home with her parents to go to boarding school in Auckland. It was not a good day for anyone, as Margaret recalls: "We took this child up to Auckland and it was so traumatic, parting with the dear child, that George said on the way home – I remember this distinctly – he said, 'Next year when Suzanne goes, you can take her. I'm not going back there to go through that again.' Yes, it was most upsetting parting with her."

George did not "go through that again". But when, a year later, his wife set off with her second daughter on the same traumatic mission, he made Suzanne a promise that if she didn't cry when her mum left her, he would send her a 10 shilling note. It was a lot of money in those days. Margaret takes up the story:

"Suzanne was very brave. She didn't cry that day, and she wrote home and asked for her 10 shilling note, which she got. But she cried every time I left her after that, so it was a bit of a con really."

Perhaps George should have made the same offer to Helen:

Margaret: "Oh, yes, she cried. I think she was crying from the time we left home in the morning. It was quite funny. All the children she knew were standing out waiting for the primary school bus as we went down the valley, and I remember her putting her head down in the car so that she wouldn't see them."

When this sad little party arrived at Epsom Girls Grammar, they were taken to Epsom House, the hostel which would be Helen's school-term home for the next four years. "We weren't shown round the school," says Margaret, "We took her into this little cubicle and sat with her until we couldn't sit any longer."

Helen has very little recollection of this first day other than of her mother and father driving away after they had dropped her off:

"It was very upsetting, very upsetting. In fact for most of the first two years there were always floods of tears when we went back to school."

It would be difficult to overstate how miserable Helen would be at Epsom Girls Grammar, especially in the early years. She expressed her feelings about the school to Virginia Myers in *Head and Shoulders:*

I was sent away to board at Epsom Girls Grammar in Auckland. The school draws pupils from the most affluent suburbs, Remuera and Epsom, as well as from less élite areas. It was heavy going, coming from a back-country farm where I'd never mixed with people like that. Particularly when girls from those élite suburbs perceived country girls as rough and not very civilised.

And it wasn't only the girls. The headmistress used to come across to the hostel and tell us we were country girls and we'd go back where we came from, that there wasn't much that could be done for us educationally, but we'd be better for the experience of rubbing shoulders with the other pupils. There was no sense that we were out to do great things. No one ever said anything, but I resented her attitude. I'll never forget the rotten testimonial she gave me. She said I didn't know what I was looking for in life and perhaps when I found out I'd make a contribution to something. Quite a knocking testimonial. It may have been accurate at the time, but it wasn't helpful as the final document I came out of school with. I really resented it and thought, I'll prove her wrong. I think that's characteristic of me. I developed great stubbornness as I went along.

We should perhaps be grateful then to Margery Adams, Helen's old headmistress at Epsom, for unwittingly contributing to the strong-mindedness and determination that would one day drive her former pupil to seek the highest office in the land. But was Helen's assessment of Epsom Girls Grammar fair?

There is no doubt that loneliness and desperate homesickness were major factors contributing to the unhappiness of many of the Epsom House boarders. Margery Adams says that the hostel girls occasionally spoke openly of how much they missed being at home in the country:

"I remember one girl very much impressing us at an evening held to entertain the Board. She read a poem about her homesickness and how much she missed the country life, and they all applauded her very warmly which shows that they all felt the same thing."

That girl was not Helen, but it could have been. Here was a girl who until now had been cocooned in a loving family in which, as the oldest child, she enjoyed both privilege and status; who had been raised in a sheltered rural community, which she left only once or twice a year to visit the dentist, the orthodontist or take part in Calf Club Days in Hamilton; who had attended a small country school with girls and boys from backgrounds virtually identical to her own. A shy, retiring, unsophisticated, unworldly girl with her head buried in books. And this girl suddenly finds herself in the country's largest city, totally cut off from her family, in a school with 1300 girls she has never met, most of whom come from backgrounds alien to her own. There is no great mystery about this – she was lost.

Left **Still a country girl: Helen shoulders the hind quarters of a wild pig.**
Opposite Page **Form 4CL, Epsom Girls Grammar School, 1964. Helen is at far left, back row.**

Margery Adams remembers the young Helen Clark: "She was not a happy girl at school. In fact I think she was very unhappy most of the time. That's the impression I was left with: that she was unhappy, a bit of a loner and, as she said to me herself, very shy. I didn't pick the shyness, because I didn't see much of her really. Just one of the hundred-odd girls in the hostel. I didn't go over to the hostel a great deal. I went and had a meal occasionally with them, but not very often, and I don't remember individuals."

This statement provides an insight into the cultural divide that existed between Epsom House, the hostel catering almost exclusively for girls from the country, and the rest of the school. Margery Adams says she didn't go there a great deal. But nor did any of the school's teaching staff. Professor Ann Trotter, who taught history at Epsom when Helen was there and inspired her with a love of the subject, reflects on the social alienation of the boarders within the school and the anomalous nature of the hostel:

"Epsom Girls Grammar is largely a day school and was in those days a very large school and getting larger. It was also zoned. So you have the bulk of the students coming from the zone, students who have known each other probably since they started school. It's fairly overwhelming for students from small country schools to come into that sort of atmosphere. Everybody seems to have friends and you don't know how things work, and inevitably the city girls, even at 13, seem a great deal more sophisticated. If you're a boarder it's very difficult unless you're an outgoing person who is immediately prominent in basketball or swimming or something else.

"Now in a lot of schools which have boarding establishments, there are members of staff who live in the boarding establishment as wardens. These people provide you with a link with the day school operations. But that was not the case at Epsom. I was never in the boarding establishment. I don't know of any member of staff who was, except Miss Adams, who did take an interest in these girls. But it must have been, on reflection, extremely hard for many of them. And so, as a member of staff, you didn't know who the boarders were – although sometimes you could work it out – because they were not part of the gang, the club. And I don't know of any boarder in the years that I taught, who stood out at that school. A very big girls' school like Epsom was not really geared for boarders. It was an historical accident that from the very early days there were boarding establishments at Epsom and I think at the boys' grammar school too."

Helen experienced the social isolation of the hostel girls at first-hand:

"There was never a feeling that the hostel girls were well included in the school. You were very conscious that you were a hostel girl, a country girl and you were in with the kids. We lived quite separate lives. At night they got on their bikes or their buses and went back home, and we went back into a closed world in the school hostel. So we weren't well integrated into the school community. There were very few close friendships you developed with girls in the main body of the school."

It's likely that the hostel girls, most of them from farming families, felt inferior to the more sophisticated and worldly-wise day-girls. Suzanne, who joined her sister at Epsom in 1964, says she really has no idea whether the day-girls really did regard them as country hicks:

"We never had anything to do with them. I never had a day-girl friend ever in my whole five years at the school. The hostel girls stuck together. There was a physical separation as well because of the school routine. We didn't have lunch with them. We went back to the hostel for lunch.

"I think I felt inferior, definitely inferior, because after the 3rd Form I was put in the top academic class. And I was in with all these girls whose fathers were doctors or professors, and whose brothers were at university studying top-level physics because they wanted to be doctors or professors and all this sort of thing. I just felt like rubbish, basically. I shouldn't have been put in that class, perhaps the next one down, but not that one. I couldn't cope socially and, yeah, I felt pretty second-rate and I imagine Helen did too. That's prob-ably why we were driven to our own hostel girlfriends, because we felt safe there."

Later in her school career Helen would make friends with some of the day-girls and even visit them at their

Right **Writing to your parents was mandatory at boarding school, and letters were often the girls' only contact with home during the term.**

21 Owens Rd.
Epsom,
Auckland, S.E.3
16/6/64

Dear Dad, Mum, Jenefer, + Sandra,

Hope you have not got the Flu: How is Aunty Em? — I wrote her a letter the other day. Hostel dance was on Sat. night and I was one of lucky 6 4th formers chosen to be a barmaid. The rest had to go to the pictures. It was strictly a 5th. + 6th. formers dance but I'm sure some of us had more dances than them — I did anyway. We had photos taken there so I 'spose I'd better get one or two.

You know the photos of Suzi and me that we had

Cameras that day, any good, Weekly May 1.7th think there was ures of Paris think you could ently? ! ! ! ! you that last wrote for Kathryn and asked if the President of Israel could find us penpal. I got a letter from yesterday which had gorgeous stamps on it — I'll bring it home some time.

com myself. I and or a him

Love Helen.

homes on the weekend. But these occasions were rare. Clearly many of the hostel girls came to regard themselves as second-class citizens in the school. Whether they were made to feel inferior is unclear.

"It's hard to put a finger on it really," Suzanne says. "It was very real. They probably didn't make us feel like that. It was probably just a complex."

The "complex" would have been nourished by the school's academic ranking system. Students going to Epsom had to sit an entrance test and were graded into classes on the results. The grades went from A to D. Most of the hostel girls, according to Suzanne, were in the C and D classes. The grades, as Margery Adams observes, had less to do with their intelligence than with their academic backgrounds:

"They hadn't had the competition that the others had had in the intermediate schools, where pupils were graded A, B, C, D, E and so on. The country girls hadn't had that. And very few hostel girls made their way until much later, until they were right up near the top of the school. It was a long integration period, and it was usual."

The hostel girls' integration cannot have been helped by the fact that homework, which was the norm for children in the intermediates, was largely unknown in the small country primary schools. And some subjects were not taught there at all. Helen notes that Brian Freeman, the headmaster of Te Pahu Primary, was aware of the problem and, in the year before she went to Epsom, introduced homework for his Form Two pupils:

"We never did homework until the headmaster decided he'd better get us ready for this big city school. So when I came up to Epsom, it was a real shock to be put in the third layer of classes because we really hadn't had the education that the kids out of Normal Intermediate had had. These kids had learnt French for two years, had done quite advanced maths and had access to all sorts of things we never had. It took me two years to crawl up to being in the top Latin stream."

Margery Adams recognises the difficulty that girls like Helen faced when they arrived at Epsom: "She came to us from a little country school and that made competition with the abler girls in the school very difficult, because about 80 percent of our pupils were from Kowhai Intermediate, Remuera Intermediate or Normal Intermediate. And they'd all be trained in the

Left **With fellow boarders Anne Williamson, Sue Kennedy and Merilyn Craig outside the hostel at Epsom Girls Grammar School, Auckland. Helen is middle front. She was not an outstanding pupil at secondary school and did not begin to emerge academically until her undergraduate years at Auckland University.** *Overleaf* **An uncharacteristic example of defiance in the 6th Form. Beneath Helen's 'NO!!!' a friend has commented in schoolgirl French, "I say you are a naughty girl, I think, even though I don't take French."**

Russian people. His inability to recognize the importance of the popular opinion represented in the Duma was another leading factor to his downfall.

The basis of discontent in Russia lay with the working class and the peasants. For many years the Russian peasantry had been dominated by the ruling class, they had little money, and many hardships to bear. The Tzar failed to recognize the need to reform completely the ~~lot of the unfortunate poor~~ who therefore inevitably turned ~~to communism~~ No. It was never supported by the peasants. as a means of securing equality, rather than making futile appeals to their traditional leader. Once the Tzar had the mass of peasants against him there was little hope for his survival for the bulk of Russia's population lay is the peasantry and their opinions counted for a lot against the small proportion of aristocracy. Peasant and working class discontent was therefore another step towards the decline of the Tzardom.

War with Japan can be counted amongst factors leading to the Tzar's downfall. ~~During any war~~ Russia suffered a complete and disastrous defeat and showed herself quite unready for a full-scale war. The war brought the realization to the Russian people that their government was decadent and incompetent, and discontent increased. The war was regarded as being the Tzar's private affair and was generally felt to have been unnecessary; it had exposed complete inefficiency of the Tzardom. With the defeat of the ~~mavana~~ thus exposed Russian feelings against the government were risen and soon after the defeat the unsuccessful revolution of 1905 ~~out bringing~~ displaying ~~expensing~~ popular sentiment clearly.

3

Helen Clark.

Many other smaller causes of decline may be found, but these are numerous, and mostly arising from examples of the Tzar's foolishness and incompetency. Thus one may conclude that the monarchy had served its feeble purpose ~~policy~~ in Russia, and the people were ready to progress to a higher, more democratic ~~and~~ form of government in which they all could share.

Bibliography?

Sketchy & inaccurate. Did you do any reading at all? NO!!! I say vous êtes une mauvais jeune fille! je pense même que je ~~ne prends pas~~ le français

type of thing you got in entrance tests. Groomed, as it were, to go into the better classes. Well, she had to meet that competition when she first came to the school and she didn't get into one of the highest third forms. I think she started in 3C Latin. There were four Latin forms, which were the best of the girls, and then another four or five or six that didn't take Latin. She moved up year by year, working hard, but I don't remember much about her. In her 6A year she was still shy, a bit of a loner, obviously highly intelligent. She didn't stand out prominently in anything like sport. She wasn't a house captain or a prefect or anything like that. She was a good, sound, solid student. It wasn't until she was in 6A that we fully realised that she had tremendous potential."

Epsom House was no Dotheboys Hall. There was no Wackford Squeers to terrorise the students. But the hostel matron was, according to Suzanne, "a right little shrew, an absolute dictator":

"She was really strict. If you wore your slippers into the dining room you got a detention. There were inspections every morning. She'd go right through the hostel at about a quarter to 7 and rip the curtain open to make sure you were out of bed. 'Get up! Get up!' I still remember that because I didn't like getting up. And if you heard her coming, you'd leap out of bed.

"You either showered at night or in the morning. There was always a queue for the showers. You had to have your bed made, everything tidied and be ready for breakfast at eight o'clock. Then you wandered over to the school grounds in time for school to start.

"We were well fed most of the time, though I was always hungry. We never used to have any afternoon tea. Mum used to send us up tuckboxes. Maybe we farm girls had healthier appetites."

Boredom rather than starvation seems to have been the main problem for her sister Helen. There was very little for hostel girls to do after the teaching day ended – have dinner, do your homework, go to bed. There was some relief on Wednesday afternoons when you were allowed to go shopping in nearby Newmarket and once a month to venture as far as Queen Street:

"But you had to be back for dinner at 5:30. So it was a crazy sort of battle to get a bus into Queen Street by four o'clock and be on the bus by five to get back in time for dinner."

Sunday provided a further opportunity for the hostel girls to escape the confines of the school grounds. On Sunday you went to church. Suzanne recalls that this weekly outing wasn't entirely pleasurable:

"It was a torture for us. We had to dress up in these absolutely ghastly hostel uniforms which were sort of fawn dresses with buttons all down the front and beige stockings. The various religions would be grouped according to what time they were going to what church service. The Catholic girls got out at such-and-such a time, the Anglicans at such-and-such a time. The Presbyterian girls used to leave the latest. That was us.

"And then we were marched off in crocodile to St Lukes in Remuera, this great big old grey stone church. We had to sit through the service, all these hostel girls sitting in a pew. No one would ever put any money in the plate. We didn't have any spare money, and if we had, we took it down to the dairy and bought 10 cents worth of chips because everyone was so hungry. And because the Presbyterian service was always late, we wouldn't get back in time for Sunday lunch. That was important because Sunday was the one day you didn't have to sit at your fixed table, you could sit with your friends. And we never got back in time to book a table to sit with our friends. And that was a big disaster. So in the end we used to go off with the Anglicans because they had a 9 o'clock service."

Helen confirms hers sister's version of the Sunday church outing and even admits to an uncharacteristic bit of personal sinning:

"As you got a little older and bolder, you worked out that if you slipped out of the crocodile you could go and see your friends for an hour, and then you would rejoin the crocodile and go back to the hostel for lunch."

Aside from these relatively short excursions at the weekend and one day a month when they were allowed out for the day, the hostel girls were not permitted to leave the confines of the school. Even the headmistress, Margery Adams, thought this regime, "a bit restrictive, as it was bound to be. I can always remember the matron, who died about a year ago, once saying, 'Look, I think these girls should be allowed to go out for a walk sometimes,' and they were allowed to go out, two or three at a time, for a walk. But apart from that they were not allowed out of the grounds."

"A bit restrictive" is too weak a term for Helen: "We felt incarcerated actually. But then if you think of the times and the fact that you had country parents sending their kids away, they want to know they are properly under lock and key. I expect parents feel much the same today. And the city is much worse and more violent than it was in the 1960s."

On their one day of real freedom each month, Helen, and later Suzanne, would be picked up by their Aunt Fay or occasionally Aunt Marian. Fay, who had been to boarding school in Hamilton and detested the experience, had enormous sympathy for her niece:

"I really felt for Helen, because I knew how I felt when I was put into boarding school. When you've run freely in the countryside and had a wonderful life, and suddenly you are shut in this place with rules all around you, it isn't easy. So I'd go and get them for an afternoon or from nine to six. The rules were strict and I'd make sure to get them back to the hostel right bang on time. They loved to get out of that place. They'd join in with whatever we were doing. Gillian says that she and Helen used to sunbathe on the garage roof, but I can't imagine my husband letting them climb onto the roof."

Helen and Suzanne lived for this treasured day off once a month, for long weekends and school holidays when they could escape back to the country. And for one week in January, usually the third week to fit in with haymaking, the Clarks would take off to the beach. The same beach that George's mother first took him to in 1926 when he was six. The same beach that he, Margaret and, till they left home, his daughters holidayed at every year. The same beach the couple retired to in 1987. Margaret and George like Waihi Beach. The Clarks are a family who do not relish change.

Helen: "Every year my parents used to rent a house at Waihi Beach and we'd pack everything for the week into the old Vauxhall and we'd drive for what seemed forever – two hours in terrible heat in January to Waihi Beach. My father had a week's holiday at Waihi Beach every summer of his life."

Margaret: "We used to ring Mr Lind, the land agent, and he'd always find us a beach house, preferably very near the sea. So we stayed in lots of different beach houses. The kids go round now sometimes saying, 'Oh we used to stay there or there or there.'"

She remembers the journey with mixed emotions: "The car laden up with children. We had to bring all our own blankets and sheets. And being thrifty people, we brought our own meat. It was darned uncomfortable, the car laden up with kids and stuff. And usually one of them wants to bring a friend. Of course in those days there were no seat-belts. You just jammed people in. The car was so fully packed coming back one year that it was hitting on the universal. George had to have another spring put in the back."

When Helen and Suzanne were small it was standard beach holiday fare – sun, sea and sandcastles on the beach. But the hostel girls were more sophisticated:

Suzanne: "We all sunbathed. We sunbathed in our bikinis. The hostel girls were very keen on sunbathing. Those were the days when everyone had to be as brown as a peanut. I don't think Helen tanned that well – a lighter skin than mine. But we swam, went for walks, played tennis, surfed – not proper surfboards of course, the generation before that, those foam-type things. They were wonderful holidays, great holidays."

But the golden weather would inevitably end and it would be back to school.

Life at Epsom was not entirely grim. Helen made close and lasting friendships with other hostel girls, including her two best friends, both of whom, coincident-ally, had parents who were teachers in country schools.

A movie was shown at the hostel on Saturday night, though Helen, who would later develop a passion for films, says she can't remember anything she saw.

There were also dancing classes with the boys at Dilworth College. Suzanne recalls that the hostel girls would line up in crocodiles (again) and march off to the College, where they would attempt to master "the waltz, the foxtrot and the maxina – all that sort of stuff". The sessions, which were apparently equally embarrassing for both sexes, were presumably intended both as a preparation for life and for the annual get-together at the hostel with the boys from Mount Albert Grammar.

The girls had to make their own dresses for this occasion. Helen, according to Suzanne, was very good at sewing and the two would trot down to Newmarket to buy a few metres of nice material which Helen would transform into dresses on the hostel's one sewing machine. Not that the dance was looked forward to with much enthusiasm. This was the only contact the Epsom House girls had with the opposite sex. They were inexperienced and awkward. And Helen hated dancing:

"I wasn't a good dancer. I loathed dancing. Still do. When people ask me to dance, I decline. I've found that men can be very persistent asking you to dance at a function. I find it quite irritating. It's harassment really and I don't like it. But I get very little of it now that I'm Prime Minister."

There was a strong emphasis on music and the arts at

Below **All dressed up for the school dance. Girls made their own dresses on the hostel's sewing machine. Helen, aged 15, is third from right. She loathed dancing and still does.**

Epsom and Helen was able to continue learning the piano. Fay's daughter-in-law Joan was also a student at the school at that time and her lessons followed Helen's. As she waited, she could hear Helen "trilling up and down the piano", playing her pieces with apparent ease. Indeed, so discouraged was she by the virtuoso before her, that she abandoned her lessons. Helen was a talented pianist.

She played the organ too, but was something less than enthusiastic about being expected to perform for the benefit of the congregation of the Presbyterian Church in Te Pahu during the school holidays:

"My mother used to book me in to play the organ when I was home from boarding. She volunteered my services. I can't say that I was always that co-operative about it. When you're a teenager, you've probably got better things to do than play the church organ."

Drama was also a significant part of the Epsom curriculum. Margery Adams describes the school productions as "the best school drama I have ever seen anywhere. All the girls looked forward to it from their 3rd Form days. It was a competition. Each form had to produce a scene of not more than eight minutes from Shakespeare one year and from a more modern play the next. They had to paint the flats, build the scenery, dress the stage, design the clothing and everything else. And what they produced was amazing. The ingenuity, the skill, the beautiful voice production that came through were something very precious."

According to Fay, Helen wanted to be in everything:

"I can remember going over to Epsom to see her acting in a play, but even in the play she seemed shy. She wanted to be in everything, but that country shyness… I remember her saying to me once it took a long time to throw away that country shyness."

In drama, as in everything else at Epsom, there was a strong emphasis on self-reliance. Margery Adams recalls that one of the first notices she had to give the school as headmistress was from Marie Goden:

"She taught speech and drama and taught it wonderfully well. She gave me a little notice that said, 'Would you please ask Five this and Five that' – I can't remember the forms – 'to bring their saws and chisels today to make their flats.' In a co-educational school that would never have happened. At Epsom the girls had to do everything themselves."

"Hostel life taught us to be very independent," Suzanne volunteers. "We basically had to do all our own washing, organise ourselves each day, do our own incidental shopping down in Newmarket, organise our outings and trips home. Most kids these days are very dependent. They wouldn't have a clue. But we had to be independent at Epsom, stand on our own feet."

Ann Trotter says that one of the things Margery Adams tried to inculcate in the Epsom girls was self-discipline:

"Often when I was in places like London and you saw people pouring out, you'd think, if there was a disaster here we'd all be trampled to death. Well, I think that at Epsom we would have filed out neatly as the building crashed around us. Self-discipline within the community, hard work, good citizenship, responsibility for one another, an affirmation of your ability to make it regardless of your gender – these are the kind of good citizen qualities that Margery tried to inculcate."

These were the values which Helen had already learnt at home and, however unhappy she might have been, she was, as she had been at primary school, a conscientious student who rarely, if ever, got into trouble. There were, of course, others who did, but Helen was not impressed: "It was my first exposure to girls who did play up. I didn't admire them. I thought they were a nuisance."

By her 5th Form year Helen was doing English, French, Latin, German, History and Maths, which she dropped the following year. Her favourite subject was History which was taught by Ann Trotter, a future Professor of History and Vice-Chancellor at Otago University. It was the human dimension of history that interested her, "the forces that shaped the world". She recalls being tremendously interested in Elizabeth I and in the origins of the two World Wars: "I never found it dull or boring, so it must have been well taught."

But the link between history and politics had not yet formed in Helen's mind. Indeed contemporary events in the outside world affected her very little:

"The first political event I remember was the assassination of Kennedy in 1963. That did impact on our boarding school. The President of the United States had been murdered. I remember in 1964-65 starting to be aware that Norman Kirk was rising to be the Leader of the Labour Party. And I remember Walter Nash dying in 1967."

But none of these events made any lasting impression on her. They were simply events, stories in the news. The Vietnam War was discussed in Ann Trotter's history class, but even that made little impact:

"I remember the war being discussed, but it was a long way away. In fact it's interesting when you think back to New Zealand and the Vietnam War, because for a lot of New Zealanders it was pre-television initially. We had no images in New Zealand of Vietnam at all. I went from boarding school into flats. I never had a television, so I had no image in my mind of anything coming back from there."

The war in Vietnam would nonetheless play a significant role in Helen's developing political consciousness. But that was still to come.

At the end of her 6th Form year, Helen left Epsom House and went boarding in Balmoral Road. There was nothing unusual in this. Very few girls stayed on at the hostel in their seventh year.

Helen biked to and from school on the pushbike George and Margaret had bought her – her very first bike. But if she felt a sense of release from her incarceration in the hostel, her new-found freedom appears to have done little to increase her general happiness.

Fay: "When Helen was in the 7th Form she was very restless and very unhappy. She hated the school and found it boring. She'd ring me up and say she was sick and she was miserable and she didn't want to go to school. I really felt then that she needed me at this time as she came to grips with her freedom. I think she was just like a prisoner who'd been let out and didn't know what to do with herself. She had all this freedom. She'd go to every film at the Film Festival and to everything that was on in Auckland, but I felt that at that time, when she got out of that boarding school, she was a bit disturbed. Perhaps it was because she'd had a lot of friends there, and then she was sort of on her own."

Helen had got School Certificate in 1965, been accredited with University Entrance in 1966 and in 1967, her last year at Epsom Girls Grammar School, obtained a 'B' bursary. It has to be said that her secondary school career was less than glittering. She did not stand out as a top student. Though the "rotten testimonial" which she got from Margery Adams may not have been helpful, it was probably, as she herself admits, "accurate at the time":

"I got perfectly credible results at school but they weren't the full potential. You wouldn't have picked from the school results that I would get a First Class Honours degree."

Margery Adams stands by her assessment of the future Prime Minister, which she says was based on reports and comments from other members of staff:

"I got the impression, and I still keep the impression, that we all felt that she didn't do herself justice, that she had far more to offer than the school ever discovered. Or else we didn't quite realise the struggle she was having. She told me once she was very shy, and I can quite imagine that."

Fay puts it more simply: "She hated the school. And she just hated the life."

Helen Clark left Epsom Girls Grammar with little idea of what career path she wanted to follow. What she was certain of was that she wanted to go to university.

chapter**four**

AWAKENING:
THE STUDENT YEARS

IT was not at all taken for granted in the Clark household that any of the girls would go to university. In *Head and Shoulders* Helen says that her parents were surprised that this was what she and Suzanne wanted to do. No one in the Clark family had ever been to university before, and primary school teaching was a more likely and more common career for intelligent young women of the time. But schoolteaching held little appeal for the 18-year-old, who wanted "something more stimulating than Training College".

And, increasingly, what Helen wanted, Helen got. Her refusal to play the organ or indeed attend church at all at Te Pahu was evidence of the emergence of a more determined and wilful personality than had previously been seen either by her parents or her teachers. George might have had occasion to think back to those "blue eyes staring at me" and his prediction that he "might have a certain amount of trouble".

No doubt some of this can be put down to that commonest cause of friction between parents and their children, teenage rebellion. But Helen had also had five years' experience of life in New Zealand's largest city, a very different existence to that of her parents in the small rural community of Te Pahu. Changes were also occurring in her thinking and in her perception of the world around her. She was becoming interested in politics, a different brand of politics to that of her parents. George and Margaret were staunch National Party supporters. They were farmers

A W A K E N I N G

and the farming community was the backbone of the Party. Te Pahu was no different from anywhere else. "In our whole area," says Margaret, "you knew just the one or two who happened to be Social Credit or Labour. The rest were just en bloc National."

The unions were the farmers' bête noir: "There was a strike in Horatiu one year and I reckon it cost me £20,000," George recalls. "You couldn't get your stock into the works, and they ate the grass others should have had, and so it went on and on down the system. That's why we were National Party."

On social and moral issues George and Margaret could also have been fairly described as conservative. Their oldest daughter, on the other hand, had begun in her final years at Epsom to see the world in a quite different light. Her ideas on the issues of the day – Vietnam, apartheid, nuclear weapons – were tending to the radical and left-wing, and she began to bring them home.

"Her ideas were diametrically opposed to ours in many ways," Margaret states. "I suppose she thought our ideas were ancient."

So Helen's visits home increasingly became occasions for arguments with her father, arguments which, Suzanne recalls, were heated and upsetting to the other members of the family:

"It was awful. They used to argue terribly, mainly at the tea table. Helen would come home from boarding school and they would argue. She was very left-wing and my Dad, at that stage, was very right. And of course he loved an argument."

No one, including George himself, takes issue with that. He genuinely loved to argue.

George: "My father would argue for the devil of it. He took the opposite side."

Margaret: "I remember a minister saying about arguments, that they're often a display of ignorance on both sides."

"No they aren't."

"Yes, they often are."

"It's dialogue. I enjoyed these debates with Helen."

"I don't agree with that. They were often quite unpleasant."

"But you can still enjoy them."

"People listening don't enjoy them."

"You didn't have to listen."

Often the family didn't listen. Jenefer recalls her reaction to this "dialogue":

"Dad can be quite an argumentative person, quite contrary. If you think one thing, he'll then try another train of thought. He just loves what he likes to call 'discussions', but for Mum and us they were arguments. Mum hated it, the arguing. She didn't take part in it. Sandra and I would leave the room. We just

didn't want any part of it. It was disrupting our normal, happy family life."

So while his wife and three younger daughters abhorred unpleasantness of any sort, George may well have been delighted when his oldest daughter returned from boarding school, spouting ideas that were diametrically opposed to his own. Here was a chance to flex his neglected dialectical muscles. And Helen was a worthy opponent, both intellectually and in her own determination not to give way. She was an arguer too.

Her father, it seems fair to say, looked forward to these "discussions" with his daughter, but to Helen it almost began to feel as if he were lying in wait for her when she came home, welcoming the opportunity to provoke another joust. Like her mother and sisters, she began to find these encounters unpleasant. Whether George was aware of it or not, a breach was developing between him and his daughter.

In 1968 Helen enrolled at Auckland University. She took History, German, English and Political Studies:

"Political Studies was sort of an add-on. A lot of people didn't do four subjects in the first year, so I added that on. I think I'd met people in the 7th Form at Epsom who said, 'Oh, Political Studies is really interesting.' And I thought, well, my family's got an interest in politics and I'll probably find it interesting. It was sort of like that."

The "add-on" was to bring Helen into contact with students and staff who would have a major influence on her thinking, her career and her life. But in this first year her concentration was almost exclusively on study:

"I've never been a morning person. I used to hate any lectures before 10 in the morning, but I'd come in by bus and spend the day at the university until the library closed at 10 at night. You would tend to take a chair in the library for the day, and then you'd pop out to your lectures, get a cup of coffee or lunch, that sort of thing."

She was a serious student. The traditional student pursuits – sex, booze, rock 'n roll – were not for her. She didn't drink, smoke, gamble or go to parties. She joined no student clubs or organisations during her first year. She was there to study, to learn and to do well. Her sole indulgence appears to have been the movies. But even here her tastes were towards the serious, the political and the instructive:

"I was always interested in anything with a current affairs perspective. So films like Costa Gavras' *Z* I found tremendously interesting. You see, when I was a student, Greece had a dictatorship. There were movies about that. And apart from that there was quite a strong cinematic strain coming out of Germany, movies looking at the German experience through the eyes of young radicals who had gone completely over the edge, the sort of 'Red Army'. I was interested in anything with a current affairs perspective, and there were a lot of movies at the time that built on those themes.

"I was also always very interested in films about what was happening in Latin America. I've always been interested in Latin America. While I was at university in 1970, Salvador Allende became Chile's first socialist president, only to be overthrown and killed in the Pinochet coup three years later. I was always tremendously interested in Allende and in the events after the coup. Which is why I took time I really didn't have last year to go to the swearing-in of the new Chilean president, Ricardo Lagos, the first left-wing politician to lead the country since Allende was murdered. It was a very emotional occasion and people from social democratic parties around the world came to support the new President. It was fantastic."

Films about political movements in remote foreign countries, films with a current affairs perspective – not most people's idea of a fun night out at the movies. Not like a good murder mystery or an entertaining comedy or romance:

"I've spent years reading about a huge range of current affairs issues, and years going to movies about those issues. And you find more than 30 years down the track, as Prime Minister, there's almost nothing that comes out that you haven't thought about, somewhere at some time. I won't say thought about at any length or in any depth, but I've read very, very widely and watched movies for a very long time. And it's paid off. And I prefer going to a serious movie. Comedy's got to be pretty amazingly good for me to go to. If I go to a film that's a bit light, it irritates me. I went to *Tea with Mussolini* and I thought it was so damn light, you just feel, god, what am I wasting my time here for? I can't be bothered."

Helen had a readymade, if not always entirely enthusiastic companion to take to the movies – Suzanne. No keener than her older sister to spend a day longer than necessary in the hostel, Suzanne had gone boarding, then flatting with Helen in her 7th Form year. Helen felt the same sense of responsibility towards her younger sibling that she had felt when the two used to travel on the bus to Te Pahu School and the boys tried to knock off their woolly hats.

"We were good mates," Suzanne says. "We never argued. I just did what I was told usually. Helen's always been a leader. She was never bossy. She just liked to organise people and I suppose I was the obvious choice. And it wasn't just organising. She looked after people and she looked after me. She was the oldest child. I think oldest children become protective of the younger ones and look after them."

Suzanne had joined her older sister at Epsom in 1964. Margaret drove the two girls to Auckland, without George who, as he had sworn the year before, was not prepared "to go through that again". After the ritual uniform-buying at John Courts, she deposited her daughters at the hostel and waved goodbye. Suzanne, determined to win her 10 shillings, did not cry, at least not till her mother had gone:

"I was terribly homesick, as I imagine Helen was. But I remember going and sitting in her room. I don't know whether I cried then, but I wasn't very happy. So I can imagine how she must have felt the year before, knowing no one. That would have been really tough."

Helen looked after Suzanne for the next four years at Epsom:

"She was always concerned with what I was doing and always kept regular tabs on me. She'd make sure she saw me every day, make sure I was alright, that things were going well. Just general caring; caring about how people are getting on. She's a very caring sort of person."

With her school years behind her, Suzanne decided she'd had enough. She didn't want to go to university. She got a job as a micro-biological technician at the Meat Research Institute in Hamilton. But this did not suit her older sister, who thought she could do better. Suzanne was not fulfilling her potential. Helen advised her to reconsider her earlier decision and go to university. Suzanne took the advice and, after a year in the workforce, enrolled at Auckland in 1970:

"Helen continued to look after me at university. The year I enrolled, she completely took me round and did everything for me. I didn't even know what I'd done.

I think the same thing happened the second year. In the third year I decided I'd better go and enrol myself, so that I'd know what to do. You see, she wasn't bossy. She looked after people. And it came out with me, Jenefer and Sandra. And now it's still coming out through all her nephews and nieces. She likes to guide people and get them to realise their potential."

This is the single most common theme to emerge in conversation with Helen's family and friends: she looks after people, she cares. It is completely at odds with the image that dominated the media from the time when she first came to prominence in the mid-1980s until well into her first year as Prime Minister, an image of a cold, hard, unfeeling woman, unnatural in her refusal to have children, distant from the everyday concerns of ordinary families, a humourless intellectual driven only by ambition for political power. Those, including the author, who know Helen well, see a very different person – warm, caring, generous to a fault and with a rich sense of humour. If the reality belies the image, and it does, it is because Helen does not wear her heart on her sleeve. While she cares deeply, her caring is not sentimental. It is practical, focused.

With her foreign language requirement now out of the way, Helen was able to

drop German in her second university year. She also decided not to continue with English:

"I actually got to concentrate on the things I was really interested in, which were History and Politics. I did Stage II History, Stage II Politics and Asian Politics, with half a year on China and half a year on Japan."

Helen's decision to continue with Political Studies was not greeted with enthusiasm at home. George and Margaret had never really regarded it as a proper subject. It had no practical application. They would have preferred their daughter to study something more useful to her future career. English, History and languages were fine, but what on earth could you do with Political Studies?

They were not alone in their thinking. The recently appointed Minister of Finance, one Robert David Muldoon, was of the view that the purpose of a university education was to provide the student with a passport to employment. Too many students were wasting their own and the country's money on airy-fairy Arts degrees when they could have been taking practical subjects such as Science, Engineering or Accountancy. He was particularly scathing about Political Studies, which was not merely pointless and irrelevant but subversive.

Left **The big catch.** *Opposite Page* **At Kawau Island, 1970.**

Helen took a different view: "In those days you weren't really that job-focused as a student. You went to university, did your Arts degree or your Science degree. You were carrying on your education. The idea wasn't that you would have a meal ticket, because everybody did get a job. So that wasn't a concern at all. I mean, you'd have thought about the job at the end of your education – what will I do now, will I train specifically for something, will I go to Teachers College or what? You weren't job-focused, you were education-focused. Political Studies was no more pointless than doing English, History, French or other Romance languages. People just didn't think about that. It was the joy of study. I guess it's different now."

George and Margaret may have had cause to be concerned about Helen's decision to continue with Political Studies in her second year. Politics was beginning to dominate their daughter's thinking and it was not a brand of politics which they themselves embraced. In a telling passage in *Head and Shoulders*, the future Prime Minister summarised her political awakening at school and university:

> I was in my element at university. I'd started to pick up more radical ideas in the 6th and 7th forms when New Zealand first got involved in the Vietnam War. When I got to university in 1968 it was the period of student revolt around the world, which rolled over into a rather wimpish response in New Zealand with student forums and other activities.
>
> Politics had a tremendous impact on me. I hadn't planned to do a Political Science degree but I started to study politics and seemed to drift naturally toward the political causes on campus, like the campaign against Omega foreign military bases. That was the first demonstration I went on and I really enjoyed it. The Vietnam War dominated my second year and had a decisive impact on student thinking. I became involved in the growing anti-Vietnam War movement. In my third year, 1970, the All Black Tour of South Africa took place. Three really important events. I thought a lot about racism and joined Trevor Richards' Halt All Racist Tours committee. During those years I had a sense of finding my identity through being politicised.

In 1970, her third year, Helen took History and Political Studies. "So I was very focused." Her extra-curricular political activities included participating in demonstrations against the Vietnam War and sporting contact with South Africa.

New Zealand had committed troops to the Vietnam War in 1965. Rob Muldoon, who had visited Vietnam in 1963, summarised the Holyoake Government's position in his book *The Rise and Fall of a Young Turk*, published a decade later:

> Let us get our thinking straight. In 1963 the communists were the aggressors.

Their apologists in New Zealand were claiming that North Vietnam was taking no part in the Viet Cong attacks, a lie that today has been shown to be absurd. The Ho Chi Minh Trail was operating then and Russia and China were supplying the sinews of war. Since that visit I have continuously studied the Vietnam situation, and I pay tribute to the United States for carrying the burden of one of the dirtiest wars in history because their leaders knew they were right.

Helen's view was somewhat different: "My position was that it was a war between Vietnamese, that New Zealand had no place to be there. And I didn't see it as part of an inexorable tide of communism sweeping down from Russia to China to Vietnam, and then to Malaysia, to Singapore and across the straits to Australia and New Zealand. People talked of that 'red tide' at the time. That was the conservative position. It was transparently ridiculous."

On one thing Helen Clark and Rob Muldoon would have agreed: the Vietnam issue had lost Labour the 1966 election. "1966," Muldoon concluded in *The Rise and Fall of a Young Turk*, "was the 'Vietnam' election. Keith Holyoake brilliantly pointed up the issues and put the Labour Party on the other side. The people voted for involvement."

The young politics student was less impressed with the National Prime Minister: "Holyoake had become a figure of fun, a caricature of himself – the booming voice, the marble in the mouth. The students had no time for him. They thought he was pompous with nothing to be pompous about."

Pompous or not, Holyoake would win the 1969 election. New Zealand troops would remain in Vietnam. Helen Clark would take to the streets:

"I can clearly remember being part of a demonstration outside the American Consulate in central Auckland in 1970, when the Americans invaded Parrot's Beak in Cambodia. But that wasn't the first one I'd been on. There were others before that. I wasn't a front-runner or banner-carrier, just one of the troops."

Vietnam was not the only issue to divide New Zealanders in the 1960s and early 1970s. Debate over sporting contacts with South Africa had raged across the country since the late 1950s when the 'No Maoris, No Tour' movement came into prominence. Despite the growing protests, the All Blacks toured South Africa in 1960. There were no Maori players in the team. Five years later the Springboks came to New Zealand where they played against teams containing Maori. But any illusions that this indicated a softening in South Africa's policies on mixed-race sport at home were soon dispelled when President Hendrik Verwoerd announced that Maori would not be allowed to play with white players during the proposed All Black tour of his country in 1967. To his credit, Keith Holyoake rejected the

invitation by the South African Rugby Board to tour without Maori players. The All Blacks subsequently returned to South Africa in 1970. The team contained two Maori and two Pacific Islanders, one of them the legendary Bryan Williams. They were officially classified as "honorary whites".

The argument now moved beyond the issue of mixed-race teams to whether New Zealand should maintain sporting contacts with South Africa at all. The conditions existed for a bitter debate that would polarise opinion in New Zealand for more than a decade, turning friend against friend, family member against family member. And nowhere did that debate rage more fiercely than between Helen and her father.

George's view was the same as that of most of New Zealand's other rugby fans: politics should be kept out of sport. Apartheid was offensive, certainly, but sanctions and isolation, far from persuading the Verwoerd Government to heed the opinion of the rest of the world, would only harden its resolve not to have its domestic policy dictated by foreigners. Dialogue and the Holyoake Government's policy of "building bridges" provided the best hope of persuading white South Africa that apartheid was an egregious breach of human rights:

"My opinion was to keep sport out of politics, just like the time when the Americans wouldn't go to the Olympic Games in Moscow. They made the wrong decision and Moscow did the same thing when the Olympics were held in America. It was wrong. It was contact between countries."

The passage fails to do justice to the depth of George's feelings on the issue. To understand that, it is necessary to look ahead.

George was passionate about his rugby, so passionate that in 1976 he joined an All Black supporters tour to South Africa. Though there were Maori on the New Zealand team, their racial status in South Africa was unclear. The timing of the tour, which coincided with the Soweto uprising and had the official blessing of the Prime Minister, Rob Muldoon, could not have been more provocative. 1976 was the year of the Montreal Olympics, and black African nations, due to take part in the Games, demanded that New Zealand be excluded. When their demand was refused, 31 nations withdrew from the competition.

In the following year, the Gleneagles Agreement, discouraging sporting contact by Commonwealth countries with South Africa, was signed by the leaders of those nations, including the New Zealand Prime Minister. But four years later, again with the tacit blessing of Rob Muldoon, the Springboks came to New Zealand. They played in Auckland, New Plymouth and Gisborne. Two games, in Hamilton and Timaru, were cancelled because of the activities of anti-tour demonstrators.

The 1981 Springbok tour saw New Zealander pitted against New Zealander in the most bitter and violent confrontations since the Queen Street riots of 1932 or the 1951 waterfront strike. And George was in the thick of it:

"We were going down Sandringham Road to Eden Park and we had to cross over the street and there was this great line of protesters going up. I was with my little brother-in-law, Marian's husband, and I said, 'Are we going to wait till they go past before we go through, Ray?' And he said, 'Like hell!' And he waddles through this lot and his hat got knocked off. And somebody picked it up and gave it back to him. So we went through these people and when we got to the other side there was a fellow sitting in a wheelchair, and I'd seen this guy before, and he said, 'I saw you knock that woman down'. And I said, 'What rot are you talking?' This was the propaganda they put through at that time. My old grandfather always brought us up, you always had to be good to women and little children."

George took a carload of supporters to New Plymouth: "And I had a hunk of alkathene up my sleeve that day too. And I went up to a policeman and said, 'You want a hand today?' And he said, 'Oh no, I think we've got things organised.' I wouldn't have minded having a bit of a go. If I had to. Never been frightened of trouble."

Then there was the cancelled match in Hamilton. Fay remembers George coming back:

"I was at my mother's house when George returned from that match in Hamilton. He came inside and my mother laughed and laughed and laughed at him. His eyes were sticking out on stalks, he was in such a fury. It was absolutely unbelievable."

Margaret: "George was at the match in Hamilton which didn't get played. He came home and he had a face like thunder and glared at me. He glared at whoever else was here, as though we were the cause of all his misfortunes at missing the match."

George: "Actually, we were sitting up in the stand and we see these people breaking in and I wanted to get out of the stand and go down and drag some of them off and my young brother wouldn't let me. I reckon I missed a day that day. I could have dragged a few off."

Margaret: "He was wild, really wild that the match had been cancelled."

But while George was getting enraged, his daughter was out there protesting. She had been protesting since 1969. First the Omega bases, then Vietnam, then sporting contacts with South Africa. Suzanne recalls being dragooned into joining her:

"I wasn't interested in politics, and I'm still not. But Helen dragged me along on a few demonstrations. I just went along because I was told to. I was a serious Science student. Politics was not my interest. And I probably also went along because I thought it would be a bit of a laugh. I remember going on two demonstrations, the anti-tour one that walked down Queen Street and one against the Vietnam War, I think. They were pretty tame when I look back. We just walked down Queen Street with these banners out that someone had made."

Tame perhaps. But the mood of those demonstrators is elegantly expressed by Trevor Richards:

"We felt determined, confident and optimistic. We were on a roll. The forces of reaction were represented by rugby tours and Keith Holyoake and Richard Nixon and the war in Vietnam and nuclear bombs. And we were fresh and new and different. And we were going to change everything, as no doubt many generations have felt. But we felt that confidently and passionately. And I think a lot of the strength that we had came from the strength that we gave each other. And when we were attacked, whether it was by a Prime Minister or by someone coming out of a rugby game, we used it as confirmation that we were right. And on we would go."

In the same year that she joined HART, Helen joined the University Labour Club. This formalisation of her growing political allegiance to the Left was influenced to some extent by the fact that she was soon to turn 21:

"You have to remember that in those days you didn't get the vote until age 21. So in my first three years at university, you weren't a participant in the political process. I didn't get my first vote until the 1972 election, when I was 22. So really I was operating outside politics in '68 and '69, which was the last election I wasn't involved in."

In the following year, 1971, she attended the AGM of the university branch of the Labour Party, the Princes Street branch, and signed up as a member. She left the meeting as Vice-President of the branch:

"I joined Labour quite consciously because it had lost four elections in a row. It was obvious that the things I'd become really interested in, like rugby and South Africa, or New Zealand slavishly following the Americans, as in Vietnam, weren't going to stop under a conservative government."

The Princes Street branch of the Labour Party had been the brainchild of Roger Douglas's father, Norman Douglas. Aware that the Party membership was aging, he believed there was an urgent need to attract and engage young people, particularly in the university. Early members of the branch included such notables as Keith Sinclair, Walter Potts and Jonathan Hunt. By 1971, when Helen was elected Vice-President, membership was dominated by university students and staff, many of them from the Political Studies Department. Ruth Butterworth, then Associate Professor in the department, was a moving force in the branch:

"Princes Street was about forming policy for the Labour Party. It was quite different from the 'Jumping Sundays' and the *Bullshit and Jellybeans* side of the scene. It was a real serious commitment to introducing policy and pushing it through. The members, including myself, wrote the policy – on education, the role of the universities, broadcasting, the environment, foreign policy and so on. The liberal issues. I wouldn't say the branch was left-wing in New Zealand terms. It was strictly central. The whole point of the exercise was to push policy into the Labour Party. You have to remember that no constituency party ever in the North Island really had the numbers to go to the Party Conferences, so the members of the Princes Street branch were on offer to all these constituency branches. That meant that they could form a bloc that could push policy. And we wrote policy."

Ruth was to be a major influence on the young Helen Clark:

"The students loved Ruth, who was also very good to the students, took a great interest in them. And not just in the M.A. classes. Ruth took tutorials on British politics at Stage II and the Stage III classes were quite small in those days. So we got to know her from the time we were 19, and she was very supportive, very sympathetic to and empathetic with students.

"She was also unusual. In those days there were very few women university teachers. It was very rare for a woman to get near Associate Professor status as she did, so she was a role model. Remember, we're talking about the days when there were only a handful of women in the Law School. When Silvia Cartwright in the 1960s was the only woman in her class in Law School in university. When Margaret Wilson and Sian Elias were among little more than a handful of women students in Law School. The girls at university were in Arts, the brainy ones in Science, but they weren't in the professional schools.

"And what also made her exciting was that she'd had a long involvement with the Labour Party. She'd served as a councillor in London. She'd travelled widely. She lived alone. She was a successful woman who never married, never had children. So that was a different option. I admired her as an independent, free spirit."

Ruth accepts the compliment: "I was a role model for a vast number of young women at that time. There were only 11 women on the academic staff of the University of Auckland in the mid-1960s. It was years and years later that I realised

Left **Helen and Jenefer at Waihi Beach.** *Opposite Page* **Out on the farm with Jenefer; Helen riding Toby.**

this, because I was accustomed to doing my own thing. But I was also a woman living alone and that was novel as far as they were concerned. And I did a weekly column for *Zealandia* and wrote for student newspapers about what I thought. So it had, I gather, an enormous impact."

Ruth's influence on her students was personal, intellectual and political:

"I taught them all about South Africa. That was my Stage III course. All that activism came out of that class. One of the things you have to remember about New Zealand at that time is that there weren't very many books in the library. So I was buying books which the library couldn't afford to buy and lending them to students. I had a lot of South African stuff and a lot on Africa as a whole. So I was giving kids things to read which they would otherwise not necessarily ever have come across."

"She was definitely influential," Helen confirms, "although I never did any work on South Africa myself for that course. There were very few books about Africa and, as she says, she probably brought them in. I remember writing an essay about Lumumba, the first President of the independent Congo and one on Nyerere and African Socialism. Ruth was also an inspirational figure, because she opened up a wider world. She was fascinating on British Politics, she was fascinating on Africa, and then there was her M.A. course, which was about Communications and the Media."

AWAKENING

The Political Studies Department at Auckland University was, it has to be said, a hotbed of left-wing activity. Its staff and students formed the core of the Princes Street branch of the Labour Party. Journalist Bill Ralston, who took Political Studies at Auckland in the early 1970s, recalls some of the people who were around at the time:

"Michael Rann, who is the Labour leader now in South Australia and may well be the next Premier, was in the Political Studies Department. Auckland University was the birthplace of a lot of Labour politicians. Margaret Wilson was in Law at the time. Ruth Butterworth obviously was there and Barry Gustafson. I was there, a couple of years behind Helen Clark and Phil Goff. Richard Northey was there. Michael Bassett was in the History Department. And there was Jonathan Hunt who was a sort of godfather and always around, very much a presence in a philosophical sense. And Mike Moore hung around the edges. In fact I can remember Phil Goff got me, Michael Rann and a whole pile of other people to go out and campaign for Mike in Mount Eden in 1972. It was very activist Young Labour.

"The overwhelming mood in that department at the time – and it was such a left-wing department – was the horror of Muldoon. He was a focal point for the hatred and distrust of virtually everyone there on a variety of levels. I was very inter-ested in French nuclear testing and his attitude towards that I found despicable. Other people found his attitude to the South African tours despicable, or the Vietnam War, or the trade union movement at the time which was under heavy attack. It went on and on and on."

Helen had gained her B.A. in 1970 and gone on to study for her M.A. in Politics. She describes the next two years as a period when she came into her own:

"You have to put it in context. I'd had a happy childhood, sort of top of the class through primary school. You go to Epsom Girls, it's a huge city school, you're always on the outside because you're a boarder. You go to university. No one in your family's ever been to university before, so you're always trying to prove something, that you're actually up to it. And by the time you become an M.A. student, you're starting to get a string of straight A's. And of course your whole perception of your-self goes up."

Her perception of herself could scarcely have been higher than her thesis super-visor's perception of her. Professor Bob Chapman, formerly Associate Professor of History at Auckland, had founded the Political Studies Department in 1964. Already a distinguished academic, he was to become in the 1960s and 1970s New Zealand's best-known and most respected political analyst appearing on the relatively new medium of television. He had a special interest in broadcasting and in 1985-86 chaired the Royal Commission on Broadcasting and Related Telecommunications in New Zealand. He was awarded the CMG in 1987 for his services to education and broadcasting.

But in 1972 he was Helen Clark's professor and the supervisor of her M.A. thesis, entitled 'Political Attitudes of the New Zealand Countryside':

"She looked at Federated Farmers and all the constituent things that went to make up a country MP and a country MP's opinions. And how experience in Federated Farmers was so frequently the key to getting a nomination, almost exclusively for the National Party. And, of course, being a country woman herself was an enormous help."

There is no doubt that Helen Clark was Bob Chapman's star pupil. And there was never any doubt that she would get her M.A:

"And a first class one. Oh, running away. She was what she had already appeared to be all the way up – a first class student throughout. As soon as she began to write essays, she shone. I noticed the main features of the mind early on and they grew more intensive in their demonstration. First was her great capacity to be able to get a mass of detail and sort it, not only into order, but into analytical order, so that it constituted a proper argument. And the argument was of the kind that you look for – straight to the point. She was one of those who looked at the question she was asked and thought about it before saying, doing, writing anything else, and it was that point that she came to – the point of her argument. No waste, no decoration for decoration's sake, thorough and a very fine grasp of the English language. She knew exactly what she wanted to say and said it concisely.

"The characteristics of the mind were, if anything, intensified with the experience of the university. I might say that when you went into her study at the university, there were piles of documents, books – a very full library – and just documents in every direction, newspapers folded so the particular thing would appear. It might have looked disordered to a casual observer, but watch her work it! If she wanted something, the hand went out to the right pile, she went down the pile, and bang, out came the document. It was one of the most perfect examples of why somebody who doesn't know a subject shouldn't interfere with the scholar's arrangements.

"She thrived on argument. But again, it was the clarity of her analysis that shone forth. She'd say, 'Aren't you forgetting such and such? There's this to consider.' She wasn't an aggressive arguer. She used clarity of analysis again and again. She clears up a field in which muddle is the stock and trade of people who are trying to agitate the question."

Ruth Butterworth agrees and adds a further dimension: "She's extremely intelligent. But she's also developed the ability to apply commonsense. So if you've got intelligence, which is very highly honed, because she reads and always has, combined with commonsense, you've got a great mixture."

Professor Barry Gustafson, then a lecturer in the Political Studies Department, has a clear early memory of the young M.A. student: "She did my course on political parties in Western democracies. And I remember she was the best student in the class. On this particular occasion she gave a seminar and Bob Chapman and Peter Aimer were sitting in on it as well. The seminar was good, but I felt she could have pushed herself harder in some of the questions, so I started to push her in the discussion. And Bob actually came to me after the seminar and said, 'Remember that Helen is a student. You pushed her very hard. She's not a staff member and you were forcing her into a corner.' And I can remember saying to Bob, 'Well, I wouldn't have done it if I hadn't thought that Helen had the ability, if pushed, to come up with a better analysis.' And I was very conscious of her, as a good student who could go a long way in academic life and also in the Labour movement."

Bob Chapman's enthusiastic approval of Helen Clark was reciprocated and their relationship went beyond that of mere teacher and pupil. He became her mentor, sounding-board and valued friend:

"Bob had a great influence on several generations of students," Helen says. "He was the dominant intellectual figure around the Arts and Social Sciences at university, there's no question about that. He was a very inspiring person, a very compelling lecturer and, with his wife Noeline, very supportive of his students. He was also a highly ethical man. He had a deep interest in and abhorrence of nuclear weapons. It took a lot of courage for his generation of academics to take a public stand on the immorality of nuclear weapons, a stand which undoubtedly attracted the interest of the Security Intelligence Service in the days of Brigadier Gilbert and the Cold War. I think it was very courageous. He also took a deep interest in Maori politics and society, personally teaching a course on it and maintaining a wide range of contacts in Maoridom, which was very unusual for a Pakeha academic at that time.

"And I remember Bob saying that when he was a student at university he never expected to be a university lecturer, that it was always his assumption and Noeline's that they would be teachers. And specifically they would be teachers in the Native School System, because they were young and idealistic, and the Maori schools or Native Schools were where young, idealistic, white liberals went.

"Bob always encouraged his students to read widely and to have a wide general knowledge. And he himself ranged very widely. He had the historical interests, the contemporary current affairs interests. And he had been a great reader of literature. I remember reading a seminal article he had written in *Landfall* in 1948 on New

Zealand literature and what it was expressing. And he and Noeline always had a great interest in the visual arts and bought an early McCahon. He was, in a way, a renaissance man."

Though he never joined the Labour Party, the "renaissance man's" personal politics were firmly on the Left. To his great credit, he never allowed this to influence his television analysis or commentary. But where his sympathies lay became clear on election night 1969. The election was a cliff-hanger. Late in the television broadcast, which was watched by the entire country on the nation's one channel, Professor Chapman became convinced that Labour had triumphed and excitedly announced, "We won!" What made this doubly unfortunate was that it was wrong. Keith Holyoake's National Government held on to power with a six-seat majority.

As they worked together and their friendship deepened, Bob became a father-figure to his young pupil. It is a term which both are happy to accept:

"I think any mentor is; that's part of growing up," he comments. "Adults have more than one friend, more than one centre. It became a warm relationship really over the thesis, but it went back a long way. It was always a happy relationship when she was going through the various stages of her degree, but you don't get into the intricacy of someone's mind in the way you do when you're acting as the supervisor of a thesis. That's when you really get to grips with the mind."

Helen agrees: "Yes. He was my father's age. He was very generous."

Brian: "But these two men were complete opposites, weren't they?"

Helen "Yes, completely. Put it this way. My beliefs in those years were shaped by Bob Chapman, not my father."

Helen would certainly not have said this to her parents at the time. But Buddy Arthur recalls that the family were worried about the Political Studies professor:

"I remember that my father, Murray, who is George's uncle, thought Professor Chapman had a very strong influence on her thinking and the way she developed. He thought she only heard one side of the story."

Buddy's husband, Eddie Hooper, puts it more directly: "Murray, or Mick as he was known, used to get quite wound up about it. He'd say, 'She won't be thinking for herself if she's coming under that prune's influence.' Mick used to call him 'an asphalt farmer. Thought he knew all about farming, but he'd only walked the footpaths and he wouldn't know a cow's backside from a tent.' That's how Mick used to explain it."

So here you have a recipe for conflict: a father who is a longtime supporter of the National Party, a daughter who is a committed supporter of the Labour Party; a father with conservative views on social and moral issues, a daughter with liberal or even radical views; a father who supports New Zealand's involvement in the

Vietnam conflict, a daughter who joins demonstrations against it; a father who has nothing but contempt for those who protest against sporting contacts with South Africa, a daughter who is one of those protestors; a country father whose daughter's social and political beliefs are being shaped not by him but by an academic in Auckland; a father who loves to argue, a daughter who will not back down.

This should put in context the breach that occurred between Helen and George in the early 1970s, a wound that would not be fully healed for more than a decade.

It seems unlikely that George saw things quite in this light. To him, arguing was a form of intellectual arm-wrestling. A test of strength. Fun. Nothing personal. That he looked forward to these rumbles with his daughter – and his daughter's friends – seems beyond doubt. The changes in Helen that had occurred at boarding school and university were merely grist to the mill:

George: "It made the arguments much more interesting,"

Margaret: "Her ideas conflicted greatly with ours, about most things. We certainly weren't left-wing radicals, let's face it. I remember once she brought this whole group home, there must have been 20 of them, the Youth Socialist Movement or something. They were from all different countries and she brought them down one day in four or five carloads to the farm, showed them around, and I supplied them with morning tea and lunch and all the rest of it. And one of them said to George…"

George: "'…How can Helen be a socialist and yet you've got all this – the farm. You've got so much.' And I said, 'If you want to work hard enough and as long as I have, perhaps you'll reach the same goal.'"

Margaret: "And she used to bring other fellows too. Doug Andrews. He got into the IMF or the World Bank."

George: "He was quite interesting. He came down to the farm one day and Doug was a socialist and he and I argued the whole weekend. And he came up to the woolshed to say goodbye and I said, 'By Jove, Doug, we've had a great time.' I said, 'I've won some and you've won some.' And he said, 'Mr Clark, I don't think I won any.' I met him down in Parliament donkeys years later, and I went up to Doug and I said, 'How do my ideas stand up after all this time?' And he said, 'You know, Mr Clark, they're still good.'"

It's possible that Helen brought her university friends home to lend her moral support or perhaps to provide her father with an alternative target. Certainly these occasions seem to have been less distressing to the rest of the family than the one-on-one arguments between father and daughter around the tea table. Sandra even enjoyed the visits from her sister's radical friends:

"She used to bring friends home. Different sorts of people who used to have

Left **With close friend René Wilson, later New Zealand's High Commissioner in South Africa.**

wonderful arguments with Dad. They were her university friends. They probably had very different views from my father in those days. I think it was interesting. We didn't have a lot of contact with those sort of people and they talked to me, and that was nice, someone different to talk to about things."

Considerably less pleasant were the arguments about South Africa. George, as we have seen, was passionate about rugby. His was the clarion call of every New Zealander who believed it was his absolute right to see the All Blacks pummel the Springboks, whether in Auckland or Johannesburg – "Keep politics out of sport!" Helen's view was that apartheid was an unconscionable crime against humanity and that to associate with evil was to condone evil. She would have none of it.

Both views were deeply and sincerely felt and neither could see the other's point of view. The irresistible force meets the immovable object.

George's view of these confrontations remains that they were constructive. He denies that they caused any breach in the family: "No. I've always said that Helen and I probably both learned from this."

"What did you learn?" Margaret asks.

"To listen to other people's views and find that yours weren't necessarily always the right ones. And I told her she'd have to learn to compromise in life, and at that stage compromise wasn't part of her nature."

Right **Suzanne finished her B.Sc. Honours in 1972, the same year that Helen completed her M.A.**

But this constructive view of the arguments between Helen and her father was not shared by the rest of the family, who found them increasingly unpleasant and divisive.

Fay: "This was a very bad time, a terrible time for the extended family. Some of the family, for example my mother and my youngest brother, hated it and usually took no part in the heated political discussions that were taking place down on the farm. My husband and I, who were Labour voters, were glad to have Helen as an ally, because up until then we were like my grandfather, Thomas Clark, fighting a losing battle against a house full of Nats. Cath Tizard once spoke to me about the conflict between Helen and her father and she told me that Helen used to return home from a weekend in Te Pahu really hurt."

Helen began to stay away from home. Reflecting on these events, she told

Virginia Myers: "The teenage conflicts I'd had with my parents became more explicitly political once I got to university. We had very serious disagreements about politics, Vietnam, South Africa, everything."

Helen's judgement of her parents in the Myers interview is in places less than kind. But it must be remembered that the interview took place in 1985, four years after the 1981 Springbok tour that had divided the country. The worst and most bitter conflicts between her and her father over sporting contacts with South Africa were still relatively fresh in her mind. Helen's first term in Parliament as an Opposition back-bencher, from 1981 to 1984, had also been bruising and she was disappointed not to have gained a Cabinet post in the Lange Government after the 1984 election. The whole Myers interview has a sour and angry tone.

Though she does not deny having said any of the things that appear in *Head and Shoulders,* Helen is unhappy with the piece which, she says, "…purported to be in the first person, but was actually so shorn of any qualification that it was quite misleading."

By the time the book was published, the relationship between Helen and her parents had also begun to mend. Though George would not bring himself to vote Labour until 1990, he and Margaret were proud of their daughter's achievements, attended her graduation ceremonies, followed her career with interest and were supportive of it.

Looking back today, Helen says both she and her parents have mellowed. She describes her father as "a good person". George still believes he was right about sporting contacts with South Africa, but the subject isn't likely to come up:

"I always talk politics with Helen if I get half a chance, and give her a bit of advice too. But we don't do anything controversial, because she's got enough problems without arguing with me."

Helen and Suzanne flatted together for most of their student careers. There were numerous flats, the early ones chosen for their proximity to a bus route. Fay remembers driving Helen round hunting for flats, but the transport situation was soon due to improve:

"They had motor-scooters and often came to visit. They always wore protective clothing, oil-proof leggings, big coats, scarves, hats. My daughter used to go into hysterics when they'd be getting ready to leave with all these clothes."

The scooter gear made an early impression on Professor Chapman too: "She was noticeable from the beginning. The leather jacket and pants. She used to ride here on her motorbike, with her leathers, and she'd park the bike by the fence. And perhaps put her leathers on the back of the bike or the front porch and come on in for her thesis supervision."

Helen wore her hair long and flowing and parted in the middle in the manner of the student radicals of the 1970s. Fay regarded it as an unattractive style:

"She wore the very drab clothes of the era. And she had metal teeth-braces for years and years. And one weekend she came out and she had a piece of stainless steel wire boring a hole in her cheek, and my husband cut it off with some pliers. Who but Helen could have put up with that, suffered that pain? She's tough."

Not everyone agreed with Fay's assessment of Helen's looks. Ruth Butterworth says that she was "pale and wan", but remembers noticing her excellent bone structure when she appeared on television at an early Labour Party conference.

Jonathan Hunt recalls that she was considerably heavier than she is today: "She was big. Oh yes. But the first thing I noticed was what beautiful skin she had. I mean it really was noticeable. She didn't dress very well but I didn't worry too much about that, because I was interested in what she was saying. But I worked out that here was a potentially very beautiful woman."

Mike Williams, now President of the New Zealand Labour Party, was doing an M.A. in History in the early 1970s, and had joined the Princes Street branch, where he encountered Helen. He found her "spunky, attractive from a male point of view, with a good sense of humour."

Barry Gustafson agrees: "Although she wasn't a fashion plate in terms of dressing up to the nines, I always regarded Helen as a very attractive young woman. I have to admit that I can actually remember admiring her, and not just her mind but as a person, and her looks and everything else. She was very attractive, a little shy at first, I think it's fair to say, and that may well have been why Bob Chapman and one or two others were a bit protective. Because she was a nice, pleasant, exceedingly shy and sensitive young woman when she was a young student."

In the *Head and Shoulders* interview Helen leaves the impression of being overly serious and obsessed with politics to the exclusion of everything else: "I became very focused. All my interests were concentrated on political activity or study. By then I was a graduate student and all my courses were in politics. I went to a lot of meetings and was out every night, mostly to do with politics. I'd found something I was really interested in and that totally absorbed me… I became so involved that politics *was* me in a sense. A symbiotic relationship."

Helen again regards the passage as having been "stripped of context":

"I actually really enjoyed political involvement, so I didn't do a lot else, apart from going to the movies at the film festival. So your friends tended to be people who were active in the Labour Party with you. Almost everything else was excluded because you were very, very busy. If you talk to other people who were around at the time, like Phil Goff, they'll tell you the same thing, that you spent your

Left **Bob Chapman and his wife Noeline. Professor Chapman became Helen's thesis supervisor and a major influence on her political thinking. They remain good friends.**

Saturdays canvassing, your Monday nights at electorate meetings and you'd always be on a planning group for something or other. I wouldn't call it obsessive, but you were very committed and you put a lot of time into it, all your spare time when you weren't preparing your lectures, writing your thesis and that sort of thing. Any spare time that you had, that was your main interest."

The impression is left that there was no time in Helen's life for fun, frivolity or even the normal student contacts that make life at university so pleasant and memorable. Bill Ralston saw Helen as a very serious person, totally committed to politics:

"She was always extremely pleasant. A little bit reserved. The classic term is 'bluestocking'. She was quite an academic woman. She wasn't a frivolous woman. She was very concerned with a whole pile of quite weighty issues as young people can be. But I wouldn't describe her as a radical in the Abby Hoffman sense of the term. She was probably still middle of the road then, but took very serious positions

AWAKENING

on those issues. You wouldn't find her at the Kiwi pub on a Friday night or at the parties. I remember that Ruth Butterworth organised for Julius Nyerere, the President of Tanzania, to come over and there was a cocktail function at the old Government House, and I remember her there. And there's Julius Nyerere, one of the most interesting figures in African politics at the time, a great socialist leader, senior government figures and possibly Norman Kirk himself. And I can remember her being there and thinking to myself, 'Boy, is she in her element!'"

Bob and Noeline Chapman paint a slightly different picture:

"She wasn't blinkered at all," Noeline says. "Bob used to invite some of the students and young staff around for get-togethers. Perhaps we'd come back from America and wanted to play them some records. She loved jazz and classical music. She would love all that."

"She had a very wide interest culturally," Bob recalls. "There's a lot of social life of a most varied sort in Labour and in the university. She certainly was part of all that. She wasn't a swot. Nor a bluestocking. In her, frivolity turns out to be a quite serious thing. She's got a very fine sense of humour. My memory of her sessions here – and I'd have two or three hours discussing what she was doing at a given time on her thesis – is a memory of smiles. We got along easily because we could both recognise the humour in a lot of situations. Particularly situations around the university. She never missed. If you made a crack, she got there. She got there instantaneously and a smile would come on. You can see it today in a lot of her interviews on TV. She doesn't miss the humour of things. She's not humourless. Quite the opposite. She has a very quick sense of humour."

Noeline: "She always reminds me of a well-educated European intellectual, and you meet them most in Scandinavia. They're serious-minded. They're well educated. They like good music. They like to go to galleries. They like to think about those things. She also could be very amused by politicians. Never talked out of court, but if something was known, we could have a good laugh about it all. My fondest memory is of her laughing with the young people around."

Bob: "I agree. We saw her at her very best when she was here socially, or when we were discussing her thesis, because it was such an active, reciprocal conversation that we'd get. I look back at her as one of the finest students I've ever seen and known, and you do know them as a supervisor."

Helen was no bluestocking to her younger sisters either. Jenefer made several trips to Auckland while she was at high school and remembers those visits as exciting and eye-opening:

"To have two older sisters at university, it was a neat feeling really. A feeling of freedom and being liberal and seeing all the things that were quite different to the

Left **Helen's student flat at 12 Elgin Street, Grey Lynn, next door to the house later featured in the television series *Pioneer Family*.**

way we'd been brought up. It was a new life in Auckland and I thought it was fun and exciting to be part of that. There were things going on, meetings to go to, shopping for floating dresses and incense and beads in Karangahape Road. It was the 70s and that was the way people dressed in those days. And we went to the pictures and Suzanne and Helen had motorbikes and they puttered round on those. They'd take us riding on the bikes, I remember that. And she actually took us, my friend and me, to see *Hair*. And to me that was just the opening of the world. I mean, to see something like that. It was really controversial at the time and it was fun. It was just such a different way of life, it was exciting. And after we'd seen *Hair*, anything went."

Taking her younger sisters to see *Hair* would have made a substantial dent in Helen's finances. Money was in short supply for both her and Suzanne, two country girls who had come to the big smoke to further their education.

Helen has strong views on the subject: "Students have become much more self-centred these days. The ferment is around their particular material position, and it's understandable to the extent that they're much worse off than we were. Well, they are and they aren't. We almost accepted vows of poverty as students – we had no money. So you accepted a very low standard of living for the period of time you were a student. That's the way it was and you accepted it, because you knew that you'd get a decent job at the end of it."

According to Suzanne, she and Helen paid 10 percent of their fees, received a boarding allowance because they lived away from home, and "some miserable amount that you gained from Bursary". But it wasn't enough to live on. George and Margaret had to dig deep, paying a considerable part of their daughters' university fees and topping up their rent.

Helen, who was in any event ambivalent about going home, remained in Auckland during the summer vacations: "I used to work right through the summer holidays. My aim was to have that carry me through the year on top of my student allowance. My parents topped up the first two years because we didn't have enough to cover. But after that I was able to earn enough to be self-supporting on this absolutely minimal standard of living through the university years.

"The first year I had a job in a jigsaw factory, interestingly owned by the Holdsworth family. Simon Holdsworth was a contemporary of mine at university. He went on to do law and in recent years has been the President of the Employers Federation. But it was through him that I got my first holiday job in his father's factory down in New North Road, Mount Albert.

"The next year I started out with a job in a handbag factory up the top of Queen Street. I've still got a horrible scar on my hand where I brought the soldering machine down on it. I shifted to another job after that, a plastics factory in Onehunga, I think. And then I had inventory jobs, clerical jobs round different places."

Brian: "Did you form any opinion on the lives of working-class people?"

Helen: "The opinion I formed was that it was critical to get a decent education, so you could get a job that didn't involve doing these things. You go into the factory, you get a 10 to 15 minute tea break in the morning, half an hour for lunch and maybe 10 or 15 minutes in the afternoon, and then you head home. It was just tedious, deadly. And the pay wasn't reasonable at all. I mean, this was before equal pay. The men got more for working on the same machine as you did. The Equal Pay Act did not come in until 1972 and I can remember, when I got my first job as a junior lecturer at university, getting a letter advising me that I'd got the job at an annual salary of $3899."

Helen's student days were over and her professional career was about to begin. The next five years would be dominated by work, study, travel and her first attempt to get into Parliament.

chapter**five**

APPRENTICESHIP

When the young man or woman from the "Youth Socialist Movement" asked George how his daughter could be a socialist when her parents had so much, he was asking a very interesting question. Here you have a rather shy young woman, whose parents are conservative Waikato farmers who, by their own testimony, have voted National all their lives. Though the odd Labourite can be found in the family, it's doubtful that Helen would have heard many left-wing ideas articulated in the home.

She goes to Te Pahu Primary School, where she associates with the children of other conservative, National Party-voting rural parents. Then on to Epsom Girls Grammar where her fellow students are either from Auckland's richest suburbs or are again from predominantly conservative rural families. She has no personal experience of poverty or deprivation. She has lived a relatively privileged and comfortable life, cocooned in a secure and loving environment, her nose buried in books.

From this cocoon there emerges in her later years at boarding school and her student years at Auckland University, if not a socialist, then certainly a left-wing activist whose views on almost everything are totally opposed to the views not only of her parents but of most of the people one might have expected to be formative influences in her upbringing. How did this happen? Where did the left-wing activist come from?

A
P
P
R
E
N
T
I
C
E
S
H
I
P

105

Political commentator Colin James draws a distinction between politicians whose politics are 'tribal' and those whose politics are learned or intellectual. In the former category can be found people whose families have voted for a particular party seemingly since the dawn of time. Their political allegiance is both genetically and environmentally determined. It is unquestioned and unquestioning. To change horses would be almost unthinkable heresy.

Then there are those whose life experience, whether of privilege or dispossession, leads them inexorably to the conclusion that this or that view of society is right or wrong. Their politics are *felt*, precisely because they are born of personal experience.

In another category, political allegiance may reflect membership of a particular interest group – Federated Farmers or the Meatworkers Union, for example.

Race and class are also tribal determinants. Though less and less can be taken for granted in 21st century New Zealand politics, Maori and the working-class are still considerably more likely to vote Labour than for any other party.

Helen Clark comes from a white, middle-class, politically conservative, rural background. If her politics are tribal, she seems to be in the wrong tribe. So what happened?

James asserts that the Prime Minister's politics are cerebral and intellectual rather than tribal, that she learned them at university and not at her parents' knee. Helen's own statement that "my beliefs in those years were shaped by Bob Chapman, not my father", would seem to support his contention.

James contrasts Helen with Party President Mike Williams and Justice Minister Phil Goff: "Williams is a shrewd, well-off, fifty-ish, retired businessman. He can talk the language of shares and property values and why business doesn't like Clark's policies. But his campaign biography for the Presidency opened with the words, 'I was born to blue-collar parents in Wainuiomata'. Williams is tribal.

"Phil Goff also comes from a working-class background. He's got instincts which are Labour. He may have adjusted those instincts through policy positions he took in the 1980s and even takes now, but that's his base.

"Helen's base is a small, conservative, farming family that went National on the back of the early 1950s wool boom. Yes, it had Liberal antecedents, but it was definitely a small, conservative, farming family – frugal, as those small families are, conservative. That's her background. She learned her social democracy."

James believes that Helen's early health problems may have influenced her later views on the need for strong social services, and that her experience as "a displaced person" at Epsom goes some way to explaining "the remarkable combination of extraordinary resilience and a certain brittleness in her personality":

"More important, however, was to land in that seedbed of liberal-left politics of the early 1970s – Auckland University. It was that that brought her into contact with the tribe. But learned attitudes can be modified by new learning. She can, if necessary, make policy shifts a birth-member of the tribe might think apostasy."

In stating that Helen's politics are intellectual rather than empathetic, James seems to imply a degree of shallowness or lack of genuine feeling, perhaps even that she is a politician who doesn't *care*. He responds:

"There are two sorts of genuine feelings. One of those sorts it is, and the other sort it's not. The sort that it's not is a deep, gut sympathy and identification, the feeling, 'I am one with you'. Deeper than empathy, it's that sort of automatic buddiness – 'You come from the same class, you come from the same background, you come from the same heart.' I never have the impression that she feels it in that way. I also don't doubt that she is genuinely concerned about others being disadvantaged. But it's not fellow feeling. I don't think she has that deep, automatic feeling. Again, it's learnt."

James finds support from others for his assertion that Helen's politics are intellectual and learnt rather than tribal and deeply felt, but it is not unqualified. Barry Gustafson accepts that she was influenced by Bob Chapman, Ruth Butterworth and others in Political Studies, but rejects the idea that she or any of the students were indoctrinated. He points to the fact that the Department's graduates include Winston Peters, Jim McLay, Murray McCully, Ross Meurant and a number of other National Party politicians, and adds:

"You know, a student's not a jug that you fill up with water and ideas. I think someone said that a student is a lamp to be lighted, and sometimes the spark of the ideas actually catches them, and I think that was the case with Helen. She started to question some of the certainties from her previous life and suddenly found more attractive ideas, more intellectually stimulating or persuasive ideas. So this was a period in which she clearly had an intellectual approach on a lot of issues."

Radio New Zealand Political Editor Al Morrison believes that James' assessment is only partially correct: "I know where Colin's coming from, but I think there's a part of the Labour Party that is 'intelligentsia-tribal', rather than the Norman Kirk version of tribal – 'I not only built my own house, but made the bricks to build it with.' There is part of Labour which is classic Social Democrat intelligentsia-tribal, rather than working-class tribal, and I think Clark comes from that. If you talk to her about defence for ten minutes, within two minutes you'll find her making references to Vietnam. She came through the university system at a time when there was an enormous interest in what we did overseas. And it fed into that whole feminist, anti-war, hate-my-parents, generation-gap movement."

Jonathan Hunt takes a similar view: "There's a tradition in the Labour Party that goes back quite a long way, to the 1940s, to people like Martyn Finlay. It's the tradition of the left-wing intellectual, a long tradition, not just in this country, but in Britain, Australia and elsewhere. Not quite as long as the Kirk tradition of the stationary engine driver who built his own house with his own bricks, but still a very lengthy tradition."

David Lange, who must himself be deemed an intellectual, sees his own involvement in the Labour movement as tribal, but in quite a different sense to Helen Clark's: "Helen's tribal in the negative sense that she didn't belong to the National Party. I am the product of an industrial suburb of South Auckland, and I embraced it. Helen's the product of rural order, and she rejected it. You know, at the time I'm referring to, National was characterised as a party which returned MPs from electorates like Piako, who would come into the House at four o'clock in the afternoon, shout into the overhead microphone, 'I reject the proposals!' and then go back to the bar. And all the farmers in Piako would go, 'Geez, aren't they doing a great job!'

"So I think that people overstate the Vietnam War influence. Helen was taking principled positions on foreign affairs issues far beyond Vietnam. And indeed she took on harder challenges than that. Vietnam became easy to oppose in the end. You were almost out of step if you didn't."

One could go on speculating on this forever. Those closest to Helen accept that her early attraction to the Left may indeed have been intellectual rather than tribal, but place greater emphasis on the core values which she learnt at home. Bob Chapman, while not denying his considerable influence on the young politics student, believes that George and Margaret played a significant role in shaping Helen's political and social philosophy:

"There's the liberalism of the home. The father and mother are decent, liberal people. The way she was treated in the home was liberally."

It's a view shared and expanded by Sandra, Helen's youngest sister: "I think she cares about New Zealand and what's happening to the country and she wants a fair system for all. Growing up in our little part of the Waikato was very egalitarian. Everyone was equal and had the same chance in life, and you didn't look at someone differently because they were a sharemilker or a landowner or just a transient worker. And then, if you look back to the grandparents, on my mother's side there's a strong Labour background and tradition, and grandfather Clark left England for a better life for his family and his children. He was a strong Labour voter."

It's likely that all of these views have a degree of validity. Helen herself speaks of the influence on her political thought of the freer and more challenging environment of the university, of the radicalism of many of her fellow students, of Trevor Richards and the Halt All Racist Tours movement, of the staff in the Political Studies Department, particularly Bob Chapman, of events in Vietnam, South Africa, Greece, Latin America and French Polynesia and the international protests that greeted those events, of the emergence of a charismatic Labour leader in Norman Kirk, of the more liberal ethos of the 1970s, of what she simply calls "the times". One can describe all of that as "learned" or "intellectual", but to it must be added a rigorous personal integrity, an innate sense of right and wrong that goes beyond the intellectual, that is felt, and that expresses itself in a deep concern for people and for social justice. If that too was learnt, then it was learnt in the home.

Helen, as we have seen, joined the Princes Street branch of the Labour Party, where she was immediately elected Vice President, in 1971. She established herself at once as a hard worker, someone willing to attend endless meetings, stuff things in envelopes or give up her Saturday mornings to go canvassing. Jonathan Hunt observes that Helen was determined and had worked out early that in order to progress in the Party you had to do those things.

And there was plenty to do. Mike Williams recalls that Princes Street was quite unlike the Victoria University branch of the Labour Party, to which he had previously belonged: "The Vic branch was largely a social club that didn't meet very frequently. The Princes Street branch was very businesslike. We were always doing remits and lining ourselves up to go to the Labour Party Conference. I remember in 1971 going to Conference representing the Waihi branch. We used to collect delegateships from all over the place and get large numbers of people going. We didn't think there was anything wrong with that. If the Waihi branch wasn't going to be represented, we'd represent them. And I remember Helen at that point, not dominating proceedings, but guiding proceedings. She knew the constitution and pathways in the Labour Party backwards, and educated us on that."

1971 was the year of the Auckland City Council elections and the Princes Street branch was heavily involved in supporting Labour Party candidates. Helen went door-knocking and her efforts may have contributed to the election to Council of Michael Bassett and Cath Tizard.

The door-knocking continued in 1972, the year that would see the election of the third Labour Government. Princes Street had thrown much of its weight behind Mike Moore in Eden, but most of Helen's work was on behalf of Michael Bassett, the successful Labour Party candidate in Waitemata:

"Every Saturday morning. Delivering leaflets, canvassing, all the usual campaign stuff. I found it very interesting. Although it was dog territory in West Auckland. Big dogs!"

Helen was elected President of the Princes Street branch in 1973 and in the same year, at Barry Gustafson's suggestion, became the Chair of the Party's Youth Advisory Council. She began to attend meetings of the Auckland Central Labour Electoral Committee (LEC), the body responsible for party organisation in the electorate and, again at Gustafson's urging, stood for the Executive of the Party's Auckland Regional Council.

Gustafson says that the Council was split between two factions: a conservative group to which he himself belonged and a more radical group, formed around Michael Bassett and Jim Anderton:

"In those days Mike and Jim had good contacts with Roger Douglas. I mean, we forget that Roger Douglas and Jim Anderton were extremely close friends and so later were Michael Bassett and Jim Anderton. And Helen was more identified with that group, which had a lot of support in Princes Street among the young students and the staff. The Council split at annual meetings and on most votes with about 70 percent on the conservative side and 30 percent on the other. I suggested to Helen that she stand, because I wanted to see a younger person and a woman on the Executive. Helen was defeated, but was top of the unsuccessful candidates. However, at the first meeting of the Executive, where the conservatives had a

Above **Two long-haired future leaders march to the Supreme Court, Auckland, in protest at an injunction against the Drivers Union, 1975. Helen at left, Phil Goff second from right.**

majority of seven to four, one of the conservatives, who had been appointed an industrial conciliator, resigned. The conservatives wanted to have another election for the vacancy, but I insisted from the Chair that because we'd just had an election, we co-opt the top unsuccessful candidate, who was Helen. And that changed the balance on the Executive and created quite a bit of comment."

Helen herself was beginning to create quite a bit of comment.

Mike Williams: "She was very competent. You knew that she wanted to go somewhere. People deferred to her. I can remember an Auckland Central branch meeting. I was the Chairman of the Auckland Central branch, and there was something we voted on which was a tie. And as the chairman I had the casting vote. And I just went with Helen. I can remember not even thinking about it – makes me sound a bit weak in the head – just assuming that whatever the issue was, Helen would be on the right side of it."

Bill Ralston: "She had a lot of respect around the place. You could look in those days and see people who were going to become Members of Parliament. Helen was chair of the Youth Advisory Council and attending the Party's Annual Conference. You could just tell she was on her way, just as you could tell that Phil Goff was on his way. They were definitely heading down that path to becoming MPs."

Political journalist Richard Harman was also a student at Auckland in the early

1970s. He too had become aware of Helen Clark: "We knew that she was very close to Ruth Butterworth and Bob Chapman, people who had a lot of mana, people who were taken very seriously, people who one thought had influence. She was a person to keep an eye on, and I remember she spoke at a Labour Party Conference, one of the first to be televised, in 1974 or '75. I remember her standing up and she was wearing blue stockings, and some rather sexist comments were made by some of the delegates."

This may have been the first occasion on which Helen appeared on television, an appearance which made a formidable impression on her former lecturer Ruth Butterworth:

"Three young people were interviewed on *Gallery* after the conference. Helen was one of them. And what came across to me was the amazing bone structure. I already knew the quality of the mind and then here was just this instant presence on screen. I knew then that she was going to be the first woman Prime Minister of New Zealand. And I was the first person on the face of the earth to say so."

Helen was a little way off becoming New Zealand's first elected woman Prime Minister. Thanks in part to the patronage of her mentor Bob Chapman, the 23-year-old was working as a junior lecturer in the Political Studies Department. Yet her sights remained firmly on politics. The Labour Party was fielding 21 candidates, led by Jim Anderton, in the 1974 Auckland City Council elections. Helen was one of them. David Lange was another, and the two met for the first time:

"We each paid $100 for an advertisement and we woke up with great excitement on a Saturday morning before the election to see our names in the paper for the Council team. And there was a huge photo of Jim Anderton and no mention of us. It taught me my first lesson in politics and probably Helen Clark's too.

"I was a fat, shambling heap; she was a vivacious, very fit, cycling, glamorous, long-haired student heart-throb really. She was. She was physically very attractive. I remember she used to wear sweaters, which were what I would describe as a young man as form-revealing. And she rode a cycle and had a general air of buoyancy and vitality about her which was very attractive. She was also very engaging in conversation. She could sit on the floor and drink a cup of coffee. And she was part of that age which was experiencing things. And one always had the feeling that she wasn't of Auckland. And I suppose she wasn't, of course.

"And we were in this rather strangely eclectic team for the Council. And the opening meeting was conducted under the chairmanship of Michael Bassett. We duly assembled and were introduced. One member of the team, Titewhai Harawira, then denounced 'your government, your party, your people' and abso-

lutely demolished the very team she was supposed to be standing for. So Helen has not seen terribly great changes in the Labour Party.

"I always remember the frustrations of that campaign and what I thought was the pointlessness of it. Eventually Cath Tizard got elected and Jim Anderton got elected, and the rest of us 19 were consigned to the scrap-heap of history."

Helen came top of the unsuccessful candidates. She would stand again in 1977. And lose again. In a revealing passage in *Head and Shoulders*, she tells Virginia Myers that she enjoyed the campaigns and found the experience positive:

But I had to force myself to get involved in speaking and public activities. The issues I was interested in required me to express my commitment and ideas to a larger audience, and I had to develop the skill to do so. It was hard work. It didn't come naturally.

I don't think you come out of the New Zealand growing-up process with the feeling that you are an individual of worth who others will want to meet. You don't come out of the education system with feelings of great esteem. I had to develop a sense of worth over time. I guess by hard work and getting better at it, I felt, well, dammit, I am as good at it as other people and I do have something to contribute.

But I still had a lot of emotional maturing to do. I've changed immensely. Probably the most difficult thing was to change my self-image from someone who was shy and didn't push herself forward, into someone more confident and more assertive. I still have some reservations about meeting people. Sometimes at functions when I have to propel myself forward to shake hands with everyone, I think, why should I inflict myself on them? Do they really want to meet me?

Though she would not have known it at the time, Helen had a soulmate in the future President of the Labour Party, Mike Williams:

"I was very shy. I was exceptionally awkward at parties when I came to Auckland. I'd be standing in the corner. I said that to her and she said, 'Yes, it's a perfectly normal characteristic to have.' And I think she's got over that, because she works a room really well now. It's gone from her. It's gone from me too. But it's a bloody hard thing to do."

Helen's poor self-esteem in the 1970s was clearly at odds with the opinion of others. Those who knew her well regarded her with a mixture of respect, admiration and affection. Some were to become life-long friends. Among them was Judith Tizard who, in what she regards as a piece of irony, would later become MP for Auckland Central, the seat for which Helen failed to get the nomination in 1975.

Judith was the daughter of Catherine and Bob Tizard. Cath Tizard, as we have seen, had been elected to the Auckland City Council in 1971. She would go on to become the city's first woman mayor and later the country's first woman Governor-General. Her husband Bob, who had entered Parliament in 1957, was Minister of Health and State Services in the third Labour Government and became Deputy Prime Minister and Minister of Finance on the death of Norman Kirk. The Tizards were a highly political family.

Judith had become aware of Helen when Helen was Chair of the Youth Advisory Council, but was first introduced to her by Michael Bassett in 1974:

"I remember being very impressed with her. She was great. She was very funny and had a wonderfully dry wit. And she could be wonderfully rude about people I was deeply in awe of at the time – Cabinet Ministers and the like. She was very clever. And it was really interesting because she was just 24 and people like Mike Bassett and Jonathan Hunt and Murray Smith treated her absolutely as an equal. It was interesting because we forget how dismissive many people were of women in those days. And Helen was a young woman who was not strikingly attractive. She was very 'dowdy university' – long hair parted in the middle, no make-up, corduroy trousers and boots. She had soft, leathery boots and a wonderful collection of truly awful fairisle sweaters, sleeveless jerkins, real bluestocking hippie, not flower-power hippie. That was how she presented herself. It was just Helen. And she made me laugh. And I've always said that anyone who makes me laugh is a friend for life, as long as they keep making me laugh. We just got on tremendously well.

"And Mum and Dad were away all the time, so I used to put on these fabulous dinner parties. I was a very good cook, so we would quite often have dinner for 12 or 14 or 20 and Helen was always willing to party. She was often in Wellington for Labour Party stuff and for some of the research she was doing. I had an office there in the Labour Research Unit where I worked for 16 hours a week. And I'd quite often come to work and Helen would be sitting at my desk. She was very much part of the scene.

"We became good friends and I introduced her to the family. Dad was a bit wary of her. He saw her as a young radical. He was just a bit impatient, as the Deputy PM and Minister of Finance probably would be. But even in those days I think he had a great deal of respect for her, though my memory of his view was that he thought she was very cold. It was about that stage that she became good friends with Mum. She and Mum got on really well. She was very shy. But she could relax with the Tizards."

1974 was to prove a disastrous year for the Labour Party and, many would come to believe, for the country. On 31 August, Norman Kirk, New Zealand's 46th Prime Minister, died in the Home of Compassion in Island Bay, murdered by the CIA, according to the future President of the Labour Party, Bob Harvey. Though few place much credence in the theory, Kirk's foreign policy had not endeared him to New Zealand's most powerful allies or indeed to many at home. He had strenuously opposed French nuclear testing in the Pacific, pulled the troops out of Vietnam and, breaking a pre-election promise, cancelled the 1973 Springbok tour on the grounds that it presented a serious threat to law and order and to the 1974 Commonwealth Games in Christchurch.

Kirk's 21 months in office were among the most exciting in New Zealand's political history, the excitement reaching its zenith when the Government sent the Royal New Zealand Navy frigates *Otago* and *Canterbury* to Mururoa Atoll in the Pacific, after France had ignored an International Court of Justice recommendation to suspend its nuclear testing there. Aboard the *Otago* was the hapless or heroic – according to how you looked at it – Fraser Colman, Member of Parliament for Petone and the Minister of Mines and Immigration. A popular urban legend at the time was that Kirk had placed his Ministers' names in a hat and pulled out "Colman". A subsequent inspection of the pieces of paper is said to have revealed that they all said "Colman".

Kirk had many faults. He was authoritarian and enormously conservative on issues such as abortion and homosexuality. Not having had a secondary, let alone a tertiary education, he was deeply suspicious of anyone who came out of the universities or could be branded an "intellectual". He trusted almost no one and had an elephantine memory for wrongs, both real and imagined, done to him by enemies and friends alike. He was reputed to have a "little black book" containing their names. Whether the book existed in reality or only in his head is uncertain, but many considered Kirk to be both paranoid and vengeful.

But he was also one of the most dynamic individuals to emerge in New Zealand's political history. A man of enormous stature, both physically and intellectually, he was a visionary with both the intelligence and the eloquence to convey his passion for social change to others and to inspire them with it. During his 21 months in office a new sense of nationhood, of national pride, captured New Zealand.

Helen remembers Kirk coming into the Political Studies Department before the 1972 election, but can't recall actually meeting him: "I mean, the Leader of the Labour Party was a grand figure. So if you were some young Party member of 21 or 22 you just didn't get near him. But I was very impressed with Norman Kirk, because I felt he spoke for a whole generation of young people on New Zealand's identity, its place in the world, its independent point of view, not just automatically adopting the attitudes of our so-called allies. That appealed to me. It appealed to a whole generation of people."

Helen was the President of 'Labour Youth for New Zealand' in 1974 when Kirk died and attended his funeral in that capacity. She can scarcely have imagined that she might herself one day be the country's Prime Minister, but her sights were nonetheless set on becoming an MP. She decided to seek the nomination for Auckland Central. She was unsuccessful. Richard Prebble got the nomination.

According to Judith, Helen was disappointed: "She realised very early that Richard Prebble had the seat sewn up, but she decided it would be a useful exercise to run anyway. And Ruth Butterworth, who was a friend and mentor, was also running. I wasn't in Auckland, but I remember her being quite disappointed that she hadn't done better. I was very aware of the process because I'd seen Dad running for seats. And a couple of times, after major boundary changes, he'd had to regroup and reorganise, and I was very aware of how you got selected and how you did the numbers. So we'd talk about how she was going to get a seat, and what seat she was going to get. I remember one night very late, it was probably about two in the morning, fairly pissed, drawing up a list of the MPs we thought might die or retire in the next five years. It was quite a long list. I was always clear even in those early days that Helen would go into Parliament. There was never any question about it. That was her aim."

Joan Caulfield, who has been Helen's Electorate Secretary in Mount Albert since 1996, was then married to Jim Anderton: "The first memory I have of Helen is a vivid memory. It's of her coming to our house to see Jim and talking about standing for Parliament. And I remember her sitting on the couch with her long hair and jeans and talking quite determinedly about wanting to stand for Parliament. That's the most vivid image I have of her, and I think it's because it was the first time I'd seen that determination to be a politician."

In pursuit of her aim, Helen sought the Labour nomination for the rural Waikato electorate of Piako. There was no other candidate. Piako was National Party heartland and an unwinnable seat. Helen, who at least had the advantage of being a local girl, got the nomination. Unlike previous Labour candidates, who appear to have regarded standing for Piako as little more than an empty gesture, a pointless formality, Helen was prepared to give it her best shot. She would campaign as if there were some prospect of winning.

Piako was the best part of 160 kilometres from Auckland, so her first priority was to get a car. Buddy Arthur's husband Eddie Hooper knew about cars, and George asked for his help to find a reliable means of transportation for his daughter: "We were living in Hamilton. George helped me look round for a car in the right price range and he picked out a Mini. So I checked it out and Helen came down to see if she liked it. And she said, 'Well, if you decide it's reliable enough, then that's what I want.' She didn't care if it was a Morris Minor or a Ford Escort or a Cortina, as long it was one her father and I thought was a good car. And that was that. And she had a good run out of it too. I did a good job actually."

But helping his daughter find a decent car was about as far as George was prepared to go. While she was campaigning for Labour in Piako, he was campaigning for National in Raglan, as Fay explains:

"George, who was Chairman of the local National Party, was going around with Marilyn Waring. Now my mother was very proud of Helen, very proud. And I was

Right **Helen's campaign Mini was thoroughly checked out by her father and Eddie Hooper, husband of her second cousin and Standard One teacher, Buddy Arthur.** *Opposite* **The first of many Helen Clark election campaign leaflets, 1975.**

down at Mum's, vacuuming the floors. And George had given Mum a picture of Marilyn Waring. And I picked it up off the floor and was chipping Mum a little bit about her son taking Marilyn Waring around for house visits when his own daughter was standing for Labour. And my mother said, 'You know, Fay, there's something about that girl I just don't quite like.'"

But regardless of her father's activities and with the Mini for transportation, Helen began her campaign:

"I used to go down two or three times a week as it got close to the election. I had industrious small groups of supporters in Matamata, Putaruru, Te Aroha and Morrinsville, and we used to do a bit of door-knocking. We had good public meetings which some of the Labour MPs would attend to support me. I remember taking Basil Arthur, who was the Minister of Works, to the Kaimai Tunnel. He was allowed into the tunnel, but I wasn't. Women couldn't go down the tunnel, because the Irish tunnellers were superstitious."

According to Judith, those hard men were impressed by the Labour candidate: "A dear friend who died recently was a tunneller at Kaimai. Helen had gone to meet them all, and they were just blown away by her energy and her vision and her intelligence and everything that she was. And they said it was great. She used to

Helen Clark . . .

- Aged 25.
- Born in Hamilton.
- Daughter of sheep and cattle farmer.
- Educated at Te Pahu Primary, Epsom Girls' Grammar and Auckland University.
- Graduated MA (First Class Honours) in Political Studies.
- Junior Lecturer, Auckland University.
- Helen Clark is young, intelligent and articulate. She speaks out on important issues and has an immense capacity for hard work. These are very important qualities for an MP.
- Since 1973, she has been lecturing in Political Studies at Auckland University. Her subject gives her a very wide knowledge for judging political affairs and keeps her right up to date with political events in New Zealand and around the world.

ELECT A
WOMAN MEMBER
FOR PIAKO

HELEN CLARK GETS AROUND THE PIAKO ELECTORATE

JOIN HER CAMPAIGN AND MAKE LABOUR'S VOICE HEARD IN YOUR AREA!

IF YOU CAN HELP—OR IF YOU REQUIRE TRANSPORT ON POLLING DAY OR SICK OR ABSENTEE VOTES RING:
JILL BROOKS, Morrinsville — 6516
BILL HESS, Te Aroha — 1237D
HEC MUNRO, Putaruru — 7464
LEN WILLS, Matamata — 6236

LABOUR . . .
TRUST IT—IT'S WORKING!

LABOUR'S
HELEN CLARK

come down every weekend. I think she arranged her lectures so that she had Fridays and Mondays at least partly free. And whatever time she had, she was down there."

The tunnellers' approval may have come as a surprise to Helen herself, who, as she told Virginia Myers, had no great expectation of getting a warm reception anywhere in the district:

"In Piako I think they wondered what had struck them. I was a left-wing student politician, pro-abortion, a woman in a farming area, as different from the people there as chalk from cheese."

Helen was all of those things, but she was also a hard-working and enthusiastic Labour candidate, something the people in the district had not seen before. And her experience campaigning in the Auckland local body elections and the 1972 General Election stood her in good stead. She knew about electorate organisation, canvassing and marshalling support.

The research which Helen had done for her M.A. thesis on 'Political Attitudes of the New Zealand Countryside' must also have stood her in good stead, as did her knowledge of psephology, the statistical and sociological study of elections. On that subject Bob Chapman was an authority:

"Everybody got some dose of that, down to Stage I. She would have heard me

on radio or on television or in a lecture. At least I hope she did. She would know my methods to the point where I'd say, 'Have you looked at the E9?' – the record of every polling booth in the country. She had worked through the E9. She knew the votes in all of the booths. And remember that memory of hers. She knew what she was up against exactly and where Labour was weakest and National most entrenched. She knew that was the groundwork you had to do, and she'd done it. Using my methods.

"And what she did was to pick the small towns and go out and face her opponents insofar as they turned up – and I think a lot of them did – and put the Labour case clearly. There was nothing offensive in the way she tackled the job, just the plain statement of what the policies were and of the consequences to the farmers, which would often have been good. And she honestly was a country woman with the full experience of country life. Her family were farmers, and successful farmers, which makes a big difference. And the effect of one of their own saying things was quite different from someone who was labelled an outsider from the outset."

The 1975 election was a disaster for Labour. In 1972 the party had won 55 seats against National's 32. The figures were reversed in 1975. The swing against the government was massive. Labour increased its vote in only a handful of electorates. Piako was one. In the face of a landslide against the government, and in National's rural heartland, Helen increased the Party's vote by a modest but significant 125 votes. She had, of course, not expected to win. Nor, according to David Lange, did she want to win:

"There's no question in my mind that Helen did not wish to enter Parliament then. She still had a lot more to do. What was the point of entering Parliament then? When I got there in 1977, I didn't know why I'd gone. We spent the first four caucuses discussing the provision of towels in the shower block and retirement allowances. That was what the Party was like, and Helen knew that. She'd sat in on these things."

Lange is no doubt correct. Helen had stood in Piako with neither thought nor hope of winning the seat. She had done it to gain experience and to consolidate her reputation in the party. Piako was an apprenticeship and a successful one.

chaptersix

OF PARTIES,
POLITICS AND PETER

HELEN now turned her mind to the Ph.D. thesis which she had begun working on before the election. 'The Role of Farmers in Political Life in New
Zealand, the United Kingdom and Sweden' was an extension of the work she had
done for her Masters and, as the title suggests, required her to travel overseas. She
was awarded a University Grants Committee postgraduate scholarship and set off
in February of 1976 for an 11-month research trip which included two months in
Sweden, six months in the U.K. and a further three months travelling.

While her friend was overseas, Judith Tizard's life was turning to custard:

"I was flatting in Wellington with Dad and Bill Rowling and Warren Freer and
Joe Walding. I was in a real mess. I had had a love affair that had ended. He went
overseas, and it was just a crazy time. Labour had lost the election. I'd discovered
that Dad was having a love affair with a friend of mine. I'd given up the university.
And I was drinking too much and really absolutely grief-stricken. I thought it was
the end of the world.

"Helen was great through all of that. It was well before you would ever think of
ringing overseas. So she would write encouragingly and would demand to know
what I was reading and what useful things I'd done. She was always very kind and
accepting, but she always demanded a lot of me. She would want detailed letters.
She would say, 'Write and tell me what happened at such-and-such a meeting.'
So I had to take notes at meetings and would send them off to Helen. And there

were huge changes happening in the Labour Party at that stage, and she always wanted information."

Judith returned home to Auckland at the end of 1976. Helen was back at the beginning of 1977 and faced the prospect of returning to her flat in Elgin Street. It was, as Judith recounts, not an attractive prospect:

"She'd lived in this grotty, god-awful flat, real student dive. And it was cold and she always had terrible asthma. She used to get quite ill in the winter. And I said something like, 'Why don't you go and stay with Mum for a while?' because Mum and Dad were living in a three-bedroom townhouse with the kids all gone. So I rang Mum and said, 'Helen's looking for somewhere to stay for a couple of weeks, can she stay at your house?' And Mum said, 'Yes, sure.'

"She and Mum just got on really well, and of course Dad was away and having this affair, which Mum didn't know about, but we did. And Helen is very protective of her friends, and I think staying with Mum was partly her way of making sure she was all right. Not that Mum would have needed that protection, if she had known."

Cath Tizard takes up the story: "So Helen moved into the upstairs bedroom and I think from memory it was sort of like the man who came to dinner. She stayed two years. It was just on an ad hoc basis to start with and then she kept saying, 'I need to pay you some board.' And I said, 'Oh, no, no, don't worry about it.' But then I said, 'Well, you're welcome to stay if you want to.' And I found that a cheque for board would be put on my dressing table. I don't think we ever formally discussed an amount.

"We were used to having people coming and going and she was pleasant company. I was working at the university and she had just been employed full-time as a lecturer in the Political Studies Department. It was convenient and I never had any problem with it. She was just re-establishing herself at the time, and I suppose we were a comfortable pied-a-terre for her and she fitted in well."

Very well. During her stay at the Tizards, Helen was to be introduced to a more hedonistic lifestyle, as Cath recalls:

"We taught her to drink. She's very abstemious now but when she lived with us a drink before dinner was a sociable thing to do. And I remember that someone had given me a bottle of Advocaat and it had sat there for heaven knows how long, a yellow, thick, eggy thing, and nobody knew what to do with it. And Judith was working as a barmaid somewhere at the time and said, 'Oh, I've got a good cocktail recipe.' So we learned to drink what I think were called 'Fallen Angels' – Advocaat and cherry brandy. Helen put on quite a bit of weight over those years living with us, eating regularly, eating well and eating more than she was accustomed to eating. She got quite chubby for a while."

Left **A dark-haired Margaret Wilson (front), on holiday in Northland with Helen in the late 1970s. Margaret gave up a distinguished academic career to stand for Parliament in 1999, and was immediately elected to Cabinet as Attorney General.**

Cath and Judith each tell the following story with themselves as the harassed cook. This is Judith's version: "Helen was very interested in food. And she loved good wine. And we used to make the most fabulous cocktails. Well, Mum had invited this chap Tony King to stay with us. He was a visiting British academic and the rumour was that he was having a relationship with Barbara Castle. And we were all scandalised and titillated by this. Anyway, it was getting towards dinner time and I remember we decided we'd have martinis before dinner. Helen had invited a whole lot of people and I was cooking. She was determined to get home, but she had a Labour Party meeting somewhere and I remember being worried because it was pouring down with rain. So this chap went up and had a shower and came down. Then Mum had a meeting and she arrived home about 8 o'clock. And Tony and I had been sitting drinking martinis, because you've got to entertain people, don't you? Then Helen got home and we watched the David Frost interview with Richard Nixon. It was about 9 o'clock by then and everybody had arrived. So I thought I'd better get the soup out. So I'm fluffing round in the kitchen – it was about half-past 9 – and this chap came and leant across the kitchen divider and said, 'My dear, I'm having an absolutely fabulous time. But tell me, are there any courses other than gin?' It was not an atypical dinner party."

There was music to go with the food and wine:

"Lots of music. Helen's interest in music was really interesting. She had very

broad tastes. It was mainly John Prine and Country Joe and the Fish and that sort of avant garde pop-rock stuff, American protest music. But she very quickly got into classical music, and I think that was part of the attraction that she and Mum had in terms of their friendship, that they were both very musical and very interested in music. But Helen always pushed the edges of everything she did. Like she came back with this ghastly Bulgarian wedding music which sounded like a cat playing the bagpipes while being crushed under a 10-ton truck. It was awful. She used to insist we listen to this while we drank Slivovitz, which was pretty awful too.

"She loved exploring the whole of things. Somebody else might be interested in good Russian vodka, but Helen had to understand where the vodka came from and what you ate with it and what you'd be talking about at the time. So you'd get into 18th century Russian literature and music. And it was the thoroughness with which she pursued things that I found really amazing. And exciting, because I think at that stage both Mum and Dad were so busy that they tended to take what they needed and move on. Whereas Helen was still at that lovely stage where she could gobble things whole. She was like a political big sister and she let me tag along to lots of things, and we used to have these frightfully elegant dinners in Auckland and I became friends with friends of hers up here and it was huge fun.

"She was always very encouraging. She always asked you what you were doing and what you were reading and she was always going to films. I remember going to lots of Japanese films and Chinese films and art films. And Helen was always doing something. She was always exploring or investigating. And she used to read these very solemn, literary sort of things. And she was always saying, 'Here read this, you'll find it really interesting.' And I would plough through it thinking, 'Oh god. I'm sure it's improved my mind vastly.'"

Helen the mentor. But there are occasions when even mentors can use a little support.

Cath: "I remember one wonderful night when my daughter Anne and her husband Steve had come back from Canada. And Steve got hepatitis and they thought initially it was hepatitis A. And Anne marched in this Sunday evening just as we were preparing dinner and said, 'Right, you lot, you've all got to have gamma globulin shots. Steve's got hepatitis and you've all eaten with him.' And she had all the gear and I said, 'Where?' And she said, 'In your backside.'

"So we dutifully down-troued and she jabbed my son Nigel who was standing there going, 'Oooooh!' And Anne says, 'I can't get the needle in. Just relax.' Nigel said, 'I am relaxed.' Anne said, 'No, you're not, but I've done it anyway.' So Nigel relaxed and then she jabbed him. Then she did me. I don't mind needles, but Helen is an absolute wimp over matters involving health. To visit anyone in a hospital is a major gift from Helen. She hates hospitals, she hates doctors, she hates the whole business, which I think is very funny, very ironic for someone who was a Minister of Health. And Anne said, 'Come on, you've got to have one too.'

"So she was very brave and got her injection and went back into the kitchen. And I was just walking past and I looked up and I saw these glazed eyes and an absolutely pallid, grey-white face and I said, 'Look out! Helen's going to faint.' And I dashed round and grabbed her as she was buckling and we dumped her into that green chair over there, it's a recliner, stuck her feet up in the air and gave her a drink. We reckoned brandy was what she needed and she did. She'd been caught suddenly with no time to think about it and she'd had an injection. And her whole body just reacted and she was ready to pass out. She's courageous about so many things."

Helen had applied for the lectureship in Political Studies when Elizabeth McLeay, now Associate Professor of Politics and International Relations at Victoria University, won a Rose Women's Fellowship to Oxford. According to Barry Gustafson, competition for the vacancy was tough:

"We had a number of applications and it effectively came down to a choice between Helen, who'd been encouraged to apply by Bob Chapman, I think, and Michael Bassett who'd lost his seat in Parliament and was teaching. Michael had been a Senior Lecturer in History of course, and we had a staff meeting and it split quite badly, almost half and half. Half were for Michael on the grounds of his experience and qualifications, and half were for Helen on the grounds that she was more a political scientist than a historian. We also wanted younger women and it was a temporary position. Bob Chapman, who was the Department Head, was really the person who finally came down strongest on Helen's side. And that made the difference."

Helen was apparently a good lecturer, her lectures well prepared and structured, with touches of humour. Bill Ralston was impressed:

"I remember sitting in on a couple of her lectures and seminars in the department. She had, and still has a fantastic analytical mind and the ability to break down problems to their core very quickly. You might disagree with how she decided to dispose of the problem, but her analysis of it was usually pretty accurate. I remember seeing her in meetings and seminars and thinking, 'She's totally in control'. She was the same chairing the Labour Youth meetings – very, very efficient, bang, bang, bang through the agenda, no time wasted. I remember thinking she'd be great in Cabinet. None of these long drawn-out Cabinet meetings that go on all day where they discuss the position of the toilets in the engineering block of Auckland University. None of that sort of trivia. She'd be driving right to the heart of it all."

The new full-time lecturer was liked by the students who found her available and sympathetic.

"She was warm to students too," says Noeline Chapman. "We heard independently from women – you know how women always get into trouble around the university – that they could go and talk to Helen. Now you don't talk to a bluestocking. You talk to people who are suffering the same sort of little setbacks as you are suffering."

But Helen's interest in politics had not waned. Having spent part of her time overseas with the International Union of Socialist Youth, she had returned to New Zealand "with a lot of ideas about how successful Labour Parties worked".

The New Zealand Labour Party was certainly not working successfully. The hopes that so many of its supporters had placed in a Labour renaissance under Norman Kirk had been dashed by his death and by the Party's disastrous polling in the 1975 election. Labour was defeated again in 1978, but the result was anything but a rout, as Bob Chapman explains:

"Remember that in 1978 and 1981 Labour won two successive elections in terms of the number of votes cast, but lost them on the distribution, that is to say, on the number of seats they actually took. That was largely the nature of distributions in New Zealand under First Past the Post. Those two successive defeats were actually triumphs. Only 1975 was the disaster it seemed to be. But '78 was disastrous because Labour lost the election, having actually won it on the number of votes cast for them. And the result was that the Party was demoralised and disorganised, the branches were in bad shape and membership numbers went down drastically."

In 1978 Helen was overwhelmingly voted onto the Party's governing body, the Central Executive, later renamed the New Zealand Council. Jim Anderton was elected to the Executive in the same year. Helen had first met Anderton in the lead-up to the local body elections in 1971, an encounter which she now describes as "a meeting of common interests":

"I particularly remember Jim from the first meeting of the Princes Street branch after the '75 election. There was enormous anger in the Labour Party as to how on earth we had lost the election. I remember Jim coming to the meeting and expressing a sense of outrage that it had been lost and saying, 'Let's face it, our organisation is absolutely pathetic.' The electorates were disorganised. The Party didn't have enough members. Not enough work had been done. And not enough money had been raised. So Margaret Wilson and I and others became involved in a campaign to help Jim to rebuild the whole membership base for the Labour Party."

Anderton was well qualified for the task. A former teacher and child welfare officer, he had worked as a Labour Party organiser and as a fundraiser for the Catholic Church. He had extensive experience of local body politics. And he was a successful businessman. After working as Export Manager for UEB Textiles, then New Zealand's largest carpet manufacturer, he had started his own manufacturing engineering company, Anderton Holdings, which he ran for 13 years until he entered Parliament in 1984. *Time* magazine had recognised him, along with Bob Hawke, as one of 150 potential future world leaders. He was precisely what the Party needed – a man with business contacts, a brilliant fundraiser and organiser.

Bob Chapman, who describes him as "a sadly under-recognised worker in New Zealand politics", claims that Anderton was "fundamentally the person who rebuilt the Labour Party":

"Jim was inspired and inspiring. He really has organisational capacity. And he's got immense chutzpah. He would go into big businesses and say, 'Look, you've contributed heavily to the National Party for years. But democracy is a two-party affair, and Labour, which you often regard as a disaster when it gets in, has not had the benefit of any support or any advice from you. How about a contribution? I don't say, give us the same as you give to National, but you'd better give us enough to survive as a sensible, moderate party.' He made huge increases in the Party's receipts simply by organising the totally unorganised."

By 1979 Anderton had been elected President of the Labour Party and both he and Helen were members of the Policy Council, responsible for the development of the Party's election manifesto. The rebuilding work continued.

Mike Williams: "Helen and Jim really now ran the Party and there were massive improvements as membership built up. Jim started business house canvassing. I invented the pledge system, which is now called the VFL – Victory For Labour. It was the first time anyone had stood up in front of an audience and said, 'Sign the automatic bank transfer form now!' And I travelled the length and breadth of the country with Jim. We must have done over a hundred meetings from Invercargill right to Kaitaia. I can just about repeat off by heart the speech Jim would give, because I heard it again and again. But it worked. And Helen was the planner, with a very clear vision of where we were going."

In *Head and Shoulders* Helen speaks of this period of rebuilding the Party:

> I'd always taken an interest in the sheer grind of organization and how to make [the Party] effective, and after joining the Executive I became part of the grass-roots movement led by Jim to rebuild the Party into a more effective political organisation. When we began there was no fundraising division, no clear defin-ition of roles, no Education Officer, no Women's Officer. It was an uphill job. I was involved in running seminars on policy and organisation and appointing people to the new jobs. All this is incorporated in the structure now.
>
> I think I have been pretty influential over those years. I provided a lot of the ideas Jim fronted with. If the hundreds of hours I'd spent counselling him had been spent on my doctoral thesis, I'd have finished it by now! He got the publicity because he was the President. But I was on the Executive and put an awful lot of time into making sure his presidency was a success. He would fully acknowledge the support I've given him and I think it's recognised throughout the Party. But I didn't really function happily in that behind-the-scenes role and I would have preferred to have a little more credit for ideas.

There is an unmistakeable feeling of grievance in this passage, a sense that Anderton was getting all the credit for rebuilding the Party, when it was very much a team effort. Helen is diplomatic on the issue today. Others are less so. Barry Gustafson, who describes Anderton as "the most divisive person I've ever met in politics", claims that the rebuilding of the Labour Party began long before Ander-ton became involved and was well advanced under the previous President, Arthur Faulkner. Jonathan Hunt agrees:

Left **Newly elected to the Central Executive, Helen addresses the Labour Party Conference, May 1978.**

"All the bullshit that's been talked about when the

Labour Party finally got big membership being under Jim Anderton! It wasn't like that at all. It was under Arthur Faulkner and Bill Rowling, in 1976 and 1977, that the membership vastly increased. I can remember in my own electorate of New Lynn the only time I ever topped 1000 members, including 700 in one branch, was 1976-77."

David Lange concurs: "Helen was unassuming. She was almost the perfect assistant to Jim because you didn't know she was there. And Jim actually was the personification of the Labour Party in resurgence. He was the fellow that did the trumpeting and the speaking and was absolutely inexhaustible in his commitment to the promotion, probably in equal doses, of himself and the Party. You never had the same feeling about Helen. Helen's commitment was actually to the goals of the Party.

"Let's be quite clear about it. If Helen had had an idea and presented it herself, she'd have had her neck cut off. That's the nature of things. Jim was a person who was advancing his patch, and did it with all the resources at his command. And Helen was a very useful resource."

Whatever the truth of the matter, there is no doubt that the combined efforts of Jim Anderton, Helen Clark, Margaret Wilson, Mike Williams and others contributed substantially in the late 1970s to the reorganisation and rebuilding of the Labour Party across the country.

Helen's trip to the U.K. and Sweden was to have an unexpected and highly significant aftermath. Back in Auckland, she was changing the remains of her Swedish currency into New Zealand dollars, when she was spotted by Tord Kjellstrom, a young Swedish lecturer in the Department of Community Health at the Auckland Medical School. Tord, who had Labour Party connections, may have seen Helen previously at Princes Street, but his attention was drawn on this occasion by the fact that she had evidently just returned from Sweden. He struck up a conversation, then invited her round to his house for dinner. Also on the guest list was a colleague at Med School, a young medical sociologist by the name of Peter Davis.

Peter had a fascinating background. His great-grandfather arrived in New Zealand as an infant with his father in 1863. He later migrated to Australia and then to China where he ran a hotel.

Peter's grandfather Roy Davis was born in Melbourne. A self-made businessman and successful entrepreneur, he hated almost everything the old Britain stood for, but decided to send his son, John Stanley Davis, to a British public school. John, who was born in Tientsin, China, in 1918, was duly dispatched to Kings School, Canterbury, where he was brought up by a farming family in the South of England. Given the travel arrangements of the time, it was effectively a banishment.

When John's education was complete, his father, who expected his son to follow in his footsteps, found him a post in a partnership on the London Stock Exchange. However, the planned return to the family stockbroking business in China was not to be. World War Two intervened and John was not naturally suited to the business. Nevertheless, it did open up a lively social life. According to Peter, his father spent much of his time "going to debutante balls and drying out in a Turkish bath – all the things that young men of social aspiration did at the time."

He also enlisted as a territorial in the London Scottish. The military was a popular option for public school types who had not gone on to university, and John may have been attracted to the kilts, sporrans and glengarries which were part of the Regiment's ceremonial regalia. Enlisting may also have been a sensible preparation for the future, given the gathering clouds of war in Europe.

"My father," says Peter, "met my mother early in the Second World War when he went down to defend the south coast of England where her family was living. Her maiden name was Lloyd. She was born in Pachmahri, a hill station in India, around 1921. Her father was a doctor in the Indian Medical Service."

The oldest of three children, Peter was born in Milford-on-Sea in April 1947. In August of that year his father went to India with the Dunlop rubber company, only to be marooned in his hotel by the riots accompanying partition. Peter and his mother joined him early in 1948.

In 1950 the family moved to Tanganyika where Peter's father was employed by F.F. Chrestien "as a kind of generic white manager". The company had been named after an Anglo-Indian train driver who saw something glisten on the ground in India, picked it up and discovered that it was mica. The company later began operations in Tanganyika.

The Davis family lived for a time in Morogoro, inland from Dar-es-Salaam, then shifted five miles out of town to Magadu, where Peter spent most of his early childhood. Each day his father went to work at the company's factory in town:

"You had all sorts of interesting characters, adventurers frankly, who were kind of marooned in Tanganyika. And these African and European miners would turn up with mica. You remember, the old toasters used to have mica in the middle as electrical insulation. It was very much a cottage industry, not like the gold mines in South Africa, where you're talking about millions of dollars of investment. These were prospectors and peasants, sometimes in little co-ops, and they'd bring the stuff in to the factory where it would be processed and put into boxes and sent off.

"I was a bit of a loner. I did a lot of exploring, going out into the bush with the dog, bird-watching and exploring. And my brother and I used to play soldiers. We had lots of little rubber soldiers, and we used to dig great big trench systems. And

Right **Peter Davis at age two, with his parents and his first tricycle, India, 1949.**

my Dad used to come back from work for lunch and he'd sort of inspect what we'd done. And then we'd do some more and he'd come back for the evening meal and inspect it again. And there'd be different phases of the battle. So we did a lot of playing with soldiers.

"We had a full range of servants. We had a head servant, a night watchman, a cook, a nanny at certain stages, a gardener, a driver sometimes and a guy who did the washing. So you had all sorts of people coming and going all the time. We were brought up with Swahili, which is very phonetic and a very easy language. But I realise looking back on it, that we weren't very good. It was just a string of commands."

When he was seven Peter was sent to a European boarding school in Lushoto in the north of Tanganyika: "I was taken up by car, probably by a servant or a nanny, and I remember turning up at the school as a little kid with what had been my mother's little black bear which she called Balu, because she grew up in India and the Indian word for bear was balu. And a little suitcase with all the clothes and

HELEN: PORTRAIT

132

bits and pieces. And that was my attachment to home. I don't remember being unhappy, but probably I was. But you adapted pretty quickly."

Boarding school in Tanganyika was followed by boarding school in England. Peter was sent to Bradfield College in Berkshire in 1960, where his education continued for the next five years. While at Bradfield he stayed in a holiday home in the same village where his mother had grown up and had met his father. Other than in the summer holidays, he did not see his parents for the best part of 11 years:

"So I've never had close links in that sense, emotional or otherwise. I mean, I always liked getting back, but in a way it was because I just liked being at home and going into the bush and all the rest of it. In a way my links with my Dad have become closer since coming to New Zealand. I guess we two boys had very little to do with our parents. But it seemed perfectly natural at the time. It's only since then that I've seen other families who are a lot closer. We were virtual strangers in a way."

In 1963 Peter's father returned with F.F. Chrestien to India where he settled in Bihar. There he picked up an interest in yoga, which he now practises and teaches in England.

Peter went on to Southampton University where he took History, Politics, Economics and Sociology.

"There was a whole ferment there in the mid-60s. And you'd go to a red brick university, as this was, and you'd probably be the only guy in your class who'd been to a British boarding school. The others were all from grammar schools and you'd lived such a sheltered existence that you'd never met people like that before. So there was quite a bit of a ferment in that sense as well as more broadly. I was also trying to work out what was what and went to a few political meetings. I wasn't attracted to Labour. It was a bit statist, either rather conventional or extreme. And I really didn't make up my mind one way or another.

"There were some politics in the family. In East Africa my mother was involved in both Town and Legislative Councils as an appointed member. And there were others in the family who'd been colonial administrators. And my great-grand-mother on my father's side was the daughter of a missionary. So there were these strands of what you might call 'public service' whose significance I wasn't aware of. So there was a bit of politics in there."

After Southampton, Peter went to the London School of Economics, where he completed a Masters degree in Sociology. He came to New Zealand in 1970 to take up a lectureship in Sociology at Canterbury University and while there took leave to do a second Masters degree in Statistics, again at the London School of Economics. He returned to New Zealand and later got a job as a medical sociologist at the Auckland Medical School, where he began teaching in 1977. It was early in that

Right **The young immigrant sociology lecturer Peter Davis, who would become Helen Clark's husband in 1981.**

year that he was invited to dinner by Tord Kjellstrom and met Helen Clark.

Ask Peter for his first impressions of the woman who was to become his wife and you get something less than a romantic answer:

"Just a lot of interests in common, essentially. In meeting Helen I met somebody who had a rigorous interest in current affairs and politics, and I can't say I'd met anybody before, certainly not in Christchurch, who was interested in those things in the same way. So it was apparent that here was somebody who had travelled and who had an interest in current affairs. So that was the principal common ground."

Ask Helen what attracted her to Peter and you get a similar response: "Intellect. Common interests. He had an interesting background, interesting things to talk about. And he was a great reader, very interested in current affairs. So basically common interests in international affairs, policy."

There are, as it happens, some fascinating similarities between Helen and Peter. Both came from what might be called 'liberal conservative' families. Both were raised in rural areas. Both lived relatively insular lives as children. Both were sent to boarding school which they hated, but learnt to tolerate. Both were estranged to varying degrees from their parents. Both were serious and intellectual. Both chose academic careers. Both were interested in politics and current affairs.

It is perhaps not surprising that each should have recognised the other as a kindred spirit.

Helen and Peter undertook to meet again. But, as Peter reports, their early meetings were something less than intimate.

"Helen had this strong-willed group around Beresford Street – Cath Tizard, Cath's daughters, Ruth Butterworth, and Margaret Wilson. And the way they'd relax at the end of the week was to go around to the Tizards on a Friday evening or maybe a Saturday. In those days they used to do a lot of drinking. Helen doesn't drink much at all now. But that was the way you relaxed at the end of the week. Politics in many ways in those days was lubricated. So that's what we used to do. And some of her friends were involved in local government and local body elections, so we would go out on the odd occasion to restaurants and other places, and little by little had more to do with them and with each other."

Judith recalls her reaction to the new man in Helen's life: "Helen said she'd met somebody. I think he was just living up the road in Anglesea Street and was flatting with two women. I can remember being vaguely surprised that Helen was seeing somebody who was as academically flaky as a sociologist. But he was a dear. I remember her turning up with him at one of these dinner parties – we used to call them 'ladies' nights'. We were shrieking and giggling and gossiping and networking and supporting each other as usual, and Helen turned up with this man, to our vast amusement. And he seemed good-natured and tolerant and rapidly proved that he was willing to be teased. No, he was good, he was great. And again a very shy person, very self-composed and self-contained. I think he and Helen are absolutely matched in all sorts of ways."

Cath Tizard was hostess to the 'ladies' night': "I remember the first time I met Peter. Helen had said she was bringing this fellow home. And I said, 'Well you do know who's coming to dinner tonight?' And she said, 'Yeah, he'll be all right.' And poor Peter! He was the only man there, with Margaret Wilson, Ruth Butterworth, Judith, Helen and me. I remember this slightly bewildered-looking fellow. He didn't have a lot to say. And then we tried to include him but we were all very loud. I suppose it was a trial by fire for him. But he survived it. And then he used to come round fairly regularly after that.

"He was a nice fellow, fun. He always quietly fitted in very well. If you actually asked him a question, he'd answer. But he wasn't exactly a thrustful conversationalist. I can't say his relationship with Helen was wildly demonstrative. More patting affectionate. And Helen has never been afraid to give Peter a hug in public or that sort of thing. I knew that she liked him and he obviously liked her."

Peter was gradually introduced to Helen's circle of close friends. They all liked him and regarded him as an excellent complement to her.

Joan Caulfield: "He was very quiet and he was very supportive of Helen, there's no doubt about that. And they obviously did love each other. Since then Peter has grown in everybody's affections. I think he's been a good foil for Helen."

Mike Williams: "Peter just appeared out of the blue. They were obviously always devoted to each other and they've been inseparable ever since. Absolutely normal relationship. You fell in love, you got together."

At Christmas, Peter was taken to meet Helen's parents: "It wasn't only meeting her parents. Christmases were the big events down there. So there was the whole family – Helen's sisters, her uncles and aunts, her grandmother. They were all down there with their families. It was quite a significant gathering. So it wasn't just meeting the parents, it was meeting rural New Zealand. I'd never been on a farm and I often thought that was a weakness. I thought, 'Funny, I'm in this primary producing country and I've never been to a farm, even though I was brought up in the bush.' So it was an introduction to farming New Zealand.

"And when you think about it, in the 1960s and 70s there was quite a considerable generation gap between fashionably left-wing university people and the older generation. And I was being confronted with a whole culture which was practical, close to the land, no nonsense. What I found strange was that the house was like a displaced suburban home that happened to be in the country. I was kind of expecting something like the European farmhouse where you have great big fireplaces and antlers on the wall, and it was just like a suburban home. So this was my first acquaintance with rural New Zealand, heartland New Zealand."

Helen's parents appear to have liked Peter from the start, but the culture gap was evident to them too:

Margaret: "We didn't know anything about Peter and how she'd met him at that stage, but she must have rung or written to say she was bringing a friend down. And she and Peter arrived. He had a funny little van. I didn't form any strong impression of him at the time. He was just different. He's very English, very dreamy, very intellectual, knows everything. He was a very nice chap."

George: "I tolerated him. He wasn't much use on the farm. He's a good guy. I think Helen had found somebody of her own intellectual standard."

Peter had sabbatical leave at the end of 1978. Helen, who was due to attend a conference in Vancouver for Socialists International, went with him to Britain, where it was her turn to meet the parents for Christmas. After visiting Finland, she returned to Auckland for the start of the university year.

It was in early 1979 that she moved in with Peter at his house in Anglesea Street in Freeman's Bay. The year thus marks the formal beginning of a relationship that has endured for almost a quarter of a century and the start of the campaign that would launch Helen on her parliamentary career.

chapter seven

CAMPAIGN '81

ELEN did not stand in the 1978 General Election. According to David Lange, she preferred to continue building her power base within the Party and to wait for a better opportunity in three years' time. Such long-term strategising was and is typical of Helen, whose political success rests in large part on calculating not just the next move but the entire game-plan. She had, as Judith Tizard points out, no interest at all in being a one-term MP:

"It was very clear that she wanted an urban seat, a safe seat. If you want a long-term career in politics, there's no point having a marginal seat that you're going to lose every time the Party gets unpopular. She wanted a safe seat, she wanted an Auckland seat. She didn't want to have to shift cities. And it quickly became obvious that the next seat coming up was Mount Albert."

Mount Albert was certainly a safe seat. It had been held since 1947 by the amiable and gentlemanly Warren Freer, Minister of Trade and Industry in the third Labour Government. An enormously popular electorate MP, Freer's majority had rarely fallen below two or three thousand in his long parliamentary career. The exception was 1975 when the massive swing against the Government reduced Labour's majority in Mount Albert to a paltry 247, making it briefly a marginal seat. But by 1978 the faithful had returned to the fold. Labour again had a majority of almost 3000.

Freer was now the longest-serving Member of Parliament and Father of the

House, and it was known that he intended to retire before the next election. Here was a safe seat and it was in Auckland. So far as Helen was concerned, Mount Albert fitted the bill exactly. She decided she was going to go for it, a decision she later described as "probably the most deliberate choice I've ever made".

Among Helen's strongest and most loyal supporters were the Andertons and the Tizards. The women in both families were of the firm opinion that while dedication and a brilliant mind were desirable assets in a parliamentary candidate, the condition of the outer man or woman could not lightly be ignored. The process of transforming Helen from fashion victim to fashion plate was about to begin, as Judith recalls:

"It was about that stage that my sister Anne and Mum started getting on at Helen about her clothes and her hair and telling her to wear some make-up and occasionally bloody well smile in a photograph. She was very conscious, particularly in those days, of her teeth, and would always keep her mouth shut in photographs, so that she looked very severe. And I remember Mum sitting her down one day and saying, 'For god's sake, Helen, photographs are a tool. They're a way of getting your face out amongst people. If you seriously want people to look at that face and vote for it, then you're mad. Would you vote for a face that looked like that?' And Helen was pretty, very pretty."

It was an uphill battle. Helen, according to Cath, "was totally uninterested in clothes":

"And she was timid. She had grown up in an era when it was fashionable for a certain group of people, particularly students, not to decorate themselves, an era when the natural look was the thing. And she hadn't ever done what most adolescent girls do fairly naturally – play around with make-up and clothes and that sort of thing. And I really think she lacked the confidence to buy clothes or use make-up. And, yeah, I did chivvy her along a bit and kept telling her she was a big girl now and had to scrub up a bit better. You know, in my usual tactful way."

Not surprisingly, it was Cath who first attempted to persuade Helen to cut her hair:

"She had this long, rippling, beautiful hair, but it was right down to the middle of her back, and I suggested that I should cut a bit off at one stage. And by the time I'd cut about two inches she was in tears and shrieking at me, 'Leave it alone, leave it alone, don't cut any more.' I said, 'There's no point in cutting your hair if I'm only going to take that much off it.' But the thought of cutting her hair was like cutting a limb off at that stage."

Judith believes that the reasons for Helen's early lack of interest in clothes, make-up or her general appearance are to be found in her background:

"Helen has always been incredibly frugal. She comes from a family where there wasn't a lot of extra money. Then she went to boarding school and then to university where she seemed to manage to keep herself. So she was always very careful with money. She would spend quite sensibly on the things that gave her pleasure, and on other people. But I don't think she ever thought clothes were important. She was also very sensitive about it, as most people are who are being bullied about their looks. I remember when Anne and Margaret Wilson took her to get her hair cut, she was quite traumatised by it.

"The other thing is that being the eldest in a family of girls, she didn't have older sisters to show her how to use make-up and how to do your hair and how to play with clothes. And I don't think it ever particularly appealed to her. But the thing about Helen is that she's very open to comment and suggestion. She gets pissed off sometimes when people go on about her hair or her clothes, but she will take criticism on board. And once it was explained to her that it was a tool, she became very practical about it and went out and did it. And she started wearing skirts. I remember her coming downstairs looking very sheepish in a skirt and all of us shrieking, 'Oh my god, look at the legs! Helen's got legs!'"

Joan Caulfield was one of Helen's many advisors on clothes: "As a Labour politician, not so much now, but in the early days, your supporters wanted you to look nice and be up there competing, so to speak, with the Tories. But they didn't want you to look overdressed. So we used to have little talks about that. But it was a gradual process, and in the early days I used to go with her to help her look at some clothes. And there was a transition from her wearing the jeans and leather jackets into something that was fairly conservative, but not what you'd call trendy."

Helen herself accepts that at the time she had very little interest in clothes: "But it's part of the no-frills background, isn't it, that you didn't really have an interest in clothes. For a start, when you were a student, you didn't have the money for clothes. Remember, I was a full-time student for eight years, so prior to 1977 I'd only had three years full-time employment as a junior lecturer, and we weren't paid a lot of money. It wasn't until 1977, when I got a lectureship, that I first started having a bit more money."

Today Helen distinguishes between being interested in clothes and interested in looking well-dressed: "I'm very interested in that. But would I ever go shopping on my own? No, I wouldn't. Because I've got a satisfactory arrangement now where I have a professional designer, Jane Daniels, who understands what I need to be dressed in for my job. So I consult her. Twice a year. And I get it done. So, apart from that, I never go looking for clothes. All my needs are met through that. And I rely on her professional judgment to make sure I'm appropriately dressed."

Brian: "So you're not really interested in fashion?"

Helen: "I'd never pick up a magazine, no."

Brian: "So how good is your judgment on clothes?"

Helen: "Not bad. Jane will show me something and I'll say, 'No, that's just not me. Couldn't wear that.' But she's probably got me to be a bit less conservative over the years. I mean, this year I'm probably wearing trousers more than I have before. For 20 years I never wore trousers in my public life."

Brian: "But you're not into retail therapy?"

Helen: "I hate shopping. It's partly because I'm not interested in acquiring things. I don't want anything. My wants are limited to when my watch breaks down: 'I must get a new watch.' In fact I bought it on a plane going to New York, because that's the only time I had."

Despite her hatred of shopping and her lack of interest in clothes or fashion, Helen took her supporters' advice and abandoned the jeans and leather jacket for the candidate selection meeting. Her hair was cut short and, according to Joan, she wore "a rather nice red jacket".

The candidate selection meeting was held in the Mount Albert War Memorial Hall on a Saturday night in April 1980. On the previous evening Helen, Peter, Judith and Mike Williams convened at Anglesea Street to prepare for the ordeal to come. Judith remembers the occasion – just:

"Mike Williams and I drank the best part of a bottle of whisky while Helen rehearsed her speech in the kitchen. Peter finally went to bed in disgust about midnight. The rest of us stayed up until about 4 o'clock in the morning, while Helen made the speech and I made the speech and Mike made the speech and we all read the speech. And I remember going to the loo and thinking, I've never drunk so much in my life, and then realising that Helen had been sitting on the same glass all night, because even in those days Helen was utterly focused and didn't want to be hung-over for the selection. And I remember saying to her at four o'clock in the morning, 'Look Helen, we've done everything we can. I know you can't sleep, but I'm going to die if I don't go home to bed.' It was a great speech. I think I've still got a copy of it somewhere. It really was a fantastic speech."

Before heading home, Judith ordered a taxi for Mike Williams. Mike was in no fit state to drive, but not so drunk that his memory of the evening was totally erased:

"I remember her practising her speech in the kitchen the night before the selection. And there's a phrase in that speech that sticks in my mind, which was, 'I don't think you should select me *because* I'm a woman. However, I don't think you should *not* select me because I'm a woman.' It was a very, very good speech."

Peter must by now have contemplated the possibility that his partner would win the nomination, win the seat and end up spending at least four days a week working and living in Wellington, while he worked and lived in Auckland. The prospect seems not to have concerned him greatly:

"We basically led pretty parallel lives. Helen's a very capable person and she was already really doing two jobs – a full-time political job and a full-time academic one. There's no way I could have done that. So, as always, a lot of my energy went into my work. We were often out at meetings quite independently."

There were seven candidates vying for the Mount Albert selection – Helen and six men, including Jack Elder, Malcolm Douglas (Roger Douglas's brother), and Keith Elliott, a local schoolteacher who was Chair of the LEC. Each of the seven delivered their prepared 12-minute speech to a packed hall. Mike Williams was the timekeeper:

"I wouldn't say she wowed them, but it was a very tradesmanlike, competent speech. If you were a level-headed punter without any commitment at all to any of the candidates, you would certainly have voted for her. She dominated the proceedings to the extent that I can't even remember who the other candidates were."

With the speeches out of the way a straw vote was taken among the three or four hundred Party members present in the hall. The vote would not count with the selection panel but would serve as an indication to them of the general feeling in the hall. Helen won the straw vote hands down. It was now up to the panel to choose the Labour Party candidate for Mount Albert for the 1981 General Election.

Labour Party candidates are selected by a panel or committee consisting of three members appointed by the New Zealand Council (or Central Executive as it was then called) and three representatives chosen by the local Party members. Helen, who was herself a member of the Executive, could be sure of support from that quarter. But though she had worked hard cultivating relationships and networks in the electorate, she could not be certain that the local Party representatives would vote for her:

"The selection meeting was chaired by Jim Anderton, who was Party President at the time. I can't recall who the others were from the Central Executive, possibly two of the Party Vice-Presidents. There were three people from the local committee – a man called Bill Runciman who lived in Sandringham, Bill McMillan who was the Treasurer of the LEC, and someone else whose name I can't

HELEN CLARK
Your Next MP For Mt Albert

Do you realise it is 40 years since the Auckland Region last had a woman M.P.? Not since 1941 when Mary Dreaver was elected in Waitemata has Auckland sent a woman M.P. to Wellington. Helen Clark will therefore make history when she closes that 40-year gap in 1981.

COME AND JOIN US. Send $2 minimum to Secretary Mt Albert Labour Party, P.O. Box 41 111 St Lukes, Auckland. Phone: Brian & Mary-Lytle 860-710

remember. They really went into it wanting Keith Elliott, the Electorate Chairman, but eventually one of them gave way for me. Bill McMillan refused to give way, but he later came to be a great supporter."

Helen had won the nomination. Among her cheering supporters was Cath Tizard: "Someone had arranged that if Helen got the nomination Sylvia Freer would give her a bunch of flowers. You see, Helen had been supported by Warren, and whatever people say, the incumbent's endorsement is quite important. Anyway, Sylvia was quite happy to go along with the flowers idea. But I made sure. Sylvia said, 'I'll wait till she comes down to her seat.' I said, 'No Sylvia, walk right up the front and do it so everybody can see.' Sylvia didn't have much sense of the dramatic and I knew that if this endorsement were to be seen for what it was, it had to be done publicly. And that's what Sylvia did."

In *Head and Shoulders* Helen describes winning the nomination for Mount Albert as "the peak of my career". But the gloss of that night was soon to wear off:

"It was a difficult campaign. As a single woman I was really hammered. I was accused of being a lesbian, of living in a commune, having friends who were Trotskyites and gays, of being unstable and unable to settle to anything. If you elect

Helen Clark, my political opponents said, she's for abortion on demand and our whole society will change overnight. I was fighting on all fronts."

Helen may well have had friends who were gay, but she cannot recall knowing any Trotskyites, did not live in a commune, and it would be hard to imagine anyone more stable or more focused on the task in hand. So what of the other allegations?

Helen was certainly a proponent of liberal abortion laws: "The abortion issue was quite big in '81. I remember SPUC (the Society for the Protection of the Unborn Child) making an appointment to see me. Two people came to see me at the home of the electorate chairman. He and his wife had seven children and were active in the Catholic parish. They were liberal Catholics. And I remember we had a perfectly pleasant discussion, and one of the two people became a Party member and was a good supporter. I've always believed that if you have a firm opinion you should state it. I've always been very clear that abortion is a matter of individual choice. So if I was asked a question, I answered it. I would say, 'I believe in a woman's right to choose.' Very straightforward. But as the candidate for Mount Albert, I kept very much to the basic issues which were of interest to the electorate – housing, health, education, employment."

Rumours that Helen was a lesbian had been circulating for some time and were spread not only by her political opponents, but by some who ought to have been her supporters. Joan saw a lot of Helen during the campaign:

"There were a lot of meetings at our place. And she was also very involved with the local electorate at that time, building up the constituency, the contacts. She was quite shy. And in those days she was a young woman, independent, and she wasn't married. And I can remember a Minister, a conservative Labour Minister, referring to her in my presence as 'a barren lesbian'. And I also heard rumours from a friend of my father's, who lived in the electorate. He said that Helen was a lesbian and Peter was gay and that they were living together for political reasons, to make it look good. And because Helen's always had a deep voice, people have always thought, 'Oh well, a feminine woman doesn't have a voice as deep as that.' Which is quite ridiculous. So Helen came in for a heck of a lot of criticism because of not having children and not being considered a conventional woman."

The lesbian allegations persisted: Helen was having an affair with Cath Tizard, which led to the break-up of the Tizard marriage; she was having an affair with Margaret Wilson; her relationship with Peter was a mere sham, designed to conceal the truth that both were gay. The scuttlebutt continues to the present day:

"Over the years you still get the National Party rumour-mongering, most recently that the marriage has broken up. When Peter went to Christchurch they ran that one round. It never stops. I've heard National MPs interject, 'What about your affair with so-and-so?' They never stop. They're relentlessly personally nasty. The one thing I hate is the National Party. I think they're loathsome people. I do."

Brian: "That's pretty sweeping. You're talking about a wide group of people."

Helen: "My experience has been that at the level of party campaigning they're personally very unpleasant."

Brian: "Perhaps. But there are National Party supporters round the country who are perfectly nice people."

Helen: "Oh, absolutely, and who would feel shocked and ashamed that it was ever done in their name."

Peter doesn't remember Helen being particularly upset by the rumours surrounding her sexuality during the Mount Albert campaign: "You were rather flabbergasted that they would bother. You were a bit reliant on the professionalism of the media, because there are two levels. You can have scuttlebutt at one level, but it's whether it then becomes an issue in the media. I don't ever remember any headline. Not like the headlines you have now about me and my emails. We had nothing like that to contend with. So I think it could well be that her friends were more upset than us. I don't remember being upset. I remember being a little bit concerned, because it was a little bit extreme. But I assumed that it would die down."

Though all of these rumours were absolutely untrue, Helen's unmarried and childless state was nonetheless of concern to some of her supporters. The topic was raised at the Andertons:

"What happened was that Peter and Helen were at dinner at our place. And Jim brought up the issue of the publicity about Helen and Peter living together and not being married, and what the Opposition would make of that, because New Zealand had always been a very conservative society. And some of the rumours that went around were incredible. And I remember Jim saying, 'Well, you and Peter, you should get married. You're living together, so what's the problem?' Not knowing that for Helen it was the last thing she was holding onto that was anti-establishment really.

"But she railed against it and didn't want to do it. She didn't think it was necessary, and it was only a piece of paper. And I remember saying to her, 'Yes it is only a piece of paper, and you've already made the commitment to each other, so why worry about the piece of paper?' But I don't think any of us quite realised how strongly she felt about the whole establishment thing.

"It was a pretty pragmatic discussion. There must have been another couple there – I think it was the Chapmans – who lent their weight to it. But she wasn't happy about it. She felt that she was being forced into it. But she did decide to get married."

Peter went along with the decision, as he has gone along with almost all of Helen's decisions since they first began living together:

"I didn't mind one way or the other too much. But I don't think Helen was too keen. We were involved in this larger game of politics. You were more or less ambushed into it. I didn't really mind. Helen's strong-willed and her whole life has required her to bend that will at certain times. But I think this was probably at a deeper level. It was about identity and what it means to be a woman breaking convention. And maybe in this respect she couldn't break convention entirely. But I don't remember any decision being made about it. In these things, I go along with Helen. If Helen wants to do it, I'll do it."

Five years later, Helen told Virginia Myers: "The relationship wouldn't have worked if what I was doing didn't have his total support. I couldn't stand being in competition with somebody. When the question of my standing for Mount Albert came up, I pointed out that it could be a 30-year commitment. But Peter still thought I should stand. He's always pushed me, always been supportive."

But if Helen had to get married, she was determined to do it without fanfare. A quiet registry office wedding was planned. And the guest list was extremely small. Indeed, the only people who knew about the wedding were the Andertons, Cath Tizard and Helen's Aunt Fay. Naturally, feathers were ruffled:

"She didn't even tell me, evil cow," Judith Tizard comments. "She didn't want to get married. I was aware of that. But she didn't tell me she was getting married. And

I was pissed off with her. I was really pissed off with her. We were good, really close friends."

Other good, really close friends had not been told either – Margaret Wilson, Ruth Butterworth, Bob and Noeline Chapman. And as Cath Tizard tells it, even George and Margaret may not have been on the original guest list:

"I seem to recall that we had some sort of dispute over that. I wouldn't be absolutely sure about this, but I think I persuaded her that she had to let her parents know beforehand. I said to her that I would be deeply offended if any of my daughters – and one of them did – went and got married without telling me and I found out about it afterwards. Helen could confirm this. But I think she and I had quite long serious conversations about her letting her family know before the event."

George and Margaret *were* told about the wedding before the event.

Margaret: "She rang me up on the Wednesday in the afternoon. George wasn't home and we had a conversation. And at the end of it she said, 'Oh, Peter and I have decided to get married on Friday.' I said, 'Which Friday?' She said, 'The day after tomorrow.' I said, 'Oh god!' So I told him when he got home."

George: "So then we got on the phone."

Margaret: "And that night I made her a wedding cake, a big fruitcake."

George: "And I got on the phone. I was determined to have the family together. My family's meant everything to me, and we're still a family. So we rang up Bruce and Jenefer and they arranged to come. And we got Sandra."

Margaret: "Suzanne couldn't come. She had Catherine, who was still just a small baby."

George: "But five of us got there, so at least her family were represented. We'd have been there anyway, whether she wanted us or not."

So Helen Clark and Peter Davis were married in the Queen Street Registry Office on 6 November 1981. Present, in addition to the bride and groom, were Helen's parents, her sisters Sandra and Jenefer, Jenefer's husband Bruce, Cath Tizard and Jim Anderton. The bride wore a creamy coloured suit and a tangerine blouse which Cath Tizard had helped her choose.

While Peter and Helen were getting married, Joan was at home preparing an unusual wedding reception, unusual because only one of the guests, Helen's Aunt Fay, had been told that anyone was getting married:

"I must have gone to one of her meetings and she said to me, 'I want you to come to Jim Anderton's house tomorrow night.' And I said, 'Oh Helen, I don't know whether we can.' And she said, 'Well, we're getting married.' I said, 'Oh, I'll come.'"

Snapshots from a wedding reception:

Margaret: "We stayed at a motel somewhere and went to Jim Anderton's place in the evening. I'd made a nice fruitcake and iced it and we took that, so she had a wedding cake, which wasn't too bad at such short notice. I remember Helen wasn't feeling well. She'd banged her head badly somewhere. I know she had a dreadful headache."

Right **Cath Tizard was a witness at Helen's wedding. Cath, later Dame Catherine, became Auckland's first woman mayor and then New Zealand's first woman Governor-General.**

Jenefer: "It wasn't a day of great happiness, because the fact was that she was required to get married and have a certificate of marriage and that's what she did. To oblige other people, not herself. I think we enjoyed the party afterwards."

Sandra: "Was it a happy occasion? It was an occasion. I knew she was only getting married because of what was happening, and because of how cruel people can be and what they say about you. It didn't worry me whether she was married or not. I didn't blame her for getting married, because it might have been the way she had to go. I would accept my sister however she was."

Ruth: "It took one helluva lot out of Helen to do it. She was resistant up until the last minute. I mean, she was crying on the day. It was just so awful, because it was so deeply against her principles. She didn't believe in marriage. It went so deep. And Peter is such a happy and relaxed person that he would do anything for Helen. He's got a level of naivety still, which we observe regularly, which is quite charming."

Joan: "She did get upset. When she came back from the registry office she wasn't an entirely happy camper. She'd obviously been crying. But she was fine and we ended up having a very nice party, drinking their health and everything. It was a good party. And I do have some rather awful photos, and she looked fine."

Fay: "I think there were nibbles and drinks, that sort of thing. Margaret had made a wedding cake. The cake was duly cut and handed around. I remember that Peter went off and rang his parents in England at Cath's suggestion. And Helen says she can't imagine that her mother-in-law was particularly pleased to have a socialist for her daughter-in-law. And I remember her saying that anyone who married a politician is a fool. That got a good laugh."

George: "And Helen said, 'Dad's got three sons-in-law. Alan is very good at electricity and mechanics. Bruce would be quite useful on the farm. But I don't think Peter would be any damn use to Dad at all.' We all roared."

Margaret adds: "They come from different worlds, George and Peter."

Did Helen and Peter really need to get married? Cath Tizard doesn't think so: "It was an open secret that Helen didn't think there was any reason for them to marry. But some of her supporters thought that her chances of winning the election would be better if her relationship was 'regularised'. Well that one didn't cut any ice with me. A dead duck could have won Mount Albert. Someone with her talent wasn't going to lose the seat just because she was 'living in sin'."

There is no doubt that the potential political fallout from "living in sin" was the only reason Helen married Peter. She did not want to get married, felt compromised by having to do so and railed against it privately. Little has changed in the intervening years:

Brian: "Why were you so resistant to the idea of getting married?"

Helen: "Oh well, I've never thought there was a lot of point in getting married unless there were kids to protect."

"But your resistance to it seems stronger than that."

"It's sort of an independence thing really. I always felt that your independence was compromised somewhat by being married. If I hadn't gone into politics, I would not have married. I'm sure the relationship would be exactly as it is today. But I wouldn't have been legally married."

"How did Peter feel about your not wanting to get married?"

"He was quite happy about it. If it hadn't been 20 years ago when attitudes were different, there would have been no reason to change the status we had."

"But you were in love with one another?"

"Oh yes."

"That's a term you'll happily use?"

"I suppose so. We're 24 years down the track."

"But you were crying on your wedding day."

"Yep."

"It really was a bad idea from your point of view?"

"It was a necessary evil."

"Peter wasn't offended?"

"Oh no, he wasn't offended."

"Ruth Butterworth says Peter's such a happy person, he'd do anything for Helen."

"That's right."

"Does it still rankle that you had to get married?"

"No. I've a great capacity to move on. Things happen. You move on. Never look back. No regrets. It was the right thing to do at the time. Then just move on."

In parallel with the rumours about Helen's sexuality ran the theme that it was somehow unnatural for a 30-year-old woman in a committed relationship not to have children. It was a theme that would prove more enduring than the scuttlebutt about Helen being a lesbian. In its 1999 election campaign National made great play of the fact that its leader, Jenny Shipley, was a mother of two. Though it was never overtly stated, the clear implication was that the Leader of the Labour Party was somehow not a real woman and could certainly not relate to the lives of ordinary New Zealand families.

Helen has been consistently unapologetic on the subject: "I never wanted children. I could not have done what I've done with my life, professionally, in terms of pleasure or travel, if I'd had children. It was a very deliberate choice and I'll never regret it. You've just got better things to do with your life, unimpeded."

She rejects the suggestion that couples who decide not to have children are selfish or focused purely on themselves: "There is a thing called choice. And I just think those arguments are utterly spurious. I mean, selfish about what? I don't think anyone could accuse me of being selfish. My whole life is so outwardly directed towards other people. If I were selfish I'd go into my shell and never do anything for anyone, but that's just not me. I can't understand it. I can't see any substance to it whatsoever."

Nor can she see any substance to the argument that it is unnatural for a woman not to have children or that childless couples somehow have a missing dimension in their lives:

"If indeed there is such a missing dimension I'm very happy to have it missing. I don't think it has any relevance. I'm well aware of the double burden of women with children, particularly those who go back to work. Most women with kids who go out to work are still running the home as well. It's tough. And I don't have to do it to know that. It's hard. As for the suggestion that it's unnatural for a woman not to have children, that argument assumes that we are born to reproduce. That used to be our fate; it was never our choice."

She describes those who tried to make political capital out of her decision not to have children as "small-minded and spiteful people":

"I thought it was absolutely gross, but I actually don't think the vast majority of people gave a toss. We live in an age where people respect choice."

Helen's choice not to have children was certainly respected by her friends and family. Cath Tizard recalls discussing the issue with her from time to time:

"And I would very banally point out that for women options run out, and it's something you've got to think about while you've got the chance to have children. But, on the other hand, having been married to a politician and having had children, I know that the two lives are not very compatible. And being a politician's child is not a particularly healthy way of life. So I always respected her decision. I don't think Helen ever had strong maternal urges or that it was a great imperative in her life to be a mother. But she also very clearly understood that bringing up children would involve considerable sacrifice of her political energy, effectiveness and position."

Helen was certainly not depriving her parents of grandchildren, for, as George cheerfully acknowledges, "We've got eight of the little blighters!"

Only Jenefer sounds a quiet note of regret: "It's such a shame that those brains aren't going to be inherited. I know she says she wouldn't have been able to achieve what she has achieved if she'd had children. Well, Suzanne and I have had to work twice as hard."

It's a gentle reproach, for Jenefer knows that Helen has treated both her children and Suzanne's as if they were her own.

And Peter? Well, Peter went along: "It just didn't happen. It wasn't a conscious decision made one way or another. I had no great yen for a family, but I could well have enjoyed one. I have no idea."

A final telling comment comes from Maggie Eyre, Helen's close friend and her advisor on clothes, make-up and presentation: "I don't have children and there've been many times in my life when I've wanted children and I've gone through the grieving process of not being a mother. But I chose not to have a child outside a relationship. And meeting Helen was just remarkable for me. Here is a woman who doesn't have children. And, as a childless woman myself, I need a role model like that. It's very important to me. There are times when I think, 'Oh, maybe I should have had children.' But I look at Helen and realise, 'No, it's OK.' I think women who don't have children need role models out there, so that we don't feel like freaks, we don't feel as if we've missed out, we don't feel that we did it all wrong, that we made a mistake. So that we feel that we're still whole as women. And I say that because I often have people saying to me, 'You poor thing, what a shame you didn't have a child.'"

Though they were an irritation, the issues of clothes, marriage and children were not uppermost in Helen's mind during the Mount Albert campaign. There was an election to be won and she set about it with a will. Friends and colleagues had begun to notice a change in her, a sense of absolute commitment to politics.

Judith: "As she became more focused on the political work, she drank less and less. She didn't have time for parties and yahooing to the same extent."

Richard Harman: "You saw someone who'd obviously disciplined herself to such an extent that she now seemed to me to be beginning the second stage of morphing into the complete politician. She'd got the sound intellectual and philosophical basis, now we were seeing the beginning of the development of the apparently extroverted politician."

David Lange: "An austerity had descended on her, born of commitment and discipline, and it extended across the board. By then her indulgences – this bizarre business of going off to the opera with Jonathan Hunt – were becoming extremely disciplined too. And of course she married in '81. Let's be clear about that too. It was another form of assertion of purpose which she embraced. She made deals with herself, if you could put it that way, to pursue a particular goal."

In pursuit of her goal, Helen decided that she and Peter should move out of Anglesea Street and into the Mount Albert electorate. Peter went along:

"There are things where I just trust to Helen's judgement. I can't remember how we identified the Mount Eden house or how long it took or anything for that matter. It was just in the electorate. And frankly, Judith's brother Nigel, who is a builder, always says he virtually had to rebuild the thing. You wonder what the point was in buying it, but it's stood the test of time."

The campaign for Mount Albert was long, but largely uneventful. Large teams of helpers went out canvassing and raising money every Saturday. Helen attended endless cottage meetings:

"You know what Auckland suburbs are like. They tend to be a bit anonymous. People tend not even to know their neighbour, let alone someone who's come out of the university branch of the Labour Party to be a candidate. And I didn't really know anyone in Mount Albert, because I hadn't lived there. So the cottage meetings were very important in building up a network of people who knew you.

"Labour Party people would have meetings in their homes and invite their neighbours in. There'd be between five and 20 people in the lounge, mostly Labour people or swinging voters. And the host would start by thanking everyone for coming, and saying, 'You've come to meet Helen and she's got a few things she'd like to say.' And then we'd have a general discussion. And there was certainly the feeling that people were coming to meet their next Member of Parliament. There wasn't any great doubt about the result. I must say I enjoyed the cottage meetings. I got to know a lot of people, people I still know to this day."

It's difficult to understand how Helen fitted all of this in – the campaign, her involvement in the Central Executive and Policy Council, her full-time job as a

CHECK
with us that you
are on the roll.
☎ 7h8631

our Labour party is your
Labour party

you need
HELEN CLARK
TO SAVE...

Your family...
Your job...
Your future

P
30

lecturer in the Political Studies Department. And then there was the 1981 Springbok tour:

Above **Ross Meurant's 'Red Squad' outside Helen's electorate office near Eden Park, Auckland, Springbok tour, winter 1981.**

"I went on both marches. Paradoxically, Labour candidates had been instructed by Bill Rowling and Jim Anderton as Party President not to go on demonstrations. I think they were conscious that Kirk's stopping the Springbok tour in 1975 had played a major part in Labour's defeat. Kirk was seen as breaking his word not to stop the tour. And of course the '81 tour almost certainly does explain our defeat in that year. We actually won a majority of votes across New Zealand, but couldn't carry the provincial seats. And that's what Rowling and Anderton were terrified of.

"Anyway, I ignored the instruction. Well, what could you do? This was my electorate. Eden Park was in my electorate. The demonstrations were in my electorate. And we were simply terrified. There were reasons for people in the front row to have helmets on. The police charged the demonstrators. It was very unpleasant. I saw people beaten to the ground by Ross Meurant's Red Squad in the police. It was outrageous. But I saw it. I saw people on the ground being hammered."

Labour got 39.01 percent of the vote in the 1981 General Election, against National's 38.78 percent. 702,630 people voted Labour. 698,508 voted National. But these were the days before proportional representation and National remained

Right **Jim Anderton and Joan with Helen, the new MP for Mount Albert, just after the 1981 election. Joan is one of Helen's closest friends and is her Mount Albert Electorate Secretary.**

the government with 47 seats in the House, against Labour's 43 and Social Credit's two. The candidate for Mount Albert held the seat with a majority of 3907. Helen Clark was now a Member of Parliament.

chapter eight

INTO THE
BOYS' CLUB

O N the day after the election, Helen rang Jonathan Hunt. She wanted some basic advice – how to book her fare to Wellington, when she should come down, where you went for lunch. There was no great urgency. Parliament would not be called until April. Helen used the time to set up her electorate office and to establish herself in the Capital. She billeted initially with Bob Chapman's son and daughter-in-law, then bought herself a small flat in Aro Street.

With Parliament finally in session, she spent four days a week in Wellington, returning home on Friday afternoon. To the question, "How did that lifestyle suit you – being away from your husband more than half the week?" she replies, "I can't remember it having any impact at all."

Peter seems to agree: "It wasn't a big deal. Because you got virtually a daily phone call. I can't remember whether we always did, but I was so busy at work, ridiculously so in a way, that I had my evenings full. I was trying to do a Ph.D. and a whole lot of other things. I was active in the Labour Party – we started a magazine at one time, some colleagues and I. So I was actually very busy on a host of other things. And my evenings were pretty full. I mean, if you'd had a family, you couldn't have done it either, actually."

It was probably just as well for Peter that they didn't have a family. On top of his already heavy workload, he would probably have had to look after the kids. The marriage, as Helen later told Virginia Myers, was unconventional from the start:

"My relationship with Peter is non-traditional in that he runs the house. He's always done that. He does the shopping and I pay half. I haven't been in a supermarket for years. A lot of people might say I'm the dominant one. I guess my life dominates the household, because his is the more adaptable. If we both need the car, I get it, because I have to have it. But he has four days of the week in which to do what he wants."

New Members of Parliament were regarded as fair game by the incumbents on both sides of the House and offered little advice or assistance. "You walked at your peril," Helen says. "There was always someone waiting to trip you up." Jonathan Hunt was the welcome exception:

"Jonathan was in his early 40s. He'd been in Parliament for 15 years and was developing a certain gravitas. And his seminar to new members was a feature of every post-election period. He'd get the Clerk of the House and more experienced members who'd chaired Select Committees in to talk to you. And you'd have a tour of the Parliamentary Library. It was a very basic orientation to the new workplace. So you'd have a seminar on the House and how to ask a question, how to prepare your maiden speech."

Helen delivered her maiden speech to Parliament on 27 April 1982. She paid the traditional tribute to her predecessor, then turned to the problems faced by many of her constituents – increased State House rentals, the burden, particularly on the elderly, of rises in Government charges for postage, telephones and transport, and price increases on basic foodstuffs. She spoke of the ethnic diversity in Mount Albert, of youth unemployment in the electorate and of the falling living standards of many of those whom she now represented:

"It is a basic tenet of my philosophy that a society can be judged on how it treats its weakest members – the sick, the disabled, the young and the elderly. Attacks on social provision for any of those cannot be defended in any humane society. Labour's concern has always been for the poor, and for those struggling on the margins of society. We do not seek as our first priority to make the rich richer and the powerful more powerful. Those who believe that that is what the aim of Government should be, could not support us. Our party was founded on concepts of social justice and equality. It was founded by working men and women who could see from the experience of their daily lives the injustice of prevailing social conditions. They set out to change their society to ensure that the resources of the community were more fairly distributed, so that every member of the community could share in the wealth that the community had created."

In a segment of her speech that foreshadowed the economic debate that would tear Labour apart over the next nine years, Helen turned to the Party's philosophy:

"The Labour philosophy sees the State rather differently from the way in which a conservative philosophy sees it. We believe that the State must act to correct the imbalances in our society, favouring the rich and powerful. The conservative position is the laissez-faire posture. 'The less the Government does, the better,' they say, and 'Let the market sort the matter out.' We know that if the market is left to sort matters out social injustice will be heightened, and suffering in the community will grow with the neglect the market fosters. The law of the unregulated market is, in the end, the law of the jungle, where only the strongest can survive.

"My objectives for, and demands of the Government are relatively simple. They centre on the right to work and to be adequately housed, the need for better living standards, for access to health care at a price everyone can afford, for free and quality public education, for recognition of the rights of minorities, and for tolerance and social peace within the community. All those objectives, though simple, seem very far from realisation for the people I represent. There is an immense job of social reconstruction to be done – a job that can begin only when a Labour Government, committed to social change and equality, is elected."

She turned to the evils of 'Think-Big', then to New Zealand's role in the Pacific, disarmament and the threat of nuclear war:

"I call on the Government to make every effort to ensure that New Zealand is well represented on the second special session of the United Nations on disarmament in June of this year. Government should publicise the aims and objectives of the special session in order to draw the attention of all New Zealanders to its importance. Disarmament will come about only when there is a universal conviction that it must. It will come about only after long and patient negotiations. I should like to see New Zealand, as a concerned state, play a leading role in fostering the international climate in which that will be possible."

She drew her maiden speech to a close:

"I have spoken of the concerns of my electorate, the State's role in providing economic and social security for our people, the economic outlook, and the prospects for international peace. I believe that the philosophy of my party links those concerns. It is my hope while in this House to promote constructive solutions based on equity and social justice for the great problems that challenge us today. In doing so, I share my perspective as a woman, as a member of a farming family, as one who was fortunate to have educational opportunities, and as one now privileged to represent one of the finest electorates in New Zealand for the Labour Party. My greatest wish is that at the end of my time in this House I shall have contributed towards making New Zealand a better place than it is today for its people to live in."

Helen, who admits to having been very nervous, had spoken for the permitted half hour. George and Margaret were in the public gallery:

George: "We've got a tape of it."

Margaret: "And her Uncle Tom, George's brother, and sister-in-law went too."

Brian: "What were your feelings on that day?"

George: "Very proud."

Margaret: "Yes. And she mentioned her family."

Working conditions for an Opposition back-bencher at Parliament were something less than plush. Helen had her own office, but shared a secretary with Geoff Braybrooke:

"I tended to crowd him out completely. He would end up writing his letters by hand while the typist worked full-time for me. In those early years I used to get a lot of mail from women because women MPs were so scarce, and young ones were a real novelty. So that generated quite a lot of letters. Domestic violence was a hot topic at the time. Women were also interested in issues of equality – childcare, equal opportunity and equal pay. Housing was quite big, because access to Housing Corporation loans was quite discriminatory in those days. And I remember, somewhere in my early years, getting involved in the issue of the Dairy Board marketing breast milk substitutes abroad, thus undermining breast-feeding in developing countries. So I had a range of contacts with women's groups and causes. I was one of a small group who had an interest in it."

Margaret Wilson observes that despite that interest, Helen was never associated with the feminist section of the Labour movement: "In fact, quite the reverse. It wasn't that she was opposed to feminism but she had a more mainstream, socialist analysis. And that, I suspect, was because of her prior political training and upbringing. Her analysis was in quite conventional terms. I agreed with that, but I never thought it was sufficient, in the sense that the groups I had to deal with had another dimension that didn't always fit in with that mainstream analysis. Much of my political activity was in the Women's Section of the Party, while she was very strong in the Youth Section of the Party. And that's probably because I'm a couple of years older than she is."

According to Joan, Helen's contribution to feminism lay in the example which she provided, rather than in being a member of any organisation.

"Helen was seen as being one of the hopes for women in the Party. She was never seen as a leader for women, but as a woman who could be as effective and as good as any man could be. And I think there's a difference there. She was seen as being an equal. She wasn't seen as pursuing a particularly female agenda, a feminist agenda. The reality was that here was a highly competent woman who'd managed to win the nomination for a safe Labour seat. And that was very difficult for women in the Labour Party. Lots of women stood in marginal seats, but for her to get Mount Albert was a major breakthrough."

Certainly Helen never belonged to any specifically feminist group such as the National Organisation of Women or the Women's Electoral Lobby:

"It wasn't my primary interest. I had always assumed that women could do anything and I was quite shocked to find that some people didn't think the same way."

Nonetheless, Judith recalls that Helen was constantly inviting her to read feminist texts:

"There was a criticism amongst some of the women in the Party that Helen wasn't a feminist. And Helen would say, 'Well of course I'm a feminist.' And she'd quote a large chunk out of Mary Wollstonecraft, *A Vindication of the Rights of*

Women, and say, 'Well of course you've read that.' And I'd say, 'No.' So she'd say, 'Oh for goodness sake!' And the next time she came down she'd have this pile of books for me to read about feminism. She was always giving people books or lending them books. And she was also very stern about getting them back. And you had to tell her what you thought of them when you gave them back. You couldn't skip. But she was huge fun and very challenging and very exciting. She was a very interesting woman."

But would "a very interesting woman" be welcome in Parliament? The answer to that was a resounding No. Helen quickly discovered that the institution she had worked so hard to join was little more than a boys' club. And the boys were not interested in having girls as members, particularly not capable, intelligent and assertive girls. She found herself isolated, treated with suspicion and hostility. In the *Head and Shoulders* interview, given at the start of her second term, she poured out her feelings of despair at the chauvinism of her male parliamentary colleagues:

"The main block to being a woman in Parliament is not being one of the boys; not being in the networks they operate; not hanging around the same quarters as they do. There's a lot of social life I'm not part of, a lot of late-night drinking in the rooms. I'm sure a great deal of business and strategising is done there. That's where things happen, where people are told who to vote for the next day, who's lining up with whom.

"Every night after dinner I walk back through the Members' Lounge and there they are playing billiards, four of them at each of the three tables. Each time I walk through during the evening they're still there. Very seldom do you see a woman with them – if you do it's a kind of joke."

Helen's isolation from the social life of Parliament was in part self-imposed: "I think I was quite marginalised in that there was only a very small group that I could actually identify with. There were quite a lot of new MPs but they were mostly blokes and they got on with others in a blokesy sort of way. Very nice people like Philip Woollaston and Bill Jeffries. They accommodated to the new order better than I did. I didn't play the boys' way. I tended to get on with work. I probably wasn't very clubbable at all. I didn't have a drinks cabinet. I just wasn't part of that group. I was a serious-minded person not being taken seriously, and that was the ultimate insult."

Barry Soper, Political Editor for Independent Radio News, soon became aware that the new Member for Mount Albert was not one of the boys: "It was interesting in the early days. Card schools were a big thing in the early 80s. Late night, after the sessions were finished. You'd have regulars from the Labour Party as well as from National. Norman Jones was a regular from National, John Kirk from Labour, and

Ann Hercus. You'd never see Helen Clark at one of those late-night sessions. She'd never sit down. She probably doesn't even know how to play cards."

Dick Griffin, then Radio New Zealand's Political Editor and Bureau Chief, formed a similar impression: "I thought she was very guarded and for a while, when she was first in the House, she seemed quite reserved. She didn't seem to have a lot of friends. She didn't seem to be part of a gang. And in those days, if you weren't part of a gang in Labour, the others looked at you somewhat askance. And it was obvious even to an observer from the Parliamentary Gallery that a number of her colleagues, particularly some of her back-bench colleagues, didn't like her."

Helen's voice and appearance were also the subject of comment, not all of it uncomplimentary.

Bob Harvey: "I knew Helen in the 1980s and I remember watching her once. And she had a presence which I thought was quite remarkable. She had a serene beauty, if you like, an unearthly beauty for a politician. She seemed not quite of this earth, if I remember rightly. She seemed angelic. And for some bizarre reason I thought of Queen Elizabeth I. She was very Shakespearean. Ophelia, if you like. And we were at a meeting with some politicians and talking about Bill Rowling. And she made some really beautiful observations about Bill. Kind and generous observations."

Geoffrey Palmer: "Parliament was sexist to a high degree and all the women members who came in then faced an uphill struggle. A lot of them became rather easy to disconcert because it's a real bear pit in there and interjections are very destructive to your speaking capacities. But Helen was blessed with a deep voice and she was hard to interject on because of that. She was always a strong debater and a strong speaker from her earliest times in Parliament."

Dick Griffin: "The first Labour Party Conference I went to was in Wellington in the late 1970s, early '80s. She spoke at that conference and I remember thinking, 'Attractive woman, different voice.' I could almost swear that she was talking about Nicaragua, because the Labour Party in those days seemed to be obsessed with things South American. She was speaking very eloquently but she didn't seem to be connecting with her audience. And I thought, 'Wow, this is really a bluestocking'.

"She was always well turned out though. I mean, she never looked scruffy. In those days, and still today to a much lesser degree, there always seemed to be an element of very scruffy people in the Labour Party. Helen was never among those. She always seemed quite elegant, but distant. I thought she looked extremely attractive and she was and is. She's a very handsome woman, not pretty in the sense that she'd be a cheerleader, but the sort of looks that are striking and, in a very superficial sense, very attractive."

Barry Soper: "It was hard not to notice her when she came into Parliament – an attractive 30-something woman. I think the first thing you noticed about Helen was her voice. She's got the most incredible voice. Not long after she was elected PM there was a comment from Buckingham Palace referring to the New Zealand Prime Minister as 'he'. They'd obviously just heard her and not realised that in fact it was a woman."

Helen's surprise at the male chauvinism of Parliament was not shared by her friend Margaret Wilson: "I think the difference was that I had a feminist analysis, I had a context. It was just another case study. Whereas for both her and Ann Hercus, who also didn't really have a feminist analysis, it was really awful. And they were also asserting an authority that wasn't normally associated with the women who'd been in Parliament. There was Whetu Tirikatene-Sullivan, there was Mary Batchelor, there'd been Dorothy Jelicich. These were not women who threatened those men, but both Helen and Ann Hercus did threaten them because they both had powerful intellects and were articulate and not get-at-able women. But the personal attacks were pretty awful and I doubt that it would have been any less hurtful."

David Lange offers an interesting perspective on how Helen and her supporters within Parliament and in the Party were perceived by their more conservative colleagues: "I think we used to regard them as a self-appointed think-tank, that was a sort of wrecker's ball for the old, and moving in with the new. But Helen was never simply a sloganeer. If she advanced something it was meticulous. And that meant she became formidable within the Party and became the object of some considerable apprehension and hostility amongst older members. Remember that we're dealing with a period when the lights of a lot of these people were simply going out. Many had already packed it in and you saw some of those remaining looking askance at the emergence of the women's lobby in the Labour Party.

"You have to remember that the nature of the membership changed significantly in those years when Jim and Helen were working to rebuild the Party – from union-appointed men who wore Chicago vests and attended monthly meetings, to the most extraordinarily aggressive women of a younger age, from Labour Party women's branches whose members were older and superannuitant and would stagger round to meetings at half-past 10 on a Wednesday morning.

"Helen had no truck with any of that. She was part of a crowd which produced women activists in the Party who were frankly terrifying to a lot of older members. And among these older, socially conservative factions she was regarded as a rampant abortionist, a rampant homosexual activist, a rampant peacenik. She had every label that you can hang on her hung on her."

Left **Life was not easy for the new MP for Mount Albert. She was treated with indifference or disdain by the boys' club at Parliament.**

Lange is certainly not overstating the position. Geoffrey Palmer describes the difficulties faced by a young woman MP in those days as "hellish" and the institution as "a gentleman's club of a not very respectable sort".

Dick Griffin says that Parliament was "totally, totally chauvinistic": "To a degree that even women whom I respected in the Press Gallery also got marginalised from time to time. There would be tears before bed often. And that was in the Press Gallery. God knows what it was like on the front line down in the House or in the caucus. It was an environment where a Women's Libber (sneer, sneer), someone who wasn't married with children, didn't appear to come from middle-class suburbia, and was regarded as a bit of an intellectual, which was a slur in itself, must have found extreme difficulty. This is not a woman you ever saw near to tears, or certainly not publicly, but she was grim-faced for a good deal of the time."

There were tears. Helen recalls leaving the caucus on more than one occasion, going back to her room and having a good cry, "because they were very, very

BOYS' CLUB

vicious". She contemplated leaving after three years, but rejected the idea as a sign of defeat.

For Lange, the sexism and hostility which Helen experienced in her first term in Parliament may have been less difficult to bear than the peremptory rejection of her opinions and ideas:

"The worst thing is the abrupt, pre-emptive dismissal, the resigned need, conveyed by your parliamentary colleagues, of having to listen to some crap that they aren't going to take any notice of just because this woman is articulate. And she had a couple of things against her. First of all she was a woman, and secondly she was comparatively young. And so, having found a place of some assurance within the confines of the Party hierarchy, she was then released into the wilds, as it were, of the parliamentary environment. But by dint of her commitment and energy she absorbed all of that, betrayed no outward sign of irritation, except that she tended to contract in essential bearing."

Helen's association with Jim Anderton and the intellectual Left of the Labour Party also provided ammunition to those who wished to disparage her. To them, she was a socialist, a friend of the Cubans and Russians, a communist. Fay recalls listening to Parliament on the radio one day and hearing the Prime Minister, Rob Muldoon, refer to the Member for Mount Albert as a communist:

"And I was really upset because I knew she wasn't a communist. So I rang Fred Gair, George Gair's father, and I said to him, 'Do you know what I've just heard on the radio?' And he said, 'Don't be upset about it, Fay.' And we talked for a little bit and then I hung up. And later on he rang me back and he said, 'Fay, I've been thinking about what happened in Parliament today, and about Mr Muldoon calling Helen a communist.' And he said, 'My son George suffered something much worse than that. One day someone called him a bastard. You know, Fay, there's absolutely nothing wrong with the principles of communism, but there was something very wrong with my son being called a bastard.'"

Helen may have unconsciously invited some of the hostility towards her, as David Lange observes: "You can't live like that, fighting a cause in an alien environment without putting these appalling defensive shields in place. And in her case it was a sort of strangely quizzical look in engagement, the greeting of the absolutely stupid argument with a look of waiting for the opponent to say something next, which older members found completely intimidating. She would invite a comment by a look, and they had no comment to make, and it just simply added to the fire. She didn't set out to put people off, but that was the effect she had on some of them."

Bill Ralston recalls listening to Helen in Parliament during her first term. Her speeches, he says, were always effective and well-done: "But she could be extremely cutting. Her remarks weren't necessarily derogatory, but they could be extremely cutting. Say Allan Highet was talking about something he wanted to do in the Arts area. Helen would stand up and have a real go on a facet of the legislation that she saw as wrong or unfair. And it could be quite cutting intellectually. You were left with no doubt at the end of the speech that she didn't have a lot time for that person's ability to figure out what was going on. And I can see why at the time she was seen as a little intellectually arrogant, a little overly academic, particularly by the grassroots Labour Party back-benchers who were around her. I think they all sensed that she was someone who was on the move. Her roots were in the Party and she had good support within the Party."

Helen's support within the Party was a mixed blessing. The Labour movement in New Zealand had been riven with factionalism since the election loss of 1975. Two further losses, in 1978 and 1981, had served to deepen and entrench those divisions, and the Labour caucus, which she first attended in early 1982, had become a forum for blame and recrimination.

Much of the dissension centred around the leadership of Bill Rowling. Bill, everyone agreed, was a nice man. But that was part of his problem. He was totally unsuited in temperament to the brutally adversarial, Muldoonist-style of politics that dominated the 1970s and early 1980s. Where Muldoon's belligerence was interpreted as strength, Rowling's quiet, gentlemanly style was seen as weakness.

David Lange recounts an incident which he believes conveys the spirit of the time: "Jim Anderton hired a company to produce a film on Bill Rowling. You see Bill was Jim's Trojan Horse. Jim was determined to have Bill there until Jim could be there. I'm not quite sure that Helen actually agreed with that strategy, but that was it. And the film promoted Bill. And Anderton hired a company called Albatross. And they produced this film. And I can always remember feeling bad about it, because it showed Bill walking up a hill near Wellington, and it was getting harder and harder the higher he got, and when he got to the top he said, 'Anything's possible…' as he gasped for breath. And I said, 'Look, can you speed that film up about 20 percent and drop the voice about an octave.' And this was in front of Bill. This was the bizarre sort of thing that they were doing."

Attempts were made to fortify Rowling's image, particularly on television. He was encouraged to speak with greater emphasis and authority, to punctuate his delivery with manly gestures. But the effect was merely to give the appearance of a weak man trying to appear strong. Unlike his opposite number Rob Muldoon, Rowling was a disaster on a medium which was increasingly dominating political discourse. Both were short men, but while Muldoon somehow seemed large and menacing on the box, Rowling appeared slight and ineffectual. He was not helped by his somewhat reedy, high-pitched voice. Millionaire property developer Bob Jones, who would play a major role in the election of the fourth Labour Government, was particularly contemptuous of the Labour leader:

"It was a huge negative for Rowling that he looked wispy and insignificant and spoke with a high voice. These are realities. If you're presenting yourself as a leader, someone who wants to lead the nation, you do have to look a bit like a warrior king."

During the 1975 election, Jones, then an admirer and supporter of Muldoon, had begun referring to Rowling as "the mouse". An inveterate practical joker, Jones even succeeded in gatecrashing a live television interview with Rowling, accompanied by a local radio celebrity dressed in a mouse suit. The duo pranced around the studio with the mouse squeaking, until they were removed by security guards. Rowling thought the episode amusing. But it was a classic example of effective political satire. The "mouse" appellation stuck and was undoubtedly a factor in Labour's election loss that year.

By the end of 1981 Rowling, who had inherited the leadership mantle, perhaps unwillingly, on Norman Kirk's death in 1974, had led his party to three election defeats, each to his nemesis Rob Muldoon. Yet remarkably he still had the support of Labour's grassroots members in the Party.

But this was not the case in caucus. There, Rowling's leadership was being eroded and undermined by Roger Douglas, Richard Prebble and Michael Bassett, the flag-bearers for a group determined not merely to replace the current leader, but to move the Labour Party in precisely the philosophical direction that the new Member for Mount Albert had so roundly condemned in her maiden speech. Rogernomics was waiting impatiently in the wings.

Bill Rowling was on the opposite side of the ideological divide. His politics were the mainstream Labour politics of Savage, Fraser, Nash and Kirk, his economic philosophy fundamentally Keynesian. Rowling would have approved of Helen's maiden speech. Roger Douglas would not.

And Douglas had personal reasons for wanting to see the back of Rowling. In 1980, when he was Opposition Finance spokesman, Douglas had produced and distributed an alternative budget, not approved by the Party or its leader. In the same year he wrote and published *There's Got to be a Better Way*, subtitled *A Practical ABC to Solving New Zealand's Major Problems*. The book's thinking was a foretaste of Rogernomics and completely at odds with Labour's stated economic policy. Rowling had no alternative but to sack him as Finance spokesman. And he did.

The in-fighting led to a leadership spill which Rowling is said to have survived by a single vote – his own. But the attacks on him continued and, not surprisingly, increased in intensity after the 1981 defeat.

David Lange: "That's about the time the Party decided to have two Labour caucuses and go-away caucuses and all these other things to avoid decision-making. Caucuses were filled with overseas travellers who were going to do all sorts of derring-do. They'd say, 'Yes, yes, yes!' and they'd go away and plot. Remember that we'd increased the numbers by 1981 and the bigger the caucus the more likely that you'll get factionalism. And the chances of becoming an isolated minority become even stronger."

Lange had been Deputy Leader of the Labour Party since 1979 when an earlier palace coup had failed to win him the leadership, but successfully unseated Bob Tizard from the Deputy's chair. He recalls the attacks on Rowling:

"He was dismissively treated in caucus. Brutally, actually. Dismissed and laughed at and jeered at. Douglas and Prebble would say things like, 'Don't be ridiculous, Bill!' The same thing happened to Geoffrey Palmer with Richard Prebble. Geoffrey would say, 'We've got a priority to deal with this by doing one, two, three…' And Richard would say, 'Mr Chairman, that is absolute, bloody crap.' To which Geoffrey would respond, 'Oh, well, we'd better revisit it then.'

"One of the problems that I had was that I was sitting up the front with Bill, and every caucus I'd be there and he'd be there, and I was always supportive and never contested him at any stage. But Bill had by then developed the internal politics of desperation. The game was up for him. He had clearly done his dash and I sent out all sorts of messages to people saying, 'Look we're not going to rock this boat, Bill will work it out.'"

Jonathan Hunt recalls that the disparagement of Rowling went on behind his back as well: "They were scathing about Bill privately and Moore and Bassett had all these little cartoons about Rowling and Tweety Bird on their doors. Moore had them inside. I can remember them describing him at functions as 'the most hopeless leader'. He really got a terrible time."

Hunt was a supporter of Rowling and had voted for him in the attempted coup in 1980. Helen was also in the Rowling camp: "I liked him, I always thought that he had much more going for him than was generally portrayed. I didn't think he was a weak man. I thought that was a great disservice to his public image. He was a gentleman in an era when Muldoon was king, and it just didn't work. He probably also wasn't a television-age politician, whereas Muldoon was a master of the medium. Muldoon was his problem. In different times he could have starred. He was by nature a mild-mannered man. So I guess it wasn't his time."

In aligning herself with Rowling, Helen stood in opposition to the increasingly powerful Douglas faction in caucus. Her position on the Central Executive of the Party merely made matters worse. David Lange explains:

"Helen was alone for a great part of her personal life in the parliamentary environment and comforted only by her Party support. And the minute you make the transition from one to the other, you start to erode your base down the road. The Party was extremely suspicious of the Parliament, but nothing like the paranoia the parliamentarians had about the Party. So she was between two stools for a lot of the time, because you end up being bound by what is essentially the collective of your caucus colleagues and that is in turn regarded as a sell-out by Party activists.

"And to a certain extent that weapon was sharpened by Jim and Helen themselves, because they had recruited to the Party people whose mission in life was to be exactly like that. A lot of those people had not the slightest intention or desire or reasonable hope of ever being in Parliament. But they wanted to be self-appointed consciences for everyone who was. And that meant that the tribalism of the Party was very acute and it was an act of treachery to go and get yourself into Parliament."

Helen might not accept that analysis, but she was acutely aware of the conflict between the Party's controlling body and the Parliamentary wing:

"I was on the New Zealand Executive at the time and this right-wing group in caucus hated the New Zealand Executive, which they regarded as 'the loony Left'. And they used to try to demand absolute loyalty to sitting members and their re-selection. And we had some sitting members who really weren't very good. So I remember being attacked over that, even before I was in caucus."

Left **In 1983, Helen (left) represented New Zealand at a Socialist International Conference in Portugal.** *Opposite Page* **In Portugal with Barbara Wiese, an Australian representative and later South Australian Minister of Tourism.**

But the divisions in Labour went beyond leadership and the traditional and ongoing struggle for supremacy between Party and Parliament. A much wider battle was being waged behind the scenes for the philosophical heart of the movement:

Mike Williams: "I was dimly aware of it, because it spilled over a bit into the New Zealand Council. Douglas was running something called the Monday Club or the Wednesday Club, inviting businessmen and basically promoting his New Right agenda. And I can remember that Jim and Helen tried to head this off by an alternative viewpoint. And we tried unsuccessfully to get John Kenneth Galbraith, the liberal American economist, to a conference, because it had to be fought at that intellectual, philosophical level. This was Thatcherism they were talking, there was no doubt about that in my mind."

Bob Chapman: "The forum for this philosophical debate was inside the party organisation. The branches were hearing parts of it, but the main arena was the Policy Council. People like Douglas, Prebble, Bassett and so on – their forces are over here; and the representatives from the branches and divisions and so forth – their forces are over there. And by and large, whenever anything gets referred to the Party as a whole, it comes back in favour of Jim; and when it gets referred to the parliamentary Labour Party, it comes back much more Rogerish. But none of this was advertised to the outside world. The Douglas side didn't want the debate brought out in public. They feared it might go against them, and I think it would have. Because there were so many principles which the Labour Party had exemplified for decades and with which they were themselves associated, which were going to be dumped."

What the Douglas faction needed was a frontman with an acceptable face. And that was David Lange:

"I often say that Roger didn't have a secret agenda for many of the things he did, and that's true. He didn't plan huge income tax reductions. He certainly didn't plan GST. But in terms of their strategising to get control, that was clearly going on, I would say from 1979, when I was elected Deputy Leader. I was their hostage in that sense, right from way back. I was their boy. I was their man. I was their candidate. I worked very hard not to be pushed. When you look back on it now, it's quite obvious that I was calculated to be the flag-carrier for this particular homicidal attack, but I didn't actually fit there.

"In a funny way, I resented it. I considered by '81 that I was completely unfit to be a leader. I was in some physical danger. And that's why I said, 'Shut up, I'm not doing anything. I'm going to go to hospital. I'm going overseas.' And I called them off.

"I didn't have much to do with the philosophy, I didn't have much to do with Roger. I've never been to his house. I don't know where he lives to this day. I haven't seen him for four years."

At first sight Lange seemed an improbable frontman for a New Right group, as Helen observes: "There was nothing about David in his rise to power that suggested he would give neo-liberalism its head. He never spoke like that. You know, David was a Methodist. He was for Chapel. He was a big civil liberties lawyer. He identified with the undertrodden. But I think the group around Roger saw David as the vehicle to win the election. I think they used him, and of course the whole thing eventually flew apart. Really it was flying apart by 1987, because David did not want to front for it. I don't believe he was ever an apostle for the things Roger believed in."

Margaret Wilson believes that Lange didn't really know what he was getting into: "David doesn't have an analysis. As a socialist you need an analysis. But David's an emotional and intuitive thinker and actor. So I can see why he would have thought, 'Oh, this sounds like a good idea.' And of course there were good elements in it, no question about that, we needed to get some change. But you had to be grounded to see the consequences that can follow and you have to be aware that there are some complicating factors there. I never got the feeling David saw the complications until he was quite a way into the process. But Roger needed someone to carry the message. And David was just such a gift, he carried the message, and he didn't involve himself actively in the policy."

So David would be the frontman for the Douglas faction, the acceptable face of Rogernomics. He would win the election, a feat which Rowling was patently incapable of, and take the prize. He would be Prime Minister of New Zealand. Douglas's prize would be the Finance portfolio and the opportunity to realise his vision of New Zealand as a model of the market economy. Providing no one blew the gaff, everything was in place for a restructuring of New Zealand society, the like of which had not been seen since 1935.

Towards the end of 1982 Bill Rowling announced that he was standing down as Leader. Under the Labour Party's constitution an election on the leadership would be held in the first caucus of the mid-term year of the parliamentary session. David Lange and Russell Marshall put their names forward for Leader, Geoffrey Palmer and Ann Hercus for Deputy. None of this came as a surprise to Helen:

"David was always seen as someone who was positioned to knock Bill out when the time was ripe. And there had started to be a feeling that David was very associated with the group around Roger Douglas. That became very marked after the '81 election. It was really just a matter of time as to when Bill would go."

Lange was apparently not entirely comfortable with his role as frontman for the Douglas faction: "I couldn't stand it. I remember the night Bill Rowling stood down and I contested the leadership. And I was so much in captive, ringed by this little corral, that I actually left my flat and I stayed in Joe Walding's flat in the office, sleeping on the couch, just to escape the telephone ringing."

On 3 February 1983 David Lange was comfortably elected Leader of the Labour Party, with 31 votes to Russell Marshall's 12. Geoffrey Palmer would be his deputy. Helen had voted for Russell Marshall "who was seen to be the heir to Bill's tradition, the whole tradition of Labour in that area." She would carry the scars of her loyalty to the former leader and to the philosophical traditions of the Labour Party for the next four years.

With Lange's ascension to the leadership of the Party, Labour's fortunes at once began to improve. As frontmen go, he was without peer. His formidable intellect, unrivalled powers of oratory and searing wit made him more than a match for the politically ailing and increasingly inebriated Rob Muldoon. Whatever her personal views of the new Leader, Helen could see that any hope which the Party had of revival now lay with the Member for Mangere:

"Unquestionably, the confidence of the Labour Party that it could win an election increased. But for those close to the action there was some apprehension about what an election victory might deliver."

Helen's own difficulties were more immediate than that. She was now identified with a minority faction in caucus which had voted not merely against the new Leader, but against the new Leader's now powerful supporters and the philosophic direction in which they meant to take the Labour Party. According to Jonathan

NEW ZELAND HERALD

Above **Members of the "fish and chip brigade" meet in David Lange's office on 13 December 1980: David Lange, Michael Bassett, Roger Douglas and Mike Moore.**

Hunt, Helen was increasingly marginalised:

"It was apparent that Anderton was going to get a nomination for a seat in '84. And the fish-and-chip brigade had decided that there were some people they didn't want in the Cabinet, if Labour won the election. Helen was one and Anderton was the other."

The "fish-and-chip brigade" had derived its name from a photograph which appeared in the *New Zealand Herald* of Lange, Douglas, Bassett and Mike Moore eating fish and chips in Lange's office in Parliament. Moore, according to Jonathan Hunt, was not actually a member of the brigade, but had got himself in the photograph by accident. But he was certainly a sympathiser.

The brigade began meeting in Lange's office some time after the 1978 election and was instrumental in the abortive coup against Rowling the following year. But they had had partial success. Lange was now Deputy Leader, the meetings continued and, according to Lange himself, grew in numbers.

Bill Ralston describes the fish-and-chip brigade as "a little informal caucus which decided to roll Bill Rowling and got the numbers together and did it... Helen stood, I think more out of loyalty, alongside Rowling, and she was punished by Lange and the rest of them for taking that position. Certainly the right wing and the centre-right sidelined her mentally, I think, more than anything else."

In *Head and Shoulders* Helen describes her deep sense of alienation at the time: "I felt very bruised. There were very few people I could identify with and I became very conscious of working as a group because those first three years in Parliament were so hard… The team which promoted Lange to power is incredibly sexist and I don't see any way that a woman could ever have got admission to it… Part of my being overlooked for any office is because I belong to another faction in the Party, but part is also that I'm a woman. I remember one colleague flying off the handle at me in a row in caucus. He muttered, 'Don't be such a silly…' and he clearly wanted to say bitch – it was on his lips – but he shrieked, 'Don't be such a silly *woman!*' It was an extraordinary explosion.

"After a very difficult caucus meeting I often have lunch with friends – other MPs. My way of dealing with a really bad time is by talking to people. We go as a group to a pizza bar up the road and talk things through. Or I ring up Peter, or sometimes Margaret Wilson, or a woman friend of mine who is a close confidante. I ring Peter every night, about 11 p.m.

"It's been really important to me to have good friends. They are numbered in a handful and are all political people or indirectly linked to politics. Women like Cath Tizard, Margaret Wilson, my lawyer friend, and Jim Anderton's former wife, Joan. I haven't had a mentor in the Party, but I've had long political friendships, as with Jim Anderton."

Helen's association with Jim Anderton had been both long and close. She had described her first encounter with him in 1971 as "a meeting of minds". The two had been involved in campaigns to elect Labour candidates to the Auckland City Council and had worked tirelessly together to rebuild the Party after the debacle of 1975. Helen assisted and supported Jim. Jim encouraged and supported Helen. In Labour Party circles their names were linked, often to Helen's disadvantage.

But if Helen was close to Jim, she was closer still to his wife Joan who became her friend, counsellor and, it sometimes seemed, surrogate mother. She was a refuge in times of trouble.

In 1982 Joan had her own troubles. Her husband was about to end the marriage. In describing Helen's response to these events, Joan reveals a side of her not seen by the general public, but familiar to anyone who knows her well – Helen is there when things go wrong:

"My marriage broke up in 1982 and I remember Helen coming to see me, which I never expected. But she found out that Jim had left and she came and made a visit to me and I thought it was so nice of her really. Even now I feel quite emotional about it, because it was a terrible time. And Helen took the time out. She came over and visited me. And I know how hard Helen finds some of those things to do. So I look back on it as being, I suppose, the beginning of our friendship. Because in the period up until then I had been Jim's wife. I had been the one who cooked the food, who provided the coffee. Our house was an open house and there was

Right **Election campaigning for the third time, 1984. The Party was in buoyant mood. The smell of victory was in the air.**

always food and I just thought that was my job to do.

"Helen and Margaret were well educated, very bright women. I thought they were wonderful, and secretly used to wish that I was there with them. But my role was different. At least I could do some nurturing. And I remember feeling that quite strongly about Helen, that what I could do was nurture, make sure that if she did come round there was soup or something to eat.

"So that when Jim left I felt bereft. I felt that a lot of the friendships were Jim's friendships, they were not my friendships. But Margaret and Helen both made it clear in their own ways that they actually saw me as a friend. I wasn't just Jim's wife. And that actually had a profound impact on me. I was so grateful to Helen for taking the time. Whatever had gone on beforehand, she obviously felt strongly enough to come and see me. I'd forgotten how emotional I felt about that. I've never talked about it. I've never talked about Helen coming to see me and how I felt about it. But it cemented my absolute loyalty to her."

Barry Gustafson believes that the breach between Jim and Joan may have contributed to the later breach between Helen and Jim: "Helen is actually a very moral person, not a religious person of course, but a very moral person in many ways. And she was very, very friendly with Joan. And in fact I think that might be one of the keys to why she and Jim fell out. It wasn't just the political thing. I think her sympathies were very much with Joan. She was supportive of Joan and helped her. And she was very angry with Jim. And I think Jim felt she made her choice, and went with his former wife."

Helen had reason beyond her friendship with Joan to feel annoyed with Jim. The irony was not lost on her that it was Jim who, only a year previously, had persuaded her for political reasons and very much against her will, to get married. He had now walked out of his own marriage, with no apparent concern for the effect of his actions on his own political career.

1984 was election year and the National Government's hopes of being returned to office for a fourth term were looking increasingly fragile. The 1981 election had given National 47 seats in the House to Labour's 43 and Social Credit's 2. But National's majority had been reduced to one as a series of disgruntled MPs on both sides of the House played musical chairs. Two Labour members, John Kirk and Roger MacDonnell, unhappy that they had lost their nominations for the upcoming election, had effectively become independents and were voting with the Government on critical issues.

But the Prime Minister was unable to benefit from these defections. Within his own party a number of disaffected members, including Mike Minogue, Marilyn Waring, Derek Quigley, Simon Upton, Dail Jones and Ruth Richardson, had crossed the floor on a number of occasions and voted against the Government on major economic matters. Muldoon had been saved only by the votes of the two Social Creditors and of Kirk and MacDonnell.

By mid-1984, however, his position had begun to look increasingly tenuous. Social Credit had announced it would no longer vote with the Government, leaving National with an uncertain majority of one. National Party President Sue Wood was dispatched by the Prime Minister to warn those who had crossed the floor that if any of them voted against the Government again, he would call an early election.

In response, Marilyn Waring announced that she was leaving the Government caucus. She would continue to vote with the Government on confidence motions and on anything other than the issue of nuclear warships entering New Zealand waters, or women's issues.

On 14 June 1984 a drunken Rob Muldoon appeared on television to announce to the nation that he could no longer be confident of a majority in Parliament. A General Election would be held in one month's time, on Saturday 14 July. He may or may not have been aware of the significance of the date. The 14th of July was Bastille Day.

Helen did not see the television broadcast: "On the night Muldoon called the snap election, I'd been at home with a terribly bad headache. And David Caygill and Kerry Burke, who had flats in the same old block as I did, came and beat my door down about midnight and said, 'The House has risen, it's gone.' I said, 'What? No Parliament tomorrow?' 'No, it's all collapsed, there's an election.' It was pure revelation. And there was great excitement because it was clear that Muldoon couldn't write a budget, he had completely run out of options. And there was certainly a feeling Labour was going to win, no question."

The excitement was tempered to some extent because, as Bob Chapman observes, Labour had no manifesto in place and was deeply divided on major policy issues:

"In the period leading up to the '84 snap election a struggle was going on for control of the Policy Council, which was quite a new institution. Fundamentally the branches and the Party were with Anderton, while the parliamentary Party tended to be much more on Douglas's side. And the lines were more or less evenly drawn between the forces of Jim and the forces of Roger. So much so, that when Muldoon announced the snap election, it was not possible to produce an economic policy that was at all specific. And it was given over to the master of choice words, Geoffrey Palmer, to be in charge for a short time, and he produced a document which literally could be read any way, as though either side had won or both sides had won."

It was, according to Jonathan Hunt, a considerable achievement in the circumstances: "I've always said that the reason we did so well to start with was that Lange espoused Rogernomics and Geoffrey Palmer organised it. And I'll never forget a very revealing comment that Geoffrey made, 'I don't give a damn what the policy is, I just want to *know* what it is, so I can go out and sell it.' So there was no specific 1984 election policy in the end because the snap election happened so quickly, and quite a few of the decisions taken after the election had never been discussed in caucus or at Conference or any of the forums where such things are normally debated and decided."

The snap election thus came as a boon to Roger Douglas, restored since Lange's election to the leadership to his former position as Opposition spokesman on Finance. He was not required to commit to paper the economic policies which he intended to pursue if Labour became the Government. The point was not lost on Helen:

"The fundamental divisions within the Party would have been very obvious to anyone on the inside in '81 and '84, because we couldn't produce an economic policy. And in the end Geoffrey Palmer, who used in fact to run the Policy Council, went away and wrote a policy that could have meant anything, in order to satisfy both sides. But everyone knew that we were going into an election where the Minister of Finance was eventually going to run rampant."

The snap election thus gave Roger Douglas carte blanche.

Rob Muldoon and David Lange were both given 10 minutes on radio and television to present their opening addresses. The Prime Minister chose to use less than half his time, devoting much of that to the widespread support which he claimed he had from those "ordinary New Zealanders" whom he liked to call "Rob's Mob".

David Lange sensibly made use of his full 10 minutes to deliver a plea for an end to the divisiveness that had characterised political life for the previous nine years and to articulate the same core Labour values that the Member for Mount Albert had embraced in her maiden speech. His television address was written after a late-night brainstorming session with Douglas, Prebble, Moore, Palmer and others, at which the general thrust of the address was hammered out. It contained not one hint of Rogernomics.

Mike Williams was watching the broadcast with Helen Clark: "We were very cynical about Lange. We just didn't think he had it. And we both sat and watched. And I turned to her and said, 'That was very good.' And she said, 'It was very good.'"

Lange had got off to a flying start. Richard Long, then Political Editor of the *Dominion*, had been observing the Labour Leader's progress:

"Lange grew up so quickly during that campaign. It was just phenomenal the way he matured from having been almost a back-bench yokel to a statesman who could wipe the floor with Muldoon. And I think Muldoon knew that he daren't let Lange develop any further. He could just see the pace at which Lange was developing and he knew that by November it would be too dangerous.

"And I still to this day refuse to accept that it was Marilyn Waring who forced Muldoon into a snap election. There were two reasons for that. Firstly, he couldn't put together a budget. There was no money left and the economic policies were barmy. And, second, he saw Lange growing so phenomenally in the job, he knew he had to nail him before he grew up. So he thought that by calling an early election he was acting quite cleverly. And they had a leaked report from Douglas saying that Labour was planning to devalue. And they launched that pretty quickly but didn't get any traction. And then, in the campaign itself, Lange just grew up so fast that Muldoon couldn't match him."

Within a week of the television openings, it was becoming clear that Labour was in a strong position to win the election, not least because of the extraordinary rise in the polls of Bob Jones' New Zealand Party which was taking votes almost exclusively away from National. Jones had formed the party in October 1983. Within months official membership had grown to more than 20,000. The party would win almost a quarter of a million votes in the coming election, an extraordinary 12.25 percent of the votes cast. Under MMP it would have had more than a dozen seats in Parliament.

As the campaign continued, David Lange continued to dominate on television. In the last moments of the final leaders' debate, he informed the Prime Minister that under Labour's consensus style of government, he would not be excluded from the decision-making process. There would be a role for him to play. A bewildered Rob Muldoon replied, "I love you, Mr Lange."

Labour swept to power in a landslide victory, winning 56 seats against National's 37 and Social Credit's 2.

New Zealand had a new Prime Minister. And Helen Clark was now a member of the Government.

chapter nine

MARKET FORCES

THE immediate aftermath of Labour's victory was four days of political high drama. In his book *Nuclear Free – The New Zealand Way*, David Lange recounts what happened:

> The election took place on 14 July, a Saturday. Under New Zealand's constitution the new administration could not formally take office until nearly two weeks later. Convention had it that the outgoing administration would act, in the meantime, in accordance with the announced intentions and, if necessary, the direct instructions of the incoming government. But the conventions of the constitution did not allow for a wrecker like Muldoon. In his book, convention was there to be flouted. On the Sunday he threatened economic crisis. On the Monday he refused my instruction to devalue the currency. With the foreign exchange market suspended, the crisis was real enough. New Zealand was on the brink of defaulting on its international debt.

Almost $1.4 billion dollars had left the country since the beginning of the election campaign as speculators gambled on an imminent devaluation. New Zealand's liquid reserves were depleted to a precarious level.

On Tuesday Muldoon reluctantly agreed to implement the incoming Government's economic instructions and on Wednesday devalued the currency by 20 percent. The immediate currency crisis was over.

Against this background of drama and financial chaos, the fourth Labour Government's first Cabinet was elected. Helen Clark was not in it. There are two versions of how this came about. According to David Lange, Helen knew that she would be unacceptable to the powerful Douglas faction and had the good sense not to put her name forward:

"Because she was told she wouldn't get in, I imagine. I've got no proof of that, but I know there were lists compiled, and I know that only the reckless would put their name up if they knew they were going to lose. If you put your name forward under those circumstances you merely confirm that you're a cooked goose. Remember that you're dealing with a caucus which was greatly enlarged, so you had a lot of new boys and new girls who were susceptible to lobbying pressure and inducement.

"And there'd been a great tradition since I'd been in the caucus to have the lists confirmed before the vote. So the chances of Helen being on the '84 Cabinet list were zero. Because they didn't need her then and they regarded her as a threat – Roger and all that sort of mob, the Prebbles, the hard boys. And I'm pretty sure that Helen didn't put her name forward. It would be uncharacteristic of her to be nominated and lose."

Helen's version is somewhat different. While conceding that it was "pretty much a foregone conclusion" that she would not get into Cabinet, she maintains that she did in fact put her name forward:

"I was actually in on the ballot for the 20th place and the other side swung their votes in behind Margaret Shields. It was the luckiest thing that ever happened to me. Because I was 34 at the time and there's absolutely no question that I benefited from having another three years' experience before I became a Minister. And I wasn't tainted by the first three years."

Helen's account of events is undoubtedly the correct one. David Lange's version, which removes him from the equation altogether, is contradicted by Jonathan Hunt:

"I suffered because of the fact that I went three times to Lange asking for Helen to be given even an under-secretaryship or something like that. And Lange was desperate that Anderton wouldn't get straight into Cabinet. And the absolute relief on Lange's face when he didn't get in. But Helen lasted right through to the last ballot. And then it was Helen Clark and Margaret Shields. It was a difficult position because both were good friends of mine and I'd voted for both of them up to that point. But in the end you had to vote for ability.

"Phil Goff, who had come into Parliament at the same time as Helen, got into Cabinet. Goff was helped by the fact that he was mates with quite a lot of people and had been a very effective new back-bencher. Helen had also been a very effective new back-bencher, but she had enemies. And in the end she lost by only two or three votes. She was very disappointed. She came into Bob Tizard's office, I think it was, and she was in floods of tears. I was very upset. I went three times to Lange and in the end he got really irritated."

From this account it becomes clear that Lange was not a disinterested observer in the matter of Helen's election to Cabinet, as his version of events would seem to imply. He was positively antagonistic to the idea and, according to Dick Griffin, made his antagonism widely known:

"I remember David Lange making it very clear to anybody who was prepared to listen that, if he had his way, Helen and two or three other Labour Party women weren't going to make it into Cabinet. Of course it was a caucus decision, but at that stage Lange was riding high. This was a man who'd gone from the Auckland Labour Party Conference when he'd just been made Leader, and sat out in the back room eating biscuits most of the afternoon, to a remarkable victory in 1984. And he was riding high and certainly not inclined to speak well of Helen Clark or one or two other Labour Party women who were seeking at least junior Cabinet positions.

"And the implication was that these women were a bit flaky, some were even neurotic, and did you need them in Cabinet? Like a hole in the head you needed them in Cabinet! And he put Helen in the same sort of category as Fran Wilde, which was unkind in the extreme because Fran was strident and annoying and irritating, and Helen was anything but. However, to many of us in the Gallery he seemed to associate Helen with Fran, which we found very peculiar. I'm sure he will deny it, but the involuntary rolling of the eyes and the body language were enough to give you the distinct impression that she was one of a number of people he didn't want to have a bar of, as far as Cabinet was concerned."

The reasons for Helen's exclusion from Cabinet are clear: she had been a Rowling supporter and she was closely identified with the left-wing Anderton faction in the Party. But as Geoffrey Palmer observes, she certainly deserved a place:

"In the run-up to the 1984 election, Helen was thought by those on the Right to be rather too influential. And she was, I think, kept out of Cabinet by deliberate actions that were taken by some who thought she'd be too effective in it. So she wasn't in the '84 Cabinet, even though there was no doubt that on merit she should have been."

Helen's observation that not getting into Cabinet in 1984 was "the luckiest thing that ever happened to me", is wisdom in hindsight. It was certainly not what she felt at the time, as her comments to Virginia Myers in 1985 make clear:

"The post-1984 election period was probably the lowest point in my career. I wasn't selected as a ministerial under-secretary, which was personally quite hurtful – and it was meant to be hurtful. I was as deserving as anyone, but I was left out for factional reasons, and there was intense antagonism towards me personally. My morale went right down. What was the point of it all? Why the hell was I doing this stupid job? What rewards were there?"

These were undoubtedly her true feelings at the time. But Helen is someone who likes to appear staunch. Suggest to her today that she must have found a situation or event upsetting, let alone have been reduced to tears by it, and she is inclined either to minimise her distress or deny it altogether. Her attitude is perhaps understandable when one considers the field day which the media and her political opponents had over her tears at Waitangi in 1998. But she is also highly conscious of the double standard that is applied to politician's tears. When a male politician weeps, it is seen as a sign of sensitivity. When a female politician weeps, it is taken as a sign of weakness.

So we can accept Jonathan Hunt's account that Helen was "in floods of tears" over her omission from Cabinet. She shared her feelings with Judith Tizard:

"She was very distressed not to get into Cabinet and even more so not even to get an under-secretaryship, as they were called in those days. She was so upset she was shaking. They'd had a real go at her in caucus and the attacks were savage. I was driving, and I remember stopping at the top of Masons Avenue and saying, 'Now listen Helen, you've been re-elected and you're not going to resign. Don't be so bloody stupid.' And she said, 'You know, I don't have to put up with this. I could get a job at the U.N. I could get a job in any university in the world.' And she could. She absolutely could.

"So I said, 'Listen, the buggers have given you three years' sabbatical leave. Use it. As a senior back-bench Government MP, you'll be able to chair a committee. Go and front up to them. What do you want? You want Foreign Affairs. This is your opportunity to grab the area and make it your own. Be the chair of the Foreign Affairs and Defence select committees. Get into all of the studies you want, do all the travelling you want, have a ball. What's the point of playing their game? They're boys, they'll burn out.'

"And I think those three years were actually the making of her politically. If she'd been in Cabinet for those first three years they would have forced her to do things that would have compromised her in the public view."

Peter Davis also takes the view that his wife's exclusion from Cabinet wasn't a bad thing:

"She had, in a way, to find her place a little bit more. You had this juggernaut progressing and she might have been shredded. And I think she was more able to be her own person outside Cabinet."

According to Peter, Helen never discussed with him the possibility of resigning. He doubts that she would ever have seriously considered it:

"I don't think so. Because Helen had been steeped in the Labour Party's traditional and philosophical foundations for so long through people like Bob Chapman. There's almost a tribal induction there that I don't think she could have abandoned."

Helen did not dwell long on her distress or sense of injustice at having been omitted from Cabinet. She took Judith's advice, or possibly her own counsel, focused on her area of interest and expertise, Foreign Affairs, and travelled:

"Actually I had quite a good time, a better time than the first three years, because I chaired the Foreign Affairs and Defence select committees and I travelled quite widely. I mean, there was nothing to do at home. I had no influence. I had no relevance. I was so marginal it didn't really matter whether I was there or not. So I did a lot of travelling. I went to anti-nuclear conferences in the States and all over the place. I went to the Philippines to watch a general election. When Peter had sabbatical leave I took three months in 1985 and went with him. I went to the U.N. End of the Decade for Women Conference in Nairobi. I was about a month in Africa, which was fantastic. I went to the Socialist International Congress in Peru in 1986 and had about a week in Nicaragua and some time in Argentina. I just travelled enormously; I had a wonderful time."

David Lange describes this period, from 1984 to 1987, as "Helen's years of indulgence, probably the only happy times that she had in Parliament." But Helen's concentration on Foreign Affairs and her travels overseas were purposeful. She was, as Judith had suggested, "making the area her own" and, in the process, gaining the respect of her parliamentary colleagues. She was laying the foundations for future political advancement.

There were other reasons to be buoyant. Since her arrival in Parliament, things had improved between Helen and her parents. George and Margaret were genuinely proud of their daughter's achievements and took a lively interest in her career. She told Virginia Myers that in the last five years she had made an effort to put her differences with her parents aside and not be drawn into conflicts:

"I still have to say to myself when I go home that I mustn't be baited. My father and I had terrible arguments over the Springbok tour and didn't speak for months. But I've got over rejecting my parents. I look for the good things about them rather than thinking they're impossible. I don't avoid going home for the weekend just because we're likely to argue about something."

A cause for disagreement in the Clark household was, however, provided by Fran Wilde's Homosexual Law Reform Bill. Wilde had introduced the Bill to Parliament in March 1985. Its intention was to decriminalise consenting homosexual acts by males over the age of 16 and to outlaw discrimination on the grounds of sexual orientation. There was considerable public interest in the Bill and feelings ran high. A petition opposing the legislation attracted 835,000 signatures. More than 2000 letters and submissions on the Bill were considered by Parliament's Justice and Law Reform Committee.

The Bill was finally debated in July 1986 and passed on a conscience vote by 49 votes to 44. It should go without saying that Helen was one of those who voted in favour. George and Margaret were not impressed:

"My father was apoplectic about Fran Wilde's Homosexual Law Reform Bill. Mum and Dad actually signed the 'anti' petition in the main street of Hamilton. And I remember saying, 'What on earth did you do that for?' And they couldn't really articulate why. They didn't like it. And I said, 'For god sake, the fact you don't like something isn't reason enough to sign a petition wanting to keep it against the law.' But you ran up against a quite basic belief. I don't think they would do it again today. The world has changed around them, and changed them as well. But I found it very hard to understand. But then they would never in their lives have met a person who was gay or who they knew was gay – ever."

Certainly not in Te Pahu. George and Margaret were country people and associated with country people. And even if there were homosexuals among their friends or acquaintances, they would certainly not have declared it. To engage in male homosexual acts had, after all, been a crime punishable by imprisonment.

Margaret doesn't recall the family ever discussing the issue. George does:

"Oh yes we did. I said to Peter one day, 'I think they should all be drowned or something or other.' And he said, 'George, you're looking at about seven or eight percent of the population.' It's abhorrent to me. That's it. I was so angry with George Gair. His casting vote could have turned the outcome one way or another, and he voted for it. We live on a farm. We live in a clean society. This sort of thing didn't come into our thinking."

The reform of the homosexual laws, though it changed the lives of tens of thousands of New Zealanders for the better, was minor compared to the economic reforms instituted by the fourth Labour Government under its Minister of Finance, Roger Douglas. Douglas had signalled many of these reforms in his "alternative budget" in 1980 and in *There's Got to Be a Better Way*, published in the same year. They included: an immediate 20 percent devaluation; substantial cuts in personal and company income tax; heavy penalties for tax evasion; the introduction of a

Left **Margaret Wilson served as President of the Labour Party from 1984 to 1987. She has been Helen's friend and colleague since university days.**

universal retail sales tax, later known as GST; the abolition of import licensing, export incentives and agricultural and industrial subsidies; a single Social Security benefit; increased competition in Broadcasting, including the setting up of two competing television corporations; turning Railways into a Corporation; deregulation of the economy; encouragement of foreign investment; tight controls on government spending and inflation; and an assault on government bureaucracy.

Douglas introduced *There's Got to Be a Better Way* with a quotation from Friedrich Nietzsche: "A nation usually renews its youth on a political sickbed; and there finds again the spirit which it had gradually lost in seeking and maintaining power."

The subsequent text was appropriately provocative and direct:

Any reshaping of New Zealand's institutions should start by challenging every facet of central Government. Make departments justify everything they do. If a department cannot justify something, cut it out. (See Killing Things.)

Ask – are Government departments necessary? Are they doing the job? Can they be trimmed? How can the workload be simplified? What are they trying to achieve? Should they be undertaking any additional functions in the interests of overall efficiency in New Zealand?

Be ruthless with the answers.

Make trading departments charge other departments for work they do on the same basis as private enterprise. Start with architects and surveyors. Move on to the Government Printer.

If they make a profit, is it because they're more efficient than private enterprise or is the private enterprise system just a rip-off?

If they make a loss, turn the work over to private enterprise…

KILLING THINGS (The case for departmental euthanasia)

The most important Minister in the Cabinet should be the Minister in Charge of Killing Things.

To put it in words of one syllable, for every dollar spent on doing something new, three old dollars for doing old things must go.

If you're hankering after a revolution, try that one for starters.

Douglas would be as good as his word. As Colin James observes in 'The Policy Revolution 1984-90', published in *New Zealand Politics in Transition*, edited by Raymond Miller:

"In speed and extent, the economic liberalisation which took place after the 1984 election was unmatched internationally, except in former communist bloc countries after 1989, and it made the New Zealand economy among the freest in the world."

The bywords for this revolution were deregulation, de-control, efficiency and the primacy of the market.

James again: "[The key incoming ministers] were predisposed to deregulate. They were reform-minded, risk-welcoming liberals, middle-class products of a secure upbringing and for the most part veterans of political activism in the late 1960s and early 1970s. Though their origins were mostly working-class or modest-income families, their attitudes and lifestyles increasingly diverged from those origins. They were an educated élite, used to a sophisticated lifestyle quite unlike that of the bulk of Labour's wage-worker support. For the most part, these techno-cratic liberals saw the economy as a technical problem, the technical solution to which would enable them to carry through the 'real agenda': improved social services, a more equitable society and a more independent foreign policy."

The mechanisms for this were tax reform, including the introduction of GST and the halving of the top rate of personal and company tax to 33 percent; divesting the government of some of the businesses it owned or part-owned and corporatising others; creating efficiencies and controlling expenditure in the State sector; freeing up the financial and foreign exchange markets; removing govern-ment subsidies, regulations on business and import licensing; lowering protective barriers and cutting tariffs; and mandating the Reserve Bank to control inflation. The importing of second-hand cars was permitted and shop-trading hours were greatly relaxed.

James: "This vast and sudden programme of reform sent the economy on a roller-coaster ride. The freeing of financial and foreign exchange markets encouraged wild speculation and a frenzy of takeovers, followed by spectacular collapses (including the mainly Government-owned Bank of New Zealand, the country's biggest bank), the loss of control of many companies to overseas buyers, some for a song, and then a sharp retrenchment in bank lending and productive investment. Inflation and interest rates soared initially, carrying the currency with them, putting exporters under pressure and blowing out the balance of payments deficit."

Unemployment increased; net emigration rose to an average of 17,000 a year; the crime rate burgeoned.

Against this, James writes, "There were dramatic efficiencies in the corporatised and privatised government businesses which went from near-universal loss-making to profit."

The government also dramatically increased social spending on Health, Education, Housing and Welfare. But the net outcome of 'Rogernomics' for many New Zealanders at the lower end of the socio-economic scale was a deterioration rather than an improvement in their circumstances.

James: "While some people became very rich and the educated élite also did well out of the reforms, incomes for ordinary New Zealanders stagnated or, if they lost their job, dropped. Between March 1984 and March 1990, the real disposable income for the top quintile went up 6.4 percent while that of the bottom quintile fell 0.3 percent. This was not a traditional Labour picture. Instead of the dignity of independence envisaged by early Labour politicians, the fourth Labour Government presided over a big rise in the numbers dependent on the state for their income."

A deep sense of betrayal began to surface among Labour's traditional supporters. The rich, it seemed, were getting richer and the poor poorer. And the Government seemed intent on selling the family silver, often to foreign buyers. This was not what they had voted for. And none of it had been presaged in Labour's election manifesto. There was no manifesto, only a deliberately vague statement of policy, crafted by Geoffrey Palmer.

Though Helen, through her experiences on the Labour Party Executive, on the Policy Council and in caucus, could not have failed to be aware of the Douglas faction's agenda, her sense of betrayal must have been as acute as any. This, after all, was the woman who had declared in her maiden speech:

"The Labour philosophy sees the State rather differently from the way in which a conservative philosophy sees it. We believe that the State must act to correct the imbalances in our society, favouring the rich and powerful. The conservative position is the laissez-faire posture. 'The less the Government does, the better,' they say, and 'Let the market sort the matter out.' We know that if the market is left to

sort matters out social injustice will be heightened, and suffering in the community will grow with the neglect the market fosters. The law of the unregulated market is, in the end, the law of the jungle, where only the strongest can survive."

That this was precisely the direction in which her Government was moving affected Helen deeply. Barry Gustafson witnessed her despair on several occasions: "Helen used to come in during the mid-80s and literally cry sometimes in the common-room. And we'd have a cup of coffee and she'd talk about what was happening in the fourth Labour Government and whether she wanted to remain part of it or retire from politics and go back to academic life. She found the '84-'87 period particularly, absolutely hell."

But, in public at least, Helen did not rock the boat. If she disapproved of the economic direction in which the Minister of Finance was taking the country, she gave no public expression to that disapproval. She did not, according to Jonathan Hunt, speak out against any of the Douglas initiatives. "And I imagine if she'd been in Cabinet, she'd have gone along with the general thrust. Well, look at her actions as Prime Minister."

Gallery journalists, according to Dick Griffin, interpreted this silence on economic matters as support for the Government's policies or at least as tolerant acceptance of them. But it was a misinterpretation. There were two reasons for Helen's public silence on Labour's departure from its historic economic and

philosophical path: she was uninterested in damaging the Government's chances of remaining in office; and she was biding her time.

Nigel Roberts observes that, in not wanting to undermine Labour's chances of a second term, Helen was very much in tune with her colleagues in Parliament and in the Party: "One of the driving forces behind the first term of the fourth Labour Government was a huge determination that encompassed the entire Party not to be another one-term government. They looked back to the one-term Kirk-Rowling Government from '72 to '75 and to Nash's one-term government from '57 to '60. And if there was any ghost they were fighting, it wasn't the ghost of Rob Muldoon, it was the ghost of a one-term government. And so there was a determination that the fights wouldn't break out. There was not going to be a public massacre within the Party."

This was certainly Helen's view. She might disagree fundamentally with aspects of the new economic and philosophical direction. But, if she expressed it at all, she would keep her disagreement within the confines of caucus. She was not going to throw the baby out with the bathwater.

Lange: "She was totally meticulous in terms of not rocking the boat. Anything she said that might rock it, she said to herself for years. That meant that by '87 she had ceased to be perceived as a threat to the new orthodoxy. There's a double-handed compliment there. It's potentially detrimental to be viewed that way, but

MARKET FORCES

the truth was that she'd got through quarantine."

Brian: "Implying a lack of principle?"

Lange: "Rather moving towards a goal."

Brian: "Calculating?"

Lange: "Oh yes. But calculating has connotations. It's not that. It's a view of life. We live in an age where instant gratification is deemed to be a political necessity, where the next public opinion poll is critical, where the three-year electoral cycle is where you either haemorrhage or triumph. And here we've got a woman who is almost Chinese in her approach to time. She actually has an agenda. I don't know the detail of that agenda today. But it will be there. And it will be still maturing."

Brian: "So she was into delayed gratification."

Lange: "She certainly wasn't into premature gratification."

Colin James is also uncomfortable with the word "calculating":

"'Calculating' is not a word I would use. Extremely disciplined, in her work habits, in the way she deals with people. Very few politicians are as disciplined. She is prepared to wait, prepared to take the long route if necessary. And I think we're seeing that in the Government now. She wants three terms and she will put things on hold for as long as is necessary to get those three terms, because only by staying in long enough can she achieve her long-term goals. That's her argument. And yes, she is definitely calculating in that way."

There is common ground on this among Helen's friends, colleagues and the political commentators. Helen is a strategic player. At the core of her political advancement lie discipline, pragmatism, endurance and extraordinary patience. But, in her, pragmatism does not imply lack of principle. It is, rather, the servant of principle.

In assessing today the individual roles of the principal players in the fourth Labour Government, Helen draws a clear distinction between the Prime Minister and his lieutenants:

"I think David was a man with a big vision. He had a genuine social conscience and a very good heart. And he went into Parliament and a funny thing happened on the way to the Forum. I don't think he ever had any great knowledge of the economy. What happened was that he wanted to deliver on the social issues. But how was that to be done? The route Muldoon was on was doomed. There was no 'third way' as we know it today. And so he opted for Roger as the alternative. And it was always his view that this would enable him to deliver the sort of society he believed in. Hence the Royal Commission on Social Policy which actually set out the sort of world David would have liked to preside over. But the Royal Commission was absolutely sabotaged by Roger and others. David saw what Roger was offering as a means to an end. But in fact of course the means utterly perverted the end. That was tragic.

"David was more than a frontman. He was always better than that, but he didn't have the people around him to bring out the best in him. He would have been the ideal 'third way' politician if someone had been there to give him the ideas, to strengthen his own good heart and good intentions with a clear philosophy and direction. He was the right man in the right place. His background and motivation were very, very good. But I think that if you get to the top too quickly and too easily, you haven't had the experience which enables you to tough out tough times."

Helen's view that David was "the right man in the right place", is supported by Lange himself: "Most of us have been opportunist creatures of our time, responded to public clamour. We're all situational leaders. Churchill was one. I was very clearly a situational leader."

What distinguishes Clark from Lange, then, is that Helen would put in a 25-year political apprenticeship before becoming Prime Minister, while David's apprenticeship was less than 10. Helen had done the hard yards. David had not.

Nigel Roberts: "It seems to me that that's where Helen Clark had it all over David Lange. I don't think Lange did the homework. He didn't know the policy detail, didn't know the facts on a lot of issues. But he was brilliant. John Henderson, the former director of the Prime Minister's office, talked about his time working for Lange when Lange was Leader of the Opposition. Henderson would brief Lange walking through the corridors, Lange would go into the House and slay Muldoon on facts he'd been given 20 seconds beforehand. He was a great synthesiser, a natural orator, whereas Helen Clark knows the policy details and so did Muldoon.

"And the Douglas faction were promoting him because they had to have a leader and it was not going to be Rowling for the fourth time. And David Lange, the 'situational leader', as he rightly calls himself, was talked about as a potential Prime Minister from the night he won the Mangere by-election nomination for Labour. And why? Because they were looking back to the dead Kirk."

There was one thing that Helen and David did have in common – when they entered Parliament neither had a firm grasp on economics. That, and his ignorance of the details of policy may absolve Lange to some extent from the charge of complicity in the Douglas revolution. Bob Chapman says that David may have been "a sheep in wolf's clothing":

"Because he didn't pretend to know about economics, and this was all about economics. And he had been enthused early on by Roger Douglas, who at that time was picking winners, and by the apparent logical simplicity of the whole thing. But this was at a time when Douglas's ideas were radically different from what they turned out to be in the end. Nonetheless, Lange got carried along by it and joined in with what was seen as inevitable, the devaluation. And that delivered the whole situation into the hands of the Minister of Finance. And from then on Lange's part was to stress the older ideas and mix them in with some of the new, to put a human face on these policies."

Bill Ralston takes a similar view: "I'm not sure Lange ever got his head around the full extent of what Douglas was about, and you've got to remember that it was a snap election. And in the speed of the election, policy fell by the wayside. I can remember covering Lange's speeches at the time. You'd roll the camera and he had some great sound bites, and then you'd play it back later and it meant nothing. He was an empty vessel of wind in those days. But he said it so eloquently he could carry audiences with him. But the policy vacuum that existed in Labour in the run-up to the '84 election was huge.

"I don't believe Douglas ever colluded with Lange saying, 'Now what we're going to do is actually rip apart the New Zealand welfare state.' And I don't know if it even fully dawned on Richard Prebble until he was heavily involved in it. Remember his 'Save Rail' campaign? I'm sure he believed he was saving Rail right up until the moment he sold it, because that was just the way that things went."

Jonathan Hunt takes a more basic view of Lange's failings: "David is a very interesting person to comment on and talk about. His huge problem was that he didn't like long periods of work. He wanted others to do all the hard things. A very disappointing man. He's probably the sharpest and most acute mind that you could ever want to meet."

A gentler summation is provided by Tom Scott: "I think Lange ran on charm. Charm was the largest component in his personality. And he was funny and endearing. He was Prime Minister for about four years and he probably had two good years, but they were wonderful."

None of the family silver was in fact sold during the Government's first term. That would come later. Economic deregulation was at the top of its agenda from 1984 to '87 and was pursued at breakneck speed. 'Blitzkrieg' was the tactical approach favoured by the Minister of Finance – catching the enemy unawares with pre-emptive strikes. Before you knew what was happening, the battle was lost.

In matters of social and foreign policy, however, the Government was responsible for a series of positive and far-reaching reforms. Colin James in *New Zealand Politics in Transition*:

One unshakeable policy Labour brought into office was to ban nuclear-armed and nuclear-powered ships and aircraft. After some hesitation by Prime Minister David Lange, the government implemented that ban in the face of heavy pressure from the United States which cut off defence ties as a result. Defence policy refocused on the South Pacific.

Foreign policy was widened from an obsession with trade to a more political role. This was especially evident in rebuilding links with southern Africa, coupled with the reimposition of a ban on rugby tours by South Africa and the ejection of the South African consul-general.

[The Government] appointed a much higher proportion of women and Maori to official bodies, including the country's first Maori and female Governors-General, Sir Paul Reeves and Dame Catherine Tizard. It established a Ministry of Women's Affairs, funded women's sport and refuges more generously and passed 'pay equity' legislation to benchmark pay in female-dominated occupations against pay in similar men-dominated occupations. Help was given with trade union education... The fourth Labour Government was also considerably more sympathetic to environmentalists' campaigns to halt or slow logging of native forests and mining on the Coromandel Peninsula.

A Bill of Rights was passed which proved effective in blocking legislation inimical to civil rights. The use of cannabis was partly decriminalised and a Labour back-bencher, Fran Wilde, successfully piloted a bill decriminalising homosexuality through Parliament. Generally the Government permitted a generous interpretation of the Official Information Act which has made government policy making far more transparent.

An even more important change concerned the status of the Treaty of Waitangi. The Treaty had been declared a 'simple nullity' by the Supreme Court in 1877 and thereafter had no legal force. This was changed by a combination of the Treaty of Waitangi Amendment Act (1985) – which gave the Waitangi Tribunal jurisdiction to hear, establish the facts of and recommend redress for claims in respect of injustices back to 1840 – and a series of court decisions which took their cue from that amending Act... The net effect was that the Treaty regained legal force. It also gained moral force.

James observes that the initiatives in foreign policy, the environment, race relations and the constitution helped hold Labour's support in the 1987 election. Certainly, the Government campaigned on its record in office, on what it had already done rather than what it intended to do. No manifesto would be published until after the election. The strategy may have been an early sign of nervousness on the part of David Lange about what his Minister of Finance intended to pull out of the hat next, or, more cynically, a deliberate attempt to keep the electorate in ignorance of what was to come. After all, it had worked in '84.

It was not a strategy that Helen Clark would have approved of.

Barry Gustafson: "She was upset at what was happening in the Labour Party, the way the Cabinet and caucus appeared to be saying one thing and doing the opposite. In other words, they weren't up-front. From the time she was a student, Helen's always been prepared to stand up for what she believed in and fight her corner and argue that. She's not a duplicitous person. And I think she found that there were things going on behind the scenes that she didn't like in that fourth Labour Government. She thought that if they were going to fight elections on certain policies there was a commitment to implement those policies, unless you found it impossible, in which case you had to go out and get another mandate. In '87, for example, I don't think she was at all impressed at the Lange Labour approach – 'Well, we'll publish the manifesto more or less after the election' – on the grounds that if you tell people what you're going to do, you won't get a chance to do it. In her view, that hit at the essence of democracy."

Labour increased its share of the vote in the election by 5 percent, retaining its 17-seat majority in the house. But National also increased its share, by an even greater margin of 8 percent. Both had gained from the virtual disappearance of the New Zealand Party which attracted a mere 5306 or 0.29 percent of the votes. This was perhaps not surprising. The Party's founder, Bob Jones, had largely lost interest, and many of its supporters would have found a comfortable home in the refurbished Labour Party. As Colin James notes, "The rise was partly on the votes of many better-off people who would normally have been expected to vote National, but liked the new economic direction."

But the election was not without warning for the Government. In electorates held by Cabinet Ministers, according to Helen, the blue-collar vote plunged:

"It didn't go down in Mount Albert, because I was not identified with the Cabinet. But the Ministers were definitely punished, paving the way for the big wipe-out in 1990."

Labour had in any event avoided being a one-term government. More than that, it appeared to have been given a mandate not merely to pursue the same economic direction which it had followed for the previous three years, but to go further.

The 1987 victory must therefore have appeared a mixed blessing to the Member for Mount Albert. But her day was soon to come.

chapter ten

IN CABINET

THERE were four places to be filled in Labour's post-election Cabinet. Michael Cullen, David Butcher, Bill Jeffries and Helen Clark were all elected on the first ballot. Helen was given Housing and Conservation. She had clearly "ceased to be perceived as a threat to the new orthodoxy". But David Lange's own increasing unease was also at play:

"1987 was a pretty critical time for the Government. I was at that stage struggling to find means of spiking the juggernaut. And I certainly looked to her to provide some of the intellectual contestability and rigour. I would have told her she had to defend State Housing probably. I can't remember the exact conversation. But I was concerned about things that were happening and I had gone into the election with the understanding of the Minister of Finance that we would fight in '87 to make the economy a place fit for people to live in. And that would have been the message I gave Helen – we've got to do something about Housing and stop it being eroded. And that was her brief. She was to hold the bridge."

Helen accepted the brief and set about defending her patch:

"And that's what pitched me into headlong confrontation again with Roger. A new Minister gets a whole stack of briefing papers from their Department. And when they arrived I must have had an inkling that evil was afoot. And I remember asking for a whole lot more papers. And Treasury, with Roger's driving hand behind it, had indeed been beavering away on how to sell the State Housing stock and all the mortgages. And I made it plain as Minister of Housing that this was unacceptable. And I genuinely believed I'd removed all vestiges of that from the package.

"But you were constantly subjected to sneak raids on your portfolio, because they wanted to destroy the things you were doing. When I came back from my two weeks' summer holiday I rang up the Housing Corp and said, 'What have you been doing over the summer while I've been away?' They said, 'Oh well we're working on what was in the package.' And I said, 'What the hell are you on about?' I got the stuff faxed to me and found that they'd been working on exactly the agenda that I thought I had stopped. At which point I got on the plane to Wellington and made an appointment to see David. And I went in and said, 'Look, I can't be Minister of Housing. I can't carry on. If this is what people want I'm out of here.' And he said, 'No, no, no, it's not what we want.' And he then told me that he'd spent the time looking at what Roger was on about and he was going to stop it. And shortly thereafter he made the "cup of tea" speech. So my contribution was to add to his deep reservations.

"I remember that in the end there was a working party set up which had Adrienne von Tunzelman on it with Rob Campbell and Heather Simpson, who was my nominee. And they were to look at Housing. And Heather played the most masterful game of procrastination which went on for more than a year, by which time Roger had been sacked by David and the Working Party dissolved without reaching any particular conclusion."

Helen's contribution to Housing was significant. As a result of the new Minister's efforts, spending was increased in the 1988 budget. Special emphasis was placed on those in greatest need – low income urban dwellers, especially in Auckland, Maori living in rural areas, special needs groups such as mental health patients and abused women. A new unit was established within the Housing Corporation to deal with the housing needs of women. Under the papakainga scheme, houses could be built on multiple-owned Maori land, with the house itself used as security for a loan. By the end of Helen's tenure as Minister there were almost 3000 more new houses on the Corporation's books.

Helen had won the battle to protect State Housing. But, as David Lange notes, winning involved a trade-off:

"She won that battle. But the cost of winning it meant that she did not engage in the broader philosophical debate within Cabinet. That's how she saw her mandate and that's how she discharged it. She can't be criticised for that. She wasn't there to be Joan of Arc, she was there to be the Minister of Housing.

"One of her principles was pragmatism. It's a weird combination, but she does it very well. In Cabinet you'd have arguments about the philosophical implications of decision-making. Helen never engaged in that. Never. She had her patch and she looked after it. She kept her patch, she kept her head in and she lived to fight another day."

Though the term was not in common use, Helen may also have been coming to the conclusion that between the extremes of state interventionism and laissez-faire economics lay a more rational direction, "a third way". Noting that Helen is now one of the longest serving Members of Parliament, Jonathan Hunt observes:

"She learned from the loss in '84 that she had to be a very Centre person to be leader. The most successful Prime Ministers that either party has had have been centrist in their politics. Centre-Left like Holyoake and even Muldoon in some ways. Or slightly Centre-Right like Fraser. And I think Clark's in that category."

"Keeping her head in" did not, however, mean that Helen was immune from personal attack. Judith Tizard describes the atmosphere in caucus during this time as "absolutely septic", a view endorsed by David Lange:

"The vituperation. I always remember reading a paper by Professor Jim Holt who used to be an advisor to Roger. In this particular nasty paper he described Helen Clark as 'Queen of the Mushies'. And this is the sort of thing that she collected, so there was a conflict. That was the great irony of the period from 1987, when she was Minister of Housing. She actually managed to exert her thrall over the policy and funding of her Ministry against people who'd been deeply, personally, philosophically and almost cravenly hating of her."

But, as Joan Caulfield recalls, Helen was not unscathed by the hostility towards her or by the burgeoning criticism of the Government in which she was now a Minister:

"Helen and Peter came for dinner. And I remember at that time being very irritated by what the Government was doing. And she was pretty tired. And I remember that she and Peter were sitting on that couch. They were holding hands and I was sounding off about something. And she said one or two things to me which made me realise that if I wanted to retain her friendship, this had to be a safe house. And it could not be a house where she came and was criticised for what was happening in the Government. She needed to be able to come and sound off.

"So I made a decision then never to criticise. Because I also knew of the battles that Helen was fighting on the inside with Roger Douglas and I'd seen some of the results of that. On occasions she'd been so frustrated about the fights she'd had with Roger Douglas that she'd been quite upset. And I thought, she needs places she can come where she's not going to be bombarded with criticism of what the Government is doing. So I then decided that I wasn't going to talk about politics. And if we talked about politics, I wasn't going to be critical."

Helen's image was apparently more distinct to her enemies than it was to the journalists in the Press Gallery. Dick Griffin reports that she was by now "a woman of considerable moment":

"It was absolutely necessary to get her opinion on a whole range of things on a regular basis. It was never a flamboyant opinion. In fact it was always a very guarded opinion. And you would never have known that she was prepared to do battle on the Left or Centre-Left of the spectrum. In fact she always gave the impression she was quite hard-headed about her Housing portfolio and latterly her Health portfolio responsibilities. And, as always, she wasn't prepared to treat fools gladly in any sense."

Helen was developing a reputation as a hard taskmaster. Perhaps too hard.

Richard Harman: "Her office became notorious for two things. Firstly, the high staff turnover. She went through a large number of staff and was considered to be very difficult to work for. They used to come by the Gallery and tell you this all the time. And she was notoriously difficult to please and very, very tight, very controlled."

Helen was apparently also a force to be reckoned with in her second portfolio, Conservation. Geoffrey Palmer describes her as "a deadly effective Minister":

"She was pretty ruthless. She's always been very ruthless in terms of getting the objectives she wants and she will not put up with any nonsense from public servants of any sort. She's been harder on the Public Service than any recent political leader I've known and she gets the results. I mean, there may in the end not be every favour to be gained from that, but so far it's been very effective."

Helen might well accept this analysis. In an article published in February 1989 in *National Business Review*, she told Linda Clark:

"I have actually become much more hard-headed about how we spend public money and what we spend it on, because I know it's a scarce commodity and I know more people would benefit from it, if it was well spent… When I look back to some of the policy discussions and debates I took part in as someone coming up in the Labour Party, I regret that we talked a lot about ends and not very much about means at all."

The Department of Conservation, of which Helen was now Minister, was brand new. It had been formed after a review of the environmental and conservation functions of Government:

"The review team had identified where all the green dots in government systems were. There was the Department of Lands and Survey, which was partly running farms and had the National Parks. There was the Forest Service, which had the idea that everything would eventually be milled, but had the Forest Parks which they weren't milling. And there was the Department of Internal Affairs, which had the Wildlife Division. So on the 1st of April 1987 all these green dots, including Marine Mammals, became the Department of Conservation.

"Now the Chief Executive at the time never believed he had enough money to run a department, so he then set about proving he didn't have enough money to run a department. And just before the end of the financial year in 1988 he proudly presented himself saying, 'I always said I didn't have enough money to run the department, and in fact here I am millions short.' The Cabinet went berserk and he wasn't given any more money to run the department, and a review team was put in to make it live within its budget.

"We'd constantly been getting chipping from the conservation groups about how there was more being spent on the carpet than the kakapo, and there was a huge bureaucratic structure that he'd set up. I think for a $100 million budget there was a Head Office, eight Regional Offices, 34 District Offices and god knows how many Field Headquarters. The whole thing was quite radically restructured when it was only about a year and bit old. That was what was involved in trying to deal with financial reality in a government department. It was quite tough actually. A lot of people were made redundant when I was the Minister."

Helen's supporters on the Left might have been forgiven for thinking that their flag-bearer had adapted rather too quickly and too easily to the principles of the new orthodoxy. They would not have been comforted to learn that, in order to generate revenue for the Department, trampers were to be charged for using Conservation huts. The Minister had evidently embraced the concept of "user pays".

But Helen was no friend of the developer either. She stopped the Monowai mining project from proceeding on Conservation land in the Coromandel and put paid to a new marina on Lake Taupo. In other initiatives, the new Paparoa National Park was opened on the West Coast, and a new track, the Kepler, near Milford. Legislation was passed making New Zealand a party to CITES, the Convention on International Trade in Endangered Species.

But while the Minister of Housing and Conservation was quietly and efficiently getting on with it, her Government was in the early stages of self-destruction.

October 1987 provided a stunning example of market forces in action. Wall Street crashed, followed by the rest of the world's stockmarkets. The effects of the crash were felt in New Zealand by rich and poor alike. The rich were punished most severely as their fortunes, derived from speculation, disappeared overnight. As paper company after paper company went under, the sound of balloons bursting could be heard across the nation. Nor were Labour's traditional supporters immune from the economic downturn that followed the crash. Unemployment was on the rise. The shine had been taken off Rogernomics. There was talk of a December economic package to deal with the crisis.

Helen: "We hardly got any notice of what we were going to be discussing at the Cabinet. And in fact there was actually a denial there would even be a package, as I recall. It was on, it was off, it was on. And then presumably David got bullied to the point where it was on. And the 'seven guilty men', including Lange, Douglas, Prebble and Caygill, were lined up at a press conference to talk about all the things they were going to do. Even Michael Cullen got roped in. And a number of them looked distinctly unhappy. If you ever went back to the media shots, it was all a bit bizarre really."

At the heart of the December economic package was a proposal for a flat income tax rate of 23 percent. To those on the Centre-Left such a tax was inequitable, favouring those on higher incomes. Helen also saw the proposal as a cynical piece of manoeuvring by the Minister of Finance:

"Roger couldn't persuade the Ministers or the caucus to cut expenditure and remove whole functions of the State, so what he did was quite calculating. He cut the revenue base, knowing that the tax collected would be so small he'd be able to come back and argue again for cutting State functions and spending. So we went off for Christmas having had this December economic package."

The summer break was to prove the beginning of the end for the fourth Labour Government. In January Roger Douglas went off to the new-right World Economic Forum in Davos. David Lange, uncomfortable with the December package and with the speed of the reforms generally, wrote to him expressing his discomfort. An exchange of letters followed which was leaked to the media. With Douglas still out of the country, Lange, in a speech to the Australian National Press Club in Canberra, announced that it was time for "a cup of tea", meaning a pause from the reforms. He then unilaterally squashed the idea of the flat tax.

Helen: "Roger came rushing back to heighten the sense of crisis about it all and everyone went into huddles. And eventually a number of points in the package were resiled from. The tax rate was still cut, but not to anything like the extent that Roger had wanted. David Caygill protected the Health System and the mad plans that Roger had had for the Housing Corporation, to sell off the houses and mortgages, so that there would actually be no State Houses, got absolutely nowhere, which was my main interest."

The relationship between the Prime Minister and his Minister of Finance had now deteriorated to an unworkable level.

Jonathan Hunt: "By early '88, after the exchange of letters, David and Roger had

stopped talking. And I said, 'Look, I'm going to get the two of them into the room together and let them confront each other,' because they hadn't actually been talking face-to-face. Well, the thing went superbly well and they were talking well. Then all of a sudden my back door was pulled open and Margaret Pope stormed in and pulled Lange. I said, 'Just a minute,

Above **During the late 1970s and 1980s women gained a stronger voice in the Labour Party: Jenny Agnew (Mount Albert branch), new MP Sonia Davies, Judith Tizard, Helen Clark.**

we're having a meeting.' And she pulled him out just like that. And that was the moment I knew that we were in terrible trouble. I just got this terrible sinking feeling that there was going to be a constant conflict in Cabinet from then on. And there was."

Helen was unimpressed with the attempts to reconcile Lange and Douglas: "Another thing that was so odd about this whole period was that there was a group in the Cabinet and caucus who persisted in believing that these were not fundamental differences, that someone could mediate between them. You know, these two had got on so well, they'd been the great strength of the Government, and if people could only get them together and talking again. And these people didn't seem to appreciate that this was actually absolutely fundamental. It was a major policy split with quite deep philosophical roots in the end.

"And then, in '88, the level of conflict within the Government really did escalate. We had very, very tense, horrible Cabinet meetings and there would be occasions when David would leave the room, sort of very charged up. And then Douglas would leave the room very emotionally charged up. And Geoffrey would carry on chairing the meeting. It was all quite bizarre. And it was difficult because there wasn't widespread awareness outside that circle, in the media and among the public, of just how deep the divisions were. And you went to quite considerable lengths to disguise that. I remember people coming in and doing interviews about Roger Douglas and you'd really bite your tongue, not wanting to say anything that would lead to a whole lot more queries about what was going on."

The juggernaut of privatisation was now gaining momentum. In March, Equiticorp bought 90 percent of the Crown's interest in New Zealand Steel. Petrocorp was sold to Fletcher Challenge in the same month. By November Health Computing Services and the Development Finance Corporation had both been disposed of.

The internecine warfare continued unabated in Cabinet, finally becoming public when the Associate Minister of Finance, Richard Prebble, in a television interview on *Eyewitness News* effectively accused the Prime Minister of being insane. Lange sacked him from Cabinet, but not quite instantly:

"What happened was that I sacked Richard after delaying several hours so I could savour his television performance on video. When he accused me of being insane, I enjoyed that. I sacked him about 9 o'clock that night."

Prebble's sacking was closely followed by the resignation of Roger Douglas and, in protest, Trevor de Cleene, the Minister of Revenue and Customs. Lange then appointed his Minister of Health, David Caygill, as Minister of Finance. But the burden of these two major portfolios proved overwhelming and Helen returned from a month's holiday in Argentina and Chile to be offered the Health portfolio by the Prime Minister. She was formally appointed Minister in a Cabinet reshuffle in February, at the same time giving up Conservation. Her Cabinet ranking rose from 17 to 8, making her the first woman to sit on the front bench of any New Zealand government.

As Minister of Health, Helen displayed the same hard-headed pragmatism that she had shown in Housing and Conservation. Faced with a requirement by the new Finance Minister to cut public spending by 2 percent before the 1989 budget, she demanded that Health Boards stay strictly within their budgets, even if this meant keeping wage rises to an absolute minimum and reorganising services. She sacked

WOMEN IN POWER
THE TOP TABLE

HELEN CLARK, 39
Minister Of Health, Minister Of Housing

In terms of universal respect, Helen Clark leads the other women in cabinet by a yard. A former university lecturer in political studies, she was closely associated with Jim Anderton in rebuilding the national executive of the Labour Party.

Clark married just before she stood for Parliament in the safe Labour seat of Mt Albert, in what was seen as a political move to make her long-term relationship more acceptable to voters. In this government's first term she was head of Parliament's foreign affairs select committee, promoting Labour's anti-nuclear policy.

Clark is credited with having had a major role behind the scenes attempting to mediate between Roger Douglas, Richard Prebble and David Lange's supporters prior to both former ministers being demoted. She's seen as a member of the network that works with and behind cabinet, and has no trouble getting heard by her colleagues because of the respect she has earned.

the ailing Auckland Area Health Board, of which her husband, Peter Davis, was a member. The number of institutional beds was reduced as part of a policy to return patients to a more normal lifestyle in the community.

Many of these moves were unpopular not only with the general public but with her departmental officials. But, as she told Janet McCallum in *Women in the House – Members of Parliament in New Zealand*, "I was a Minister in a hurry and civil servants have 40 years. There's inevitably a clash of agendas."

According to Jonathan Hunt, Helen's earlier problems with staff now resurfaced: "A terribly hard taskmaster, she went through about three private secretaries in a year. And the day she was elected to be Deputy Prime Minister we had to get her a PPS, because she'd had a terrible time getting someone. She had to have someone who was the doorkeeper and whom she could rely on and trust implicitly. So my job was to ring up Alec McLean and offer him the job. Alec accepted and after one day he came to see me and said, 'I can't do it. I'm not going to take any more of this.' And so I went to her and I really got her to the stage where she burst into tears. I said, 'Look, you've got to realise that you've got to have someone and you're going to have to have confidence in them. You're going to have to work with them. And this guy is good.' And Alec has done a very good job. And they're very good mates today. But she didn't suffer fools gladly and she appointed some people who didn't work out and she was very hard on them."

A different clash of agendas was being fought out in the Government caucus as the deposed Minister of Finance and his lieutenants set out to destabilise the Lange administration.

Helen: "There was always a very strong minority group for Roger and he just set about making as much trouble for David as he could. So every caucus meeting was misery. There was tremendous fighting. At one point they actually had a go at his leadership with a motion. And I remember David Caygill getting up and supporting it, which was quite devastating to David, because he'd always counted on Caygill's support and had put a lot of faith in him as the Minister of Finance."

Jonathan Hunt did the numbers for Lange: "David came to me and said, 'Well what's it look like?' I said, 'If Kerry Burke gets there on time you've got 40 votes.' And he said, 'You mean 50.' I said, 'No, 40.' He got a terrible shock when I told him that, because he thought he had 50. He thought they couldn't do without him. And that's the time I think he might have decided, 'Well, I'll go till the fifth year.' And the actual figure was 39 out of 57."

Lange kept his job, but the strain on him was horrendous:

"That was one of the things that you never really get any credit for, for keeping your head while all around were losing theirs. People slamming doors and falling over – I remember Roger slamming doors. And you've just got to realise that these people are frayed, mentally and spiritually, and it was an exhausting time. I sat there crying, just got to the point of sheer frustration, in tears on my own. And Helen was privy to all of that. And if you're talking about the process of searing your personality – and that happens – you can't live through that without being affected by it. I remember by '89 feeling that my light had gone out. I watched myself doing some television interview, and I couldn't see any vitality in my face at all. I was just absolutely an animal object, robotically reciting some mantra that I'd somehow or other ingrained in me."

According to Jonathan Hunt, David became increasingly isolated: "When I was Leader of the House in '88 he'd ring up and say, 'What's happening?' And I'd tell him. And you could hear the television in the background. Then of course he had his heart flutter and had to have an angioplasty."

There was worse to come. Helen takes up the story:

"There was this constant heightening of tension. And David, for all his many strengths, was never a party manager. He didn't really know how to mobilise support, protect himself. So there was a point, I think in July, when he decided that he would fill the two vacancies in the Cabinet that had been created with the sacking of Prebble and de Cleene's resignation the year before. And so notice was given and a Cabinet ballot was called for.

"Now, for whatever reason, he didn't exercise the power which I have used on two occasions since I have been Prime Minister, under a rule which says, 'Where a casual vacancy arises in the Cabinet, the Prime Minister shall make a nomination to the caucus for that position.' So I nominated Parekura Horomia when Dover Samuels went, and I nominated Marian Hobbs back to her portfolio after the accommodation enquiries. David didn't do that. Nominations were simply called for. It may be that he didn't think he'd get what he wanted, so he didn't bother to nominate anyone. So to the two vacancies – hey presto – the caucus elect Annette King, which was fine, but they also elect Roger Douglas. And that was the straw that broke the camel's back.

"All of this happened on the Tuesday. And my recollection is that David went home that weekend and someone had said to me, 'David seems very depressed.' And I rang him on the Saturday, I think. And I said, 'How are you?' And he said, 'Oh I think you should think about what you want to run for next week.' And I said, 'What do you mean? And he said, 'I'm standing down.' I was the first person to hear about it. And he said he expected that Geoffrey would take the leadership, but I should have a look at organising myself to be the Deputy.

"And then he went down to Wellington and told the Cabinet on the Monday morning. Roger's re-election to Cabinet was literally the week before, and David decided he just had no faith in a caucus which would re-elect someone whom clearly he could not work with. I then ran. There was a ballot for Leader on the 8th of August. Geoffrey won against Mike Moore. Then there was a ballot for Deputy and it was me versus Roger. And I won. Not by a lot. It was very divided."

Divided or not, Helen Clark, at age 39, was now the Deputy Prime Minister of New Zealand.

David Lange's resignation and the election of Geoffrey Palmer as Prime Minister and Helen Clark as Deputy, were duly announced to the nation at a press conference. Lange, freed perhaps from the onerous responsibilities of the highest office in the land, was in good form:

"I announced it at the press conference. And there's a wonderful photograph of Palmer, Lange and Clark, as Palmer launches into this great tribute to me. Very fulsome, very effusive. And I said, 'Oh Geoffrey, I've changed my mind!'"

Reflecting on Lange's last years in office, Helen describes David's mental state as "Very distressed. Not mad, insane or irrational. But very distressed. He wasn't someone who could ever organise support. He was a bit of a loner. He wasn't easy to help."

She takes issue with Jonathan Hunt's view that as Prime Minister, Lange was averse to hard work: "David was so quick and able. He'd done all those years of legal

Above **"Oh, Geoffrey, I've changed my mind!" David Lange hands over power to Geoffrey Palmer, with the new Deputy Prime Minister alongside.**

aid pleas in mitigation, where you'd walk in, pick up the brief and ten minutes later be propounding. So he had an ability to read very quickly, digest it and comment on it. He had that skill. But I wouldn't be prepared to accuse him of being lazy.

I think his whole style is so different to mine. It's completely different. I read things very thoroughly. People can't believe how I get a grip on all these complex areas, how I go to a committee meeting and say, 'Now paragraph 13 on this page…' But I do read everything. And I keep an overview and I have quite clear views.

"But David never really steered the Government, in my opinion. And that was his downfall. The others steered it. And when the others were sacked, no one steered it. And David was then in quite a distressed state not quite knowing how to steer the show forward, because the prop was taken away. When you are no longer following Roger, who do you follow? At that point David actually needed to lead, but he didn't have a clear path. He didn't quite know what to do. I'm very reluctant to be hard on him, because I think these were weird times. The brain is there. Very able."

David Lange would remain in Parliament until 1996, serving out his time in the Labour Government as Attorney General, Minister in charge of the Serious Fraud Office and Minister of State. With Labour's defeat in 1990 his status changed:

"I was a highly paid social worker for Mangere, very much on the back-bench and increasingly mesmerised by the ability of the Leader [Mike Moore] to speak in a way that meant that when he was on television I knew there were two people who had no idea what he was talking about – him and me."

Helen's election to Cabinet in 1987, her subsequent promotion to the front bench early in 1989 and her defeat of Roger Douglas in the vote for Deputy Prime Minister, were seen by some commentators as evidence of a desire by the Labour caucus to mollify the Party's increasingly disgruntled traditional supporters on the Left. But, according to Helen, the economic policy did not change at all. The juggernaut moved relentlessly on:

"You still had Roger driving it along. You still had the legacy of the previous five years. And I had paid so little attention to any of that, that I wasn't equipped to drive a different direction. I had my hands totally full being Minister of Health. Roger came back into the Cabinet and Geoffrey made him Minister of Finance again and the manic behaviour began again. Richard Prebble came back in as well after Geoffrey became the Leader. So it was kind of like the old team was back."

The old team was indeed back, selling off more of the family silver. Post Bank, the Shipping Corporation, Air New Zealand, Landcorp and the Rural Bank were all privatised in 1989.

As Deputy Leader Helen gave up Housing in favour of the Labour portfolio. She retained Health, "one of the graveyard portfolios because no one will ever agree that enough money's been spent and there are always the shroud wavers."

Her achievements in Health were nonetheless considerable: the Smoke Free Environments Act, limiting smoking in the workplace and some public areas, and prohibiting tobacco advertising and sponsorship; the Health Research Council Act, replacing the Medical Research Council with a broader-based body charged with promoting and funding health research; the Nurses' Amendment Act, giving midwives autonomous status and allowing them to order laboratory tests, use medicines and attend births without the oversight of a doctor; the establishment of Area Health Boards throughout the country:

"Lots of things. I placed considerable emphasis on public health, setting out clear goals on how to reduce unnecessary death and disability by tackling smoking, heart disease, better management of asthma, earlier detection of melanoma. And the first big budget for cervical screening. It was a very, very busy and productive period."

Too busy, according to Fay: "When she was Minister of Health, I can remember her coming home on a Friday night exhausted. If you'd put a match to her she would have have blown up. She nearly worked herself to death. I think Peter had a bit to put up with, because she was pretty snarky just through sheer exhaustion."

In the Labour portfolio Helen's most significant achievement was undoubtedly

Above **Celebrations for the new Deputy Prime Minister: Helen arrives home to find friends, family, supporters and the media waiting for her.** *Opposite* **The new Prime Minister, Geoffrey Palmer, and his Deputy, Helen Clark, outside Parliament, August 1989.**

the Employment Equity Act. The Kirk administration had passed the Equal Pay Act in 1972, but though the Act had redressed the imbalance between the wages paid to men and women, there was still a long way to go. By 1990 women's wages were still only 80 percent of men's. Helen told Parliament:

"I believe that the gap could close by as much as six percent because of the measures in the Bill. That would still leave a pay gap that will have to be addressed through the longer-term solutions of equal employment opportunities and through expanding women's job opportunities into non-traditional sectors... No one should pretend that the gap will be closed without legislation, because without it there are only good intentions and no action."

The Employment Equity Act was passed in July 1990, only to be repealed by the incoming National Government.

It should not be thought that any of these victories, in Housing, Health or Labour, were easily won. When she was not engaged in battle with the 'forces of evil' in Cabinet and caucus, Helen was defending her portfolios against the entrenched bureaucracy of a conservative Public Service. Geoffrey Palmer was impressed by her ability to handle the departmental officials:

"I think her determination was her greatest strength and I can remember from her first tour of ministerial duty she just was immovable. A lot of Ministers give up after a while. They say, 'Oh, it's too hard, the officials don't want to do it. And they advise me this, that and the other thing. And, oh, it's just too hard. We can't do it, we'll have to do something else.' She was never prone to do that. She would make officials do what she wanted. She was pretty hard on them even then. I think it was just a sort of political conviction that you were there to do something and you were going to do it. And it was what you were going to do and not what they said you should do. I've always thought she was like that."

Helen's determination to stay and fight for what she believed in was to distinguish her from her friend and ally on the Left, Jim Anderton. Anderton, who had taken Norman Kirk's old seat of Sydenham in 1984, had quickly become disillusioned with Roger Douglas's New-Right economics. But the death of the Labour member for Timaru, Sir Basil Arthur, in 1985 provided a critical turning point in his relationship with his colleagues in Government, and particularly with Helen.

Timaru had been held by Labour since 1928. The electorate was composed of both urban and rural districts, the city itself acting as a sort of service centre for an agricultural fringe. Labour's dismantling of the agricultural subsidies in 1984 therefore had a disastrous effect on the district. The farming sector went into deep depression. Land prices crashed. Farmers committed suicide. So it was not entirely surprising that in the 1985 by-election Labour lost to National the seat it had held for almost half a century. The loss revealed a fundamental difference not only in the political strategies but in the personalities of Anderton and Clark, as Helen told Virginia Myers at the time:

"I've become more strategic about the fights I buy into. This was why I was so angry with Jim Anderton's public statements after the Timaru by-election, when he blamed the Government's economic policies for the loss of the seat. I agreed with what he said, but I was totally opposed to his saying it and strongly counselled him against it. It would have been different if he was still Party President but even then the tactics would have to be considered. I made up my mind that he'd have no help from me when it came to defending himself. It was too exposed a position. That caused some difficulties between us. But I have a strong sense of self-preservation. I didn't come this far to be burnt out in a hail of gunfire!

"These days Jim is almost getting into a maverick role, which isn't a role I see for myself. I don't mind fighting hard for issues and losing, but I don't want to be trapped in a ghetto with one or two people."

Sixteen years later, Helen's view of the aftermath of the Timaru by-election has not changed: "Basically Jim said, this is a disaster, and worked his way towards leaving. Margaret Wilson and I said, this is a disaster, but you have to hang in for a time when you might be able to make a difference. I look back on it now, 15 or 16 years later, and I still think we did the right thing.

"So, after the Timaru by-election, Jim began publicly distancing himself from the Labour Party and Government. He said the Government was doomed and there was nothing you could do to save it. And he became quite isolated. There were probably about a dozen back-benchers who would have regarded themselves broadly as on the Left of the caucus, but everyone else was prepared to hang in for another day. Jim just said, 'Look this outfit's terminal.' He stayed in, but was very critical and more or less isolated himself. I thought it was tactically wrong. I thought that the by-election was a wake-up call, but I didn't feel any great purpose was served by walking away. I mean, I never considered walking away."

Helen's observation in 1985 that Jim was "almost getting into a maverick role" was to prove prophetic. Anderton remained in the Government throughout its first term, from 1984 to 1987, and on no occasion crossed the floor. But his position was becoming increasingly tenuous. By 1988 disillusion had turned to bitterness as the Government's programme of privatisation of State assets gained ever greater momentum. Anderton began to view Helen's pragmatism as disloyalty.

Barry Gustafson: "Helen is very, very tough and determined. A weaker person would either go down with all flags flying or would crack under the strain. But Helen seems to be able neither to self-destruct nor to throw in the towel. It's a matter of character or personality. And this is where Jim hurt her. He basically said it was a lack of integrity. It wasn't a lack of integrity at all, it was a much more realistic appraisal."

In May 1989 Jim Anderton and the Labour Party finally parted company. Anderton's current biography states that he "resigned from the Labour Government because of serious breaches of policy manifesto commitments". But did he jump or was he pushed?

Bill Ralston: "He was pushed. He was unceremoniously drummed out of the Labour Party by a series of moves. They'd circled the wagons inside the Labour Cabinet and it was very difficult to tell what was going on. But they gradually alienated all of Anderton's support. And he helped alienate it too by making increasingly martyr-like statements."

Barry Gustafson: "People tried to talk Jim out of going. They said to Jim, 'If you're right then in a year or two things will have changed, the whole thing will be coming apart. These people, their policies will be discredited. The Party will swing back if you stay loyal.' But Jim could never do that. Jim could not build a team around him. As I said, he's the most divisive person I've ever met in politics. He had a group around him between '84 and '87 but by the time '87 came, he had virtually nobody. Another group comes in, another dozen MPs, Sonia Davies and co, looking to Jim as their leader. Within a short time he's alienated all of them."

Jonathan Hunt: "Jim had stood again for the Presidency of the Party at the Conference in Dunedin in 1988, but lost to Ruth Dyson. And I think that was probably when he worked out that he didn't have any future. Then, in '89, he walked away, then came back, then walked away again. He walked out of the caucus over the sale of the Bank of New Zealand. And then of course Labour didn't sell the Bank of New Zealand and Jim was persuaded to come back for a short time in '89. And shortly thereafter he set up his own party."

In *New Zealand Politics in Perspective*, Hyam Gold states that Anderton was in fact expelled from the Labour caucus in December 1988. He nonetheless stayed on the Government benches until May of the following year, when he formally resigned from the Party, having gained sufficient support from disgruntled Labour traditionalists and others on the extreme Left to form his own party, which he dubbed New Labour. In a chapter on the Alliance in *New Zealand – Government and Politics*, edited by Raymond Miller, Chris Trotter writes of the fledgling party's inaugural conference:

> With Anderton's expulsion from the Labour caucus in 1988, an opportunity arose for radical leftists of every persuasion to break out of the political ghetto within which they had been confined for most of the Cold War period. Maoists, Trotskyists, radical feminists, deep ecologists, gay-rights activists, and Maori Nationalists flocked to the New Labour Party's inaugural conference in June 1989. This sudden infusion of groups and individuals from the far left of the political spectrum caught Anderton and his supporters off guard. Instead of presenting a poignant picture of a disillusioned and disenfranchised New Zealand, yearning for 'Voice, Choice and Security' [New Labour's slogan], the NLP's first conference displayed an alarming procession of wild-eyed young men and women calling for bloody revolution. What had begun as a media triumph – over 500 delegates had gathered in the nation's capital less than a month after the Party's launch – quickly turned into a media disaster. The public perception of the NLP as a dangerous bunch of 'loony lefties' would never be dispelled.

Bill Ralston attended the conference: "I remember the first New Labour conference in Wellington, people standing up and saying, 'My name is so-and-so, I am a communist.' And you go, 'Oh whoa, I don't think this is the party Anderton had in mind.' It took him another six months to drum everyone out again, all the old Trots."

Jim Anderton was, in any event, no longer a member of the Party which he and Helen had worked so hard in the 1970s to rebuild. However disapproving she may have been of his departure, she had lost a friend, an ally and, in terms of political philosophy, if not of strategy, a kindred spirit.

In January of 1990 Helen, Cath Tizard and Jonathan Hunt set off on a trip to

Mexico. The rationale for the trip was to persuade Cath with a few margaritas to accept the position of Governor-General, though she had already made up her mind on the matter and informed the Prime Minister. The holiday was nonetheless a great success. Here is Cath's account:

"We left all the arrangements to Jonathan. Jonathan liked planning things. And I said, 'I'm happy to go on holiday and pay my share, but I don't want to be involved in planning. I'll do anything you're happy to do and I won't moan about it.' So Jonathan made all the plans. He's splendid at that. He always has the *Penguin Good Food Guide* so that we eat at the best places and get the best food. And he knows all these things.

"Jonathan travelled business. But because I could only afford to go economy, Helen chose to travel economy too, so she could travel with me. And I remember we went to Los Angeles and down to San Diego and then to Tijuana. And when we were leaving Tijuana we found that there was an absolute stuff-up with our plane tickets. Air New Zealand had done all the bookings, but their reciprocal arrangements with Air Mexico had lapsed a year before.

"So we got to the airport and our tickets weren't valid and we were going on to Oaxaca or Mexico City or somewhere. Anyhow, Jonathan and Helen were carrying on at the counter, demanding to see the manager, and behaving like a pair of chooks. And I thought, I'm not going to be part of it. So I went and sat over the other side of the two of them. And I said to them, 'Look, why fuss about this? Let's just buy new tickets on our credit cards and we'll fix them up when we get back to New Zealand.' 'No, no,' says Helen, 'we're going to have the manager.'

"And all of a sudden she's getting all stroppy. 'We *will* speak to the manager.' So we go out the back and first of all I see them pointing at me and shaking their finger at this poor fellow, and they're being very, very firm and very insistent about this. They finally see the manager off. And I was so embarrassed with the way they were behaving. It was so untypical of Helen to be stamping her foot like that.

"When they'd sorted it all out, I said, 'What on earth was going on there? What on earth were you two up to?' And she giggled like anything and she said, 'Oh, we had an hour to fill in, we thought we might as well make it interesting.' I nearly had a fit. Was this my serious-minded and dignified friend? They were creating a scene just for the hell of it.

"And they spent most of the time worrying about whether a Cabinet reshuffle would increase the Government's chances. And I kept saying to them, 'It's not going to do the slightest bit of good. Haven't you ever heard of the deck chairs on the *Titanic?*' But they didn't want to listen to me.

"Mind you, she's a great travelling companion. Jonathan had sussed out all these pyramid sites to visit. But his idea of doing a site with seven pyramids was to walk round the track, read all the notices and then go and sit in the shade. Helen, of course, immediately wanted to climb to the top of every single pyramid, and certainly the highest first. I came somewhere in between, being much more lethargic. And as I was setting off to climb one of the pyramids, I overheard the guide say to Jonathan, 'Oh, the older madam isn't going to climb right to the top, is she?' And Jonathan said, 'No, no, she'll just go up to the first platform.' And I thought, 'Bugger you!' Helen was already near the top, so I took it much more slowly and got up to the top and joined her. I told the story and she thought it was a great joke. And every time we had somewhere to go, she'd ask, 'Is madam going to climb to the top?'

"I sometimes wonder whether the Mexican tour started her off on wanting to reach the top of everything. She did no physical exertion at all to my knowledge over those years. She didn't play active sport, didn't run, didn't even walk very much. She had that little putt-putt-putt motorbike which she used, a little step-through moped or something. It's now in Motat.

"We did have a programme, but we'd always have to be back in time for margaritas in the evening and then a slap-up meal. I remember that we ended up in New Orleans. And when we'd had dinner Helen and I were all gung-ho to go and look at the jazz quarter, but Jonathan went back to the hotel to watch cricket. I mean, we've all got our ways of enjoying ourselves.

"And they were funny, those two, because they got very competitive about who could eat the hottest dish. I went through Mexico bleating 'non picante por favor' to the waiters. And they'd say, 'She doesn't like anything hot, nothing, 'non picante, non picante!' But Helen outsmarted herself one night. She asked for the hottest dish on the menu and her eyes nearly popped out. She burst out in sweat all over. Even she admitted that she'd outsmarted herself that night.

"We had lots of fun. Holidays are a learning experience for Helen, but she is able to forget her duties for a while."

With the election of the Palmer-Clark duo, the fourth Labour Government appeared to have undergone a major rebranding exercise. But the product inside the packet was still the same. With Douglas and Prebble back in Cabinet, the juggernaut rolled on. 1990 saw the sale of Government Print, the National Film Unit, State Insurance, Telecom NZ Limited and the Tourist Hotel Corporation.

The new partnership was well-received – initially.

Helen: "Well, a change is as good as a holiday And there's something fresh for the media to write about. So they write all these biographies and say, 'Oh that's nice, hasn't he got a nice wife and lovely kids.' And that is enough to hold you up for two or three months till the holes start to appear. The economy didn't improve. The policies hadn't changed. Roger was back in control. The core Labour vote was deserting us. And by January, February of 1990 it was very clear it was disastrous. It just went downhill. The party's polling was very poor, and Geoffrey's ratings which had been quite good, because people quite liked him, started to drop like a stone.

"And then there was that awful business when Geoffrey went to CHOGM in Kuala Lumpur. And he'd had journalists in for a media conference in his hotel suite and Barry Soper left his tape behind. It was left running. And when Barry got his tape back from Geoffrey's Press Secretary and played it back, there on the tape was the full dressing down which his Press Secretary, Karren Beanland, had given poor Geoffrey after the media had left. And it went along the lines of, 'You're absolutely hopeless, you're pathetic, you're not fit to be a Leader!' and Geoffrey's whimpering, 'I know. I know. I'm hopeless. I'm terrible.' And of course Barry played it. And it was things like this that just made him terminal."

Geoffrey Palmer, everyone agreed, was a decent bloke. But he had been struck with the Rowling curse. He was awful on television. Not that he conveyed an impression of weakness. Quite the contrary. But he had the wooden delivery and appearance of the dusty academic. Compared to his predecessor, David Lange, he was a cadaver on television. Jonathan Hunt recalls that an attempt was made to humanise the Prime Minister, to warm him up:

"Geoffrey couldn't communicate and he also did some very silly things. There was that business with the trumpet on the *Holmes* show. Everyone will remember it in the Cabinet if you talk to them. Geoffrey played the trumpet occasionally at parties. So they had him playing the trumpet in front of the Beehive with Holmes wandering behind him. He was trying to show the human side of Geoffrey Palmer. But it just looked so ridiculous. It was funny, but it was ridiculous. The sort of thing you never do as Prime Minister."

But if Palmer lacked X-appeal, so too, as David Lange observes, did his Deputy: "Geoffrey's image was that of a detached academic lawmaker. But at that stage Helen didn't have a great image either. What was Helen's image to the outside world? She was a woman. That was the novelty of it. The nuances of her position within the party were known to people who had been in caucus with her and the councils of the Party and the intimate ranks of the Party faithful. But she did not have a public persona in the same way that Ann Hercus had, or any of those others who courted it."

Bill Ralston believes that the Palmer-Clark combination was deadly: "Geoffrey and Helen were very much the same side of the coin. They were both academics. It was a very bad leadership match. She would always have been better in a team with Mike Moore. You needed the thinker and the populist. Helen wasn't in any way a populist until recently. I think she's developed that. She's more at ease with people now than she's ever been. But in those days she was quite reserved, she was quite stand-offish, she was quite dry. She was quite academic and so was Palmer. So the two of them made an extremely bad team."

Helen rejects this thesis, pointing to her own successful partnership with Michael Cullen, both of them former academics. Judith Tizard also regards Ralston's theory as simplistic:

"If you were looking for crude balance, then that might be true. But I don't think Geoffrey has a political bone in his body, and from that point of view I think he was deeply frustrating to work with. I think Helen's incredible background in the Labour Party, which is as profound as anyone's, meant that she understood the political process in a way that Geoffrey never did.

"But I also think she found his lack of empathy very difficult, because Helen is also very empathetic. While she has a strong policy overview, she sees how these processes affect people. And she's much less academic than Geoffrey could ever be. In fact I don't think Helen is an academic at all. She bailed out of her Ph.D. and she did it for good and sensible reasons."

Helen remained loyal to Geoffrey Palmer until mid-1990, by which time it was becoming clear that Labour could not win the election under his leadership. Jonathan Hunt records that both he and Helen had done polls of their own elec-torates: "And we were both going to lose. And I remember we had a long talk about this and we decided we had to tell Geoffrey he had to go."

Dick Griffin claims to have been given the bad news before Geoffrey Palmer: "I remember being in Helen's office and Helen has never ever been cautious about off-the-record stuff. And she said to me without any provocation, 'Well look, this man's hopeless. He's not going to make it. We can't carry on like this. We'll crash and burn at the polls. There's got to be a change to Moore. And that's just the way it is. You only have to look at the polls. And yes, I am one of those who think he's got to go, and he will go. And as soon as Moore gets back it's all over.' This is the Deputy Leader talking and what she's saying is, 'Look, this is the commonsense way of it, this is the logical progression of political thought on this. Don't be sentimental, just get a grip on reality.' And that's her to a T."

But it was Bill Ralston who was first with the news that the Prime Minister was about to be rolled: "Mike Moore had had a couple of false runs to roll Palmer. But he couldn't get Helen's support. Graham Colman was Moore's press secretary or eminence grise at the time and had a role in Moore's office as a strategist. So I cornered him one evening and said, 'I hear that Moore's making a run again.' He said, 'Yes he is. No one knows, but yes he is. It's all going to happen tomorrow.' It was the night before the caucus met. And I said, 'Have you got Clark?' thinking there's no way she's going to budge from Palmer's side. He said, 'Yes we have.' I didn't totally believe him, so I went and saw Moore. Moore said, 'Yes, I've got Clark.' Then I spoke to someone from Clark's office who said, 'Shh, yes.' And I ran the lead story on the TV3 news that Mike Moore was going to roll Geoffrey Palmer the next day and become Leader of the Labour Party and Prime Minister. And no one else had it, and there was great consternation, and it was only the next morning that it became clear.

"There must have been a special Cabinet meeting called. They met and Palmer went in and said, 'What's all this – there's a move on to roll me.' And Clark basically said, 'Well you're gone.' They'd already done a head count. And when he saw he'd lost Clark he knew he'd lost the support of his Cabinet. She was the kingmaker. I thought that was absolutely remarkable."

Helen baulks at the term 'kingmaker': "But the fact that I was the Deputy and that I supported it was pretty important. It was a very difficult position. But I became convinced that he was in no shape to go to the election at all. And I suppose it was around that time that Mike Moore started talking to me about whether anything could be done. Mike genuinely believed that he had the ability to pluck victory from the jaws of defeat. And in the end I backed him and the caucus backed him on the basis that it couldn't be worse. I mean, I look at it now and think, maybe we would have been better to stick with Geoffrey and not look like headless chooks. But it was a tough call. He had a certain integrity and dignity."

In keeping with his character, Geoffrey Palmer made a dignified exit and resigned: "Mike Moore took over eight weeks before the election. About half the Cabinet thought it might make some difference. I thought, 'Well, if you think that, fine, fellows. I'm out of here.' I don't actually think it made any difference either, but I was pleased I didn't have to be in Opposition."

Richard Harman takes a more jaundiced view of the overthrow of Geoffrey Palmer: "Well, I mean, here's the total and utter hypocrisy of Mike Moore, who was so desperate to do something that he would do a deal with Clark. And of course the whole thing's got Faustian qualities about it now. In doing that deal he undid himself. But one of the interesting things about the leadership change, which was a few very dramatic days, was the absolute fury of Geoffrey Palmer about Helen Clark. He regarded Helen as having been highly hypocritical, because she had pretended to stand, he thought, for something more than mere political pragmatism. You didn't hear Palmer get angry but he was furious about her having allied herself with Moore to depose him. Geoffrey is not a politician. He's a nice man, I think an honourable man, but not a politician. And the measuring stick that she was applying was pure politics, that this guy was going to fail at the election."

Responding to the charge of expediency in supporting Moore against Palmer, Helen later told Janet McCallum: "It was motivated entirely by the need to preserve an adequate base for the Labour Party in Parliament. I'd no doubt that we were going to do far, far worse than we did. We were looking, I think, at getting rather fewer than 19 seats in Parliament which just would have been quite hopeless. You would have been struggling very, very hard to maintain second place as a party.

"I mean, it was a very difficult thing to do, to push someone aside, particularly someone who clearly was a decent person and had contributed a lot. But at the end of the day you actually have some broader responsibility to the political movement you put your life into."

Palmer would return to academic life after the election. Mike Moore, with his Deputy Helen Clark, now had eight weeks to turn the polls around. It was mission impossible. Against the background of two leadership changes in three years, Jim Anderton's very public departure from the Party and a profound sense of betrayal among its core supporters, Labour had little or no chance of being returned to office. The National opposition, as Colin James notes in *New Zealand Politics in Transition*, had also got its act together:

"Labour's easy win in 1987 was also partly because the National Party had still to adjust to the new political environment. In the second half of 1989, it adopted the economic direction and backed the Treaty policy begun by Labour. In early 1990 it also adopted Labour's anti-nuclear policy. By proposing more reform in social services and the labour market, National attracted back its 1984 and 1987 deserters and with them came funding. It began to look like a credible alternative government. For those disaffected Labour voters who could not bring themselves to switch to National, New Labour and the Greens beckoned."

The 1990 election was a rout. Labour's share of the vote dropped from 47.96 to 35.14 percent. National's rose from 44.02 to 47.82 percent. New Labour polled a respectable 5.16 percent and the Greens an even more impressive 6.85 percent.

The electorate's punishment of Labour's most prominent Ministers was severe. In Manurewa Roger Douglas's majority dropped from 3052 to 1143. In Auckland Central Richard Prebble went down from 7355 to 3277. Michael Bassett, antici-pating the turn of the tide, wisely did not contest the Te Atatu nomination. The seat was lost. Eight-week Prime Minister Mike Moore saw his majority more than halved in Christchurch North, from 4698 to 2148. His Deputy, Helen Clark's,

HELEN: PORTRAIT

218

majority in Mount Albert plummeted from 5337 to 1230. Jim Anderton won the Sydenham seat for New Labour gaining 9821 votes and a majority over his Labour opponent of 4009, making him the first New Zealand MP ever to win a seat contested against his former party. An extraordinary achievement.

Above **With the ebullient Mike Moore, who was Prime Minister for just eight weeks after Geoffrey Palmer's resignation before the 1990 General Election.**

In the new Parliament National would have 67 seats, Labour 29 and New Labour one. The nation had passed judgement on Rogernomics.

Helen Clark's role in the fourth Labour Government remains a subject of debate. At no time between 1984 and 1990 did she publicly take issue with the Government's economic direction. As a Cabinet Minister, she did not vote against the Government's programme of corporatisation and privatisation. In the handling of her portfolios she was hard-headed, pragmatic and, according to some, ruthless. Where spending was concerned, she applied the habits of thrift she had learnt as a child. David Lange once described her as "so dry as to be combustible". Her approach to personal decision-making was prudent, political and occasionally expedient. As she herself said, "I didn't come this far to be burnt out in a hail of gunfire!" She did not rock the boat.

Yet despite the fourth Labour Government's (perhaps undeserved) reputation as the destroyer of the welfare state, the very least one can say of Helen Clark is that in her portfolios of Housing, Environment, Health and Labour, she did no harm. Her achievements in social policy were in fact considerable.

All of this makes sense if you regard Helen as a strategic long-term player, her eyes focused firmly on a particular goal, willing to bide her time. By 1990, and perhaps sooner, the goal was nothing less than the highest office in the land and the opportunity it would offer to build the sort of society she had envisaged in her maiden speech. She would wait another nine years for that.

chapter eleven

THE WILDERNESS YEARS

ELEN Clark now had a new role. She was Deputy Leader of the Opposition. Jim Bolger, the King Country farmer, was Prime Minister of New Zealand. As his Minister of Finance he had chosen the 39-year-old Member for Selwyn, Ruth Richardson, the first woman in New Zealand to hold the portfolio. Also in Cabinet was the Member for Ashburton, Jenny Shipley, now Minister of Social Welfare and Women's Affairs.

On 19 December New Zealanders got their first taste of what the new Government had in store. A 10 percent cut in welfare benefits, part of an overall spending cut of $2 billion, was announced in a mini-budget. The declared intention of the mini-budget was to reduce government spending and inflation and to raise New Zealand's international credit rating. But rising oil prices, resulting from the Gulf War, and a dramatic fall in wool prices made the Minister's task of balancing the books more difficult. Ruth Richardson told Parliament:

"It is very clear to the Government that the answer to the fiscal problems lies in social policy reform... changing the prevailing ethic from dependence to self-reliance."

The benefits cuts duly came into force on the 1st of April.

On 30 July Ruth Richardson delivered her "mother of all budgets". The welfare state was to be "redesigned":

"The great myth surrounding the welfare state is that it takes from the rich and

PHOTOGRAPH: NEW ZEALAND HERALD

gives only to the poor. In fact most taxes are raised from middle-income earners and the benefits are often given universally, to rich and poor alike."

There were changes in superannuation. The age of eligibility was to rise over a 10-year period from 60 to 65 with the current rate frozen for two years. The surcharge which had been introduced by Labour was increased, in breach of an election promise by Jim Bolger that it would be removed in National's first budget.

In other cost-saving moves, the Domestic Purposes Benefit was removed for claimants under the age of 18; eligibility for the Youth Employment Benefit was raised from age 20 to 25; parents were expected to provide financial support for their children in tertiary education; charges for public hospital care were introduced for those on higher incomes, along with increases in prescription charges and doctors' bills; lower income earners could obtain a card from Social Welfare entitling them to cheaper services, a scheme which many found too demeaning to take advantage of.

In an interview with Janet McCallum in November, cited in *Women in the House*, Ruth Richardson defended her government's breach of promise on the superannuation surcharge:

"Did we conduct policy in the public interest, or did we follow every last letter of our manifesto, when patently it was at odds with the public interest? We chose the public interest, and we'll just have to live with the electoral consequences."

She expressed pride in her achievements: "We've redesigned Health, Housing, Education to an extent, Welfare, retirement income... We've stopped middle-class welfare, and so I get more letters from the middle class who'd looked to somebody else to pay the bill for their child at university, or somebody else to pay their family benefit or somebody else to pay their superannuation... We will have done more to have lifted the burden of the state from people, and the crushing patronising notion that the Government... knows best how to spend your dollar... We're increasing the age of eligibility [for superannuation]. We're stopping this fraud of hiding people who are unemployed in accident compensation statistics. We're requiring beneficiaries to make themselves available for work. "

If those who voted National in 1990 thought they were voting against Rogernomics and in favour of a more caring and humane society, they must have been sorely disappointed. Not only, as Colin James observes in *New Zealand Politics in Transition*, were the policies of the former Minister of Finance not abandoned, they were taken further:

"The National Party in Government after 1990 acted out of character. Instead of conservatively managing the status quo bequeathed by Labour, it pushed on with reform, extending it into the social services and wages policy. In fact the first two years of the National Government can be seen as an almost seamless continuation of the policy revolution begun by Labour."

One rationale for the benefit cuts was that they would encourage beneficiaries to find work, since the benefit would be worth less than even a minimum wage. For a majority of workers, however, wages fell in real terms in the Government's first two years in office. This was largely due to the Employment Contracts Act, passed in the latter part of 1991. The Act, which amounted to a concerted attack on the power of the trade unions, replaced union-negotiated national awards with individual worker contracts, abolished compulsory overtime payments, banned strikes in support of multi-award contracts and allowed employers to refuse to enter into wage negotiations with workers. Regulations protecting workers' wages and conditions were greatly weakened.

There were major changes in social policy under the new Government: hospitals were renamed Crown Health Enterprises, contracted to provide services to Regional Health Authorities; patients were charged for staying in hospital; university funding for student fees was cut; a 0.7 percent tax on wages and salaries was introduced to help pay for accident compensation; bulk funding of teachers' salaries was introduced on a voluntary basis; State House rentals were increased to market levels; low income earners were encouraged with the assistance of an accommodation benefit to rent privately rather than wait for a State House; Housing New Zealand was set up to run state rental properties on a commercial basis.

The Deputy Leader of the Opposition watched all of this with increasing horror: "What they did was quite deliberately unpick the architecture of New Zealand, which had been constructed by the first Labour Government. The fourth Labour Government had not done that in social policy. It had unpicked the regulated economy. Labour gets quite unfairly lumped in with National, as if somehow there was a seamless Government that did these things. But the fourth Labour Government was bloody good on social policy. Had I not become Minister of Housing, had there not been David's "cup of tea", it could have been disastrous. But the reality was that the Labour Government did a fantastic job in Housing, and a pretty good job in Health and Education by and large. And it certainly maintained welfare spending. So on social policy, I think it was generally pretty good.

"But the Nats came in and just chucked all that out. In the first flush of 'Ruthanasia' they cut spending quite ferociously. There were benefit cuts, cuts in Health, cuts in Education, cuts in pensions. Shipley was the Minister of Social Welfare. She was 'Mrs Benefit-Cut'. And then she added to that in the 'mother of all budgets' by cutting the Super as well. There were disastrous changes. We saw the onset of poverty in New Zealand for the first time since the 1930s. It was a terrible period.

Market rentals for State Houses. The Employment Contracts Act. Dreadful. So the 'mother of all budgets' made it clear that this really was a loopy right-wing government driven by Ruth Richardson, not by kind Country Jim."

Observers of the political scene, as Bob Chapman notes, might have had a sense of déjà vu: "…the incongruity of a kinder, more gentle policy coming down from the leadership, and Ruth Richardson's fire and brimstone in action. Bolger plays Lange to Richardson's Douglas, a Minister of Finance quite out of his control. Bolger looks benign, he often feels benign. But National has seen the light. Douglas had the answer and their Minister of Finance is there to finish the job."

Mike Moore, the new Leader of the Opposition, proved to be something of a contradiction. Perceived, partly because of his background and partly because it was an image he had been careful to cultivate, as a working-class hero, he was reluctant to publicly renounce the policy direction of the fourth Labour Government.

Helen: "The result was that we went into the 1993 campaign not having convinced anyone that we had a product any different to the product we'd been defeated on in 1990. Mike at his best is a wonderful, engaging, warm human being, and he's got a blue-collar background. But he did tend to believe that you could win on style. And he didn't see a need for any significant policy change. So in effect we were campaigning to put New Zealand back the way it was in 1990, not to put Labour on any clearly changed course. And he thought that basically what mattered was the style, mainly communicated through television. Style, publicity, media."

Moore was a populist and an exponent of the presidential style of politics. Elections would be won less by the sweat on the brows of the Party's workers or indeed by the quality of its members in Parliament, than by the sheer force of personality of its leader. What he failed to realise was that style, though it can greatly assist a politician, is rarely enough. Style must be accompanied by at least a fundamental grasp of the issues. Moore was a sloganeer rather than an articulator of policy and in this, as David Lange, the ultimate television politician, observes, he could not have been more different from his Deputy:

"Mike is like Gordon Dryden on speed – full of ideas and full of energy. And I once made the mistake of saying to Tom Scott that he was like a pinball machine wired by a colour-blind electrician, and he wrote the damn thing. Helen had a different, unemotional support base from Mike's support base. She was a person who was involved because of careful, meticulous industry, planning and long-term assessment. Mike was an impulsive, emotional, mercurial operator who inspired by sheer novelty and had great promotion. Helen's appeal was cerebral, Mike's appeal was much more ephemeral, but nonetheless big. And the scars of that battle were there for a long time."

Judith Tizard offers a similar perspective on Mike Moore: "Mike has no analysis. He once said to me, 'When I want to understand something I write a book about it.' I said, 'But the problem is nobody understands what you're doing.' I've tried to read Mike's books and they're gobbledegook. They're a series of bumper stickers. I think Mike has developed a great deal since then, but in 1990 he was a bit like an elderly machine-gun that needed a rebore. It was firing all over the place at vast speed to very little effect."

The fundamental difference in both substance and style between Moore and Clark may have accounted for a growing perception by the Leader of the Opposition that he was being undermined by his Deputy. It's a perception which Helen rejects:

"I actually thought I was pretty bloody good to Mike. Mike was an erratic fellow. He was likable but erratic, and I did for him the job that Geoffrey did for David – I chaired the Policy Council. I was in charge of getting the policy together. Mike did a lot of touring. He did a lot of radio work, fronting work. But I reckon I was the glue that kept the show together. There were only 29 of us to run the election. It was bloody hard. It was a very small parliamentary team. And no, I don't believe I undermined him at all in that three-year period. Hand on heart, I did not. And people constantly grumbled to me about him, that he could never win an election."

There is a curious fact about Labour's performance in opposition between 1990 and 1993 – no one can remember what they did. Talk to the political pundits about Mike Moore and they move instantly to the night of the 1993 General Election, as though the previous three years had not existed at all. But there was plenty happening elsewhere.

Despite its substantial victory in the election, National had not had an entirely easy run in the ensuing three years. Ruth Richardson's hard-line economic policies did not find favour with some of the Party's back-benchers and in August 1991 Gilbert Myles and Hamish McIntyre deserted and formed their own Liberal Party. Winston Peters was sacked as Minister of Maori Affairs in October after prolonged and public disagreements with the Party on economic and foreign policy issues. In a by-election in February 1992, following Sir Robert Muldoon's retirement, the Government came close to losing the Tamaki seat to Jim Anderton's newly-formed Alliance Party. Myles and McIntyre joined the Alliance in the same year. After an unsuccessful attempt by National to prevent his renomination for Tauranga, Winston Peters resigned from Parliament in March 1993 and stood as an independent in the subsequent by-election. He polled a massive 90.8 percent of the votes cast. He then formed New Zealand First, fielding 83 candidates in the 1993 election.

Jim Anderton had meanwhile pulled off an extraordinary organisational feat, corralling not merely the Democrats, Mana Motuhake and the Liberals, but the much more electorally significant Greens as well. The Alliance had become a force to be reckoned with, as the election result confirmed. The newly-formed political party won a phenomenal 18.21 percent of the vote. National's share dropped from 47.82 percent in 1990 to 35.05 percent in 1993. Labour fell slightly. Winston Peters' New Zealand Party took 8.40 percent of the overall vote, with a remarkable 20.55 percent in the four Maori seats.

The election gave National 50 seats in the new parliament, Labour 45, the Alliance and New Zealand First two each. Jim Anderton took Sydenham for the Alliance with a massive majority of 7476 over Labour, while Sandra Lee ousted Richard Prebble in Auckland Central. Winston Peters romped home for New Zealand First in Tauranga and the Northern Maori seat went to Tau Henare. National was left with an effective majority of one, threatening a constitutional crisis which never in fact materialised.

In a supreme irony, the country also voted for the introduction of Mixed Member Proportional representation (MMP) at the next election. Had the system already existed in 1993, the Alliance would have had 18 seats in Parliament. Labour would almost certainly have been the Government.

Though few can recall much about Labour's performance from 1990 to 1993, almost everyone remembers the extraordinary performance of the Leader of the Opposition on television on election night. Moore was convinced that Labour had won the election and, in what was in effect a victory speech from his campaign headquarters in Christchurch, told his supporters and the nation: "It's going to be a long night for Mr Bolger, but it won't be as long and as cold a night as it has been for young people in this country since he was elected." The speech, whose tone Bob Chapman describes as "triumph mixed with threat", was punctuated with whispered asides from Labour Party supporters in the hall that Labour had lost the election. Moore appeared not to hear any of this.

There is no doubt that the election night speech served to undermine public confidence in Mike Moore. More importantly for him, it added significantly to the doubts which many of his caucus colleagues had been having about his ability to continue as Leader of the Opposition. Moore's fate was effectively sealed on election night.

With the election lost, Helen and Judith decided it was time to take a break: "So Helen and I went to Fiji. We had a ball. Just lazed about and snorkelled and read and drank wine and gossiped. And Peter came up and spent three days with us. Helicoptered in. You have that funny gap in the week after an election where

Left **A brief rest at Fiji's Treasure Island after the 1993 election. Helen travelled up with Judith Tizard and Peter joined them a couple of days later.**

you wait for all the final counts. And there were faxes coming through saying this electorate's count had gone up, this electorate's count had gone down. But I saw nothing that contained any suggestion of a leadership challenge."

But the leadership of the Party was already on the agenda.

Helen: "Three or four days after the election I was rung, as I recall, by Elizabeth Tennant, the MP for Island Bay. She said she had a group of MPs at her house who wanted to talk to me about whether I'd be prepared to contest the leadership. And I said, 'Well look, I haven't given this any thought', which was the honest answer. I said, 'I'm going away for a few days to Fiji to have a break after the election and maybe people can talk to me when I get back.'"

"And Judith and I then went off to Fiji, joined by Peter a couple of days later, and we actually had a complete break. And when we came back the phone started ringing even harder. From other MPs. I said to them, 'I'm not going to stand unless I know I'm going to win. So really you have to do some work to see whether that's possible.' And we had a caucus meeting, the first one after the election, where people got up and were quite critical of the result and the campaign."

Judith has a vivid memory of that meeting: "There was a lot of recrimination. There were a lot of people who took the view that if Mike hadn't been so – 'flaky' was the word that was often used – we would have won the election. And I think quite a few people were shocked that the National Party, having done the cata-strophic things they had to the welfare state, hadn't been dismissed much more firmly. So the caucus got very strong. And it became obvious then that the leader-ship was a major issue.

"Helen was quite confident that she had the numbers. But she was nervous about doing damage to the Party. And I remember her saying at the time, 'Well of course the reason the last two leadership changes were easy was that both of them agreed to go.' And she and I had long memories of the Lange attack on Bill Rowling in 1980. And we saw what was happening as very much a replaying of that."

Helen was now committed to challenging Moore for the leadership and, according to David Lange, set about her task with a will: "By that stage Helen had, for the first time that I'd seen it openly, a sort of hit squad working doing the numbers, and she became in that sense, I suppose, a rather more orthodox politician than before. And she clearly had the numbers."

Helen's principal supporters included Steve Maharey and Ruth Dyson. To Judith Tizard's amazement, Michael Cullen supported Mike Moore:

"I still find that difficult to understand. The rifts have long since healed, but when I asked him why he was supporting Moore he said it was because Mike had given him his chance and trusted him as Finance spokesperson. I said, 'Well, who the hell else was there?'"

As Senior Whip, Jonathan Hunt now had an obligation to tell the Leader what was going on: "I said to Helen, 'I'm Senior Whip. If I hear of anything, I'll have to tell Moore.' And she absolutely accepted that. I went off to a wedding in Australia and I heard about it by phone. And I immediately rang Moore and told him."

The spill was to be at the next caucus meeting. There would be two ballots, the first to decide whether a second ballot should be taken on the leadership. If the first ballot were lost, then the question of the leadership would have to be deferred, giving Moore time to marshal support. Hunt advised Moore that in his opinion the first ballot would be lost. But if it went to a vote on the leadership, Clark would win.

At the next caucus meeting, David Lange moved that a ballot be held for the Leadership and Deputy Leadership of the Party. In an extraordinary move, Moore seconded the motion which was then passed unanimously.

Helen: "I think Mike felt, if it was going to happen, it might as well happen. And he would have been conscious of the precedent with Bill Rowling in 1980 when the caucus had a go at him. Mike was in the vanguard of that. Bill managed to avert the leadership ballot by one vote, namely his own. But he then struggled right through another election. Now Mike didn't want that. I think his attitude was, 'If they're going to dump me, dump me.'"

Jonathan: "Now I was the senior person as Whip. So I said, 'Stand up those who wish to stand to be Leader.' Moore stood up, Clark stood up, and the ballot was held. And at that point David Caygill had thrown in his lot with Clark on the basis that he was going to be made Deputy, and Clark won by four or five."

Moore's dumping only a couple of weeks after an election in which Labour had actually polled almost equal with National must have seemed particularly brutal. According to Helen, he did not go with a good grace:

"He campaigned against me for the next three years. And in the run-up to that ballot he and Yvonne were making public appeals to the Party membership and saying how dreadful and unfair it was. And people were ringing the talkbacks and referring to 'Helen Clark and her lesbian friends'. And there were posters put on power poles right down the street and round the neighbourhood saying, 'Helen, why won't you ring Mike?' because he kept saying to the media, 'I haven't heard from Helen.' I mean, it was all bizarre. Completely bizarre.

"Then again, if you analyse it, was I right to back him against Geoffrey? God knows. I mean, I've felt bad about that for years. And was it the right thing to challenge him within two or three weeks of the election? I don't know. Should you have let him stay and then exit with dignity? Would he ever have gone? There was a school of thought that said, 'Mike will only leave with a stake through his heart and garlic in the mouth.' But it wasn't pleasant. It was very unpleasant."

After the caucus Helen held a press conference. Barry Soper was there:

"She had a lemon suit on and looked very smart and came in and announced that she was the new Leader. She was quite magnanimous."

The shy little girl from Te Pahu was now Leader of the Labour Party and the Opposition.

After Labour's defeat in 1990, Helen had decided that politics could not continue to be her sole preoccupation. She needed a balance in her life, other interests and activities outside politics. Judith was one of the earliest to become aware of this change of emphasis:

"I became Labour's spokesperson for the Arts in 1990 and I was talking to her about what we were trying to achieve there. And she said, as far as she was concerned, it was about having pleasure, having fun, putting some priorities back into her life and reading novels again. She had spent the previous six years reading almost nothing except departmental reports and studies on policy.

"About that time I went on the board of the Auckland Theatre Company and she got much more interested in that. She took out a subscription to the Auckland Philharmonia. I was invited to NZSO concerts, so I would often take her to them and quite quickly she decided to take out a subscription to that as well. When the opera company got up and going she would go to every opera and was very well informed on that.

"Peter's interests are much more in jazz and contemporary music. He likes

cricket, he likes music, he likes films. They really enjoyed travelling together, but I think Helen decided she needed to have lots of other things she enjoyed doing too. So she made a conscious effort.

"She was also determined to get fit. And she discovered cross-country skiing which she absolutely loved. Helen is a person who enjoys contemplation and enjoys challenge and I think it was the skiing that started it."

Helen began to travel more. Since the start of her parliamentary career travelling has been and remains her principal form of escape from the rigours of political and public life and a source of enormous interest and pleasure. Her family have been the beneficiaries of her limitless enthusiasm for seeing the world. Sister Sandra was a regular companion:

"I've made quite a lot of overseas trips with Helen. She used to subsidise my flights in the early days and fly economy so that I could afford to go. I've managed to gate-crash most of the business-class lounges around the world except for Perth. They wouldn't let me into the Perth one, but I managed to sneak into most of the others behind her and Peter.

"I think 1987 was the first overseas holiday. We went to her secretary's time-share near Surfers Paradise. I remember her ringing me up at school and saying, 'Do you want to go to Surfers Paradise next week?' And I said, 'Sure.' We played tennis, we swam in the pool. Just the two of us. We walked on the beach, we went shopping. I did a few things on my own while she did a few things on her own, and

Above **A night at the opera, Auckland.** Opposite **Helen and Peter took up cross-country skiing in the 1990s. Holidaying in Antrim, USA, 1992.**

we went shopping at Fisherman's Wharf and bought those sunhats that she wore on Kawau Island with John Howard.

"There were other trips. Peter was in Boston one year on sabbatical and we went over. That was a fun holiday. He had accommodation in an apartment building not far from Boston University. It was like one room, with a little door off for the toilet. So we only had one bed. He'd got mattresses off friends and some extra knives and forks and things and we were there for two or three weeks. In one room. And that was actually a fun trip, because the pressure was off. Helen had time to do the things she likes doing. So we visited different little art galleries and went to shows. And we went shopping in Filene's, the big bargain-basement store in Boston, where Helen bought a huge coat like a padded sleeping bag. And I remember just thinking how neat it was that no one knew her. She could just be herself.

"And I think somewhere in there during the 90s she learned to balance things, so that she could cope better. She'd probably come home more, keep in touch with family more. Take more time for herself, look at keeping her health good. I don't know, she might have had a look at things and thought, there's more to life than just working hard.

"I had a fantastic holiday in South America with her and Peter. There have only been two occasions when Helen has asked for my advice. One was because I'd already been in Argentina for a fortnight and she asked my advice on what the

exchange rate was. And she's asked my advice on clothes. She likes to know if what she's wearing looks good. How does this look? Or should I wear this blazer with that? Or are these shoes OK? This is sister stuff. This is bedroom sister stuff with not a man in the room.

"So I've been to Britain, South America, Boston. Oh, and she and I had a weekend when Jillian Anderton was singing in Melbourne in the opera. We went over to that and I took a day off school and had a weekend away. It's just not how I live. And we went down to Phillip Island to see the little fairy penguins. We had a hilarious time there, because there were all these Japanese, clicking, clicking, and it says, 'No Photos To Be Taken'.

"When she goes somewhere she usually knows about the place before she goes. I went to Africa with them a couple of years ago, to Kilimanjaro, and we had a little time in Durban and she went to every museum in Durban."

Talk to Helen's family – her parents, sisters, nephews and nieces – and you are regaled with similar stories of Helen's kindness and generosity. Most have been shouted holidays either skiing in New Zealand or travelling overseas. And invariably they remember those holidays with excitement and affection. Suzanne's big trip was to Spain:

"Helen had tickets to go to Expo in Spain in 1992, and she decided she would take me. She shouted me the trip and we travelled economy. She just organised everything. Wonderful. And we went to London and then on to Stockholm.

"We visited churches and castles and she was really good at getting round on the trains. She could read a timetable like nobody I ever knew. And we didn't waste money. We used public transport, we never got taxis anywhere. We went to Uppsala and I insisted on going and seeing Carolus Linnaeus's garden. He's the man who developed the nomenclature system for plants. He ordered all the plants into their families and genuses and gave them all Latin names – the whole modern system of plant taxonomy. I specialised in plant taxonomy, which is why I was so interested.

"And then we went to Spain where we met Mum and Dad in Malaga. We had a good time overall. We had a rental car and I was the navigator. Helen would never give me the maps till about five minutes before we were due to head out. I don't know why. Suddenly we were off and I had to orientate the map. Anyway, the Expo was very interesting. And it was all paid for, the lot. All I had to cough up was a bit of spending money each day."

There is an unofficial archive of Helen's trips around the world. It is in the form of a collection of postcards, hundreds and hundreds of them, sent to her parents, her sisters, her aunts and uncles, her nephews and nieces. The postcards are crammed with information, mini-travelogues in the sender's small, neat handwriting. Fay's collection is particularly impressive:

"She was really on a big adventure by then. Any time there was a holiday she was away. And she always sent me postcards. The postcards show how she managed to cram everything possible into those trips. My daughter Gillian thinks I lived out my dreams of travelling through Helen. I was always interested in travelling. And she once said to me, 'Don't spend your money on your house, spend it on travel.'"

No one could have been more pleased about Helen's election as Leader of the Opposition than her parents. George and Margaret, till then committed National Party supporters, had "seen the light" in 1990, and for the first time in their lives voted Labour. Their daughter had, after all, been Deputy Prime Minister in the fourth Labour Government and was Deputy Leader of the Party. But, as they both make plain, their change of allegiance went beyond parental loyalty.

George: "I used to say to a lot of Labour Party people that they were right-wing Labour and I was left-wing National. Even when I was in the National Party I remember organising telegrams down to Muldoon about the Clyde Dam. I was trying to make them a better party. But in 1990 when old Jim Bolger was making a billion dollars worth of promises to get back into Parliament, I gave up. I thought that was wrong."

Margaret: "In a land of milk and honey and plenty, every time we went to church we were asked to take basic food items. They had a big basket they put them in to give to the Salvation Army to distribute. And I thought, fancy people not even having enough food in a country like this. And I thought, it's time to change the government. That was in 1990. I thought, well fancy people in this land of ours not even having Weetbix and jam."

George: "We always vote up at Waihi, because we're generally at Helen's and I always go along and help her. And I was walking across the street, and I didn't really know who I was going to vote for, because for a farmer to vote Labour in those days was sacrilege. Anyway, we did vote Labour from then on. We adjusted and found out that Labour could probably become a good government."

Margaret: "And then, when Helen became Leader of the Opposition, we got congratulatory messages from our National Party people at home. We became famous."

George: "We had the *Waikato Times* come down here one day. They took us out on the beach. And we were walking down the beach hand in hand and our photo was all through the Waikato. And one of our neighbours said, 'Gosh, I wonder if they always walk hand in hand?'"

Margaret: "The photographer told us to."

Helen would need all the support she could get. She was quickly to discover that being Leader of the Opposition was "the worst job in the world":

"That was well and truly established by about March or April 1994. I found it a very, very difficult job. Firstly, no woman had ever done the job, so there was no image of what sort of woman could be Prime Minister and it was really quite awkward. There was a lot of very personal comment about me in those days.

Above **In the 'organised mess' that is her home office, with her mother Margaret Clark.**

"And the model of Opposition Leader we'd had was of one who is constantly on the attack. Muldoon had perfected this as a style. Bill Rowling didn't do it very well. He was an honest plodder who never really landed a blow. But he didn't communicate a positive alternative vision either. David was there next for a short period as Leader of the Opposition with the ready wit and meteoric rise. And Mike had thundered away at Bolger to some effect in the traditional style.

"Now that just didn't work for me at all. Maybe it can't work for women. I'm not sure it would work for anyone any more, because you have to be able to communicate a positive vision of what you would like to achieve as Prime Minister and in government. But at the same time, you have to be kneecapping the Government, so the case is made for their replacement. It's getting those two in balance.

"What I learned – and it took me a long time to learn this – is that the Leader needs to stand above the fray and be making positive, affirming statements, while the dogs below nip at heels and do the shin-kicking. Because none of that did me any good as Leader of the Opposition."

Helen's position was not made any easier by the bitterness of the man she had defeated for the leadership. Mike Moore, as Dick Griffin observed, seemed determined to undermine and destabilise her:

"Michael had been unforgiving during the campaign against him and continued it afterwards without any let-up at all. It was very dirty. Outlandish claims were made by people supporting Moore – questions about her sexuality, that people

couldn't relate to her, that she was a cold-hearted bitch. 'I'll never work for her. I don't want to be in a caucus with a person like that.' Now this went on and on. It was nasty, very nasty, as nasty as anything I can remember. Mike lost his temper on regular occasions and called her for everything. But she would be dismissive, often dispassionate about it. She would never ever rise to the bait, which I thought showed an enormous amount of steel, political steel. Even off-the-record she'd say things like, 'Oh, that's Mike. Of course he's totally irrational.' Or words to that effect. But she never got down there in the gutter with some of his supporters.

"It must have been a nightmare for her, because for the first year at least there was still the fag-end of Moore's supporters who resented her. And not just those in caucus, within the Labour Party too. There was a group of people who were still enormously disappointed that he'd been defeated, who saw him as some sort of Labour icon, a warm-hearted working-man's hero. And they made life extremely difficult for her."

Nor could Helen claim that she had popular support among the voting public.

She did not. Both her own and the Party's ratings in the polls were a disaster, falling as low as 2 percent and 14 percent respectively. There was, Dick Griffin says, "no traction at all in the party":

"And she was looking so bleak. And how many times did you hear people say, 'This woman will never be Prime Minister of this country no matter what.' It was axiomatic that she was never going to make it. Her confidence never seemed to waver, but in a subterranean sense it must have been a nightmare because she knew that there was a coterie of senior caucus MPs regularly meeting to discuss her leadership and whether she should continue. On three occasions at least, they were getting prepared to put it to the vote – Goff, Moore, Cullen – and she managed to out-manoeuvre them. In much the same way that she had reasoned Moore could never win an election, they reasoned that she could never win an election.

"And she didn't emanate the sort of leadership I think people were used to from the Labour Party. Those who were looking for a new direction wanted the personality of a Lange to carry the banner for them. Those who were looking for a more stable business environment, as perhaps personified by David Caygill, didn't see that in Helen Clark. And she was continually belaboured by those who described her as a bluestocking or worse. So really what was her constituency? A few in academia, cultured people in Auckland. And women, most of whom looked at her and said, 'We can't elect her either.'"

There is no doubting that this was a terrible time for Helen. Geoffrey Palmer believes that few people can have gone through "as much flak and trouble in politics as she did in those years". Colin James observes that most men would have crumbled under the sort of pressure Helen was put under in her first term as Leader of the Opposition:

"The public treatment of her in the media for being unfashionably dressed, for eschewing all the accoutrements of femininity, for being academic, for being a reserved person without much in the way of public performance, for not having children, for living a rather strange life. And on top of that the constant mutterings of challenge, the undermining by Mike Moore."

According to Judith, Helen was still not a member of the boys' club: "Many people saw her as limited and closed and as having a very tight group, particularly of women advisors, around her. A lot of the men in the caucus didn't find her approachable or easy. She wasn't hail-fellow-well-met. She didn't drink with groups. She'd never play cards apart from with family and friends. She didn't see that as part of her normal socialising."

But if Helen was indeed difficult to approach, it may have been as the result of the relentless attacks on her rather than the other way round. Colin James asserts that Helen survived these attacks through an inner strength:

"But she achieves that inner strength by blocking people out. There seems to me to be only a very small number of people who are close to Helen Clark. There's another group whom she trusts quite a lot and it takes a lot of earning to get that trust. But she trusts them operationally rather than as deep friends. She doesn't seem to have easy acquaintanceships, which most politicians do. That's part of their politics, to get on easily with people and to make superficial connections. And she doesn't do that very easily."

If things looked bleak for Helen in 1994, there was worse to come. Ruth Richardson, replaced as Minister of Finance by Bill Birch, her New-Right economic policies diluted, decided enough was enough and resigned from Parliament. A by-election was duly held in Selwyn on 13 August 1994. Labour's candidate was Marian Hobbs. Judith records this as Helen's and the Labour Party's lowest point:

"The Selwyn by-election was awful. Mike Moore worked overtly, in my view, against Marian. He was really hostile. He was so sensitive to all of this, the real walking-wounded, bleeding all over the carpet and down the stairs and out onto the concrete, and god it was awful."

Richard Harman has a similar perspective on Moore's behaviour during the by-election, but believes that it lost him support in the end: "Moore was saying that lesbians had taken over the Labour Party and the whole by-election was pitched at that level – Labour feminists versus blue-collar Norman Kirk traditionalists. And then the terrible bloody recriminations when the Nats got back in. But the Selwyn by-election was Moore's last fling. He had so ostentatiously been a wrecker that it would be impossible to take him seriously after that."

Whatever Moore's role, the Selwyn by-election was a disaster for Labour. National held the seat with a slim majority of 418. The runner-up was not Labour but the Alliance. Labour came a pathetic third. The results speak for themselves: David Carter (National) 8906; John Wright (Alliance) 8488; Marian Hobbs (Labour) 2173; Tim – "I don't mind where, as long as I'm Mayor" – Shadbolt (New Zealand First) 1165.

It was almost inevitable that all of this would undermine Helen's confidence in herself and her ability to once more rebuild the Party: "There were some quite cruel things said. Along the lines that people couldn't relate to me. Colin James wrote for years that I didn't connect with people, as if you were a foreign being who'd strayed into this game. In real life I found all this quite hard to take, because I'd been in the Labour Party for 23 years. I'd been quite a successful Minister, well thought of in the Party. I'd been Deputy Prime Minister. And suddenly it was as if none of this mattered at all. It was like starting again in a new job. And every critic was waiting

NZ WOMAN'S WEEKLY

Left **The conservatory of her Mount Eden home where Helen regularly reads and works.**

there to have a go. And of course I suppose your confidence goes with that and it becomes a self-fulfilling prophecy."

Brian: "Did your confidence go?"

Helen: "I think it was quite severely eroded. I think it was really quite a difficult position."

Brian: "There were comments about your appearance."

Helen: "Constant comments. People didn't like your hairstyle, didn't like your clothes, didn't like your voice, didn't like anything about you."

Brian: "Did the old lesbian bogey come up again?"

Helen: "That got a trot during the leadership challenge after '93, but I don't think it really surfaced again."

Brian: "And not having children?"

Helen: "Oh, there was all of that. That was why you couldn't connect with people, you see, because you hadn't had these real experiences."

Brian: "Did you find that hurtful?"

Helen: "I found it very hurtful. And I had to erect a lot of defences again."

Brian: "This was a bad period for you, from '94 to early '96."

Helen: "Yes, because it really was like starting a new job at the bottom. '81 to '84 I found quite hard. But '93 to '96 was unbelievably difficult."

Brian: "You've said you don't see yourself as tough, you're strong."

Helen: "I've always had this thing about how, when I became Leader of the Labour Party, I really faced this incredible knocking brigade. And it was because women in politics were not seen as strong, but as tough. And 'tough' has bad connotations. You wouldn't be described as determined, but as bossy. 'Tough' somehow reminded men of their mothers-in-law, whereas men with the same characteristics would be seen as strong and determined."

Brian: "You're capable of being hurt, I think."

Helen: "Oh, not much any more, to be perfectly honest. Those early years in Parliament were very, very stressful, I'll tell you that. Almost nothing moves me to that point any more. I think it's a process of aging."

Brian: "So who supported you during that period?"

Helen: "Margaret Wilson was terrific. She was outside Parliament and she was always very, very helpful. People like Ken Douglas and Angela Foulkes from the trade unions were very supportive. Steve Maharey, Lianne Dalziel, Mark Burton, Judith of course. And Trevor Mallard was always very supportive."

Brian: "Emotionally supportive?"

Helen: "I've never really looked for emotional support. But in terms of the most personally supportive, Margaret for sure. And Peter."

The extent of Helen's distress during this period is illustrated in this account by Mike Williams:

"At one point we got down to 14 percent in the polls. And I was told that when that information was delivered to Helen she shut herself in her room and burst into tears. At that point, for whatever reason, she came to visit me in my office. She just wanted to shoot the breeze, because I think she was considering flagging it away. We weren't getting any support in the polls. There was even a point at which the Alliance was ahead of us and it seemed as though Jim had made the right decision, not Helen. And we had a long, long talk. And at that point I had come to the realisation that, despite what the polls were telling me, this was prime ministerial material. I'd been out in the business world. I'd been in Australia. I'd pressed the flesh with Bob Hawke, Paul Keating and others. I knew these people. And it suddenly occurred to me that little old Helen from way-back-then had it. I don't know if she'd remember that conversation, but I certainly do. It was a long conversation and my message, which I delivered in five or ten different ways, was quite simply, 'Hang in there!' And she did."

chapter twelve

PHOENIX
FROM THE ASHES

IN response to the negative perceptions of her first two years as Leader of the Opposition, Helen displayed her now familiar resilience and determination not to be beaten. Faced with restricted access to the media, who were in any event either indifferent or hostile, she began once again the process of rebuilding the Party's and her own support from the ground up. She set about visiting the regions, talking to Labour Party organisations and community groups. Local MPs were asked to set up programmes which would allow her to meet as many people as possible, and the Party's research and publicity units were reorganised to maximise these opportunities.

Judith: "Her view was that she just had to get out and about. And everybody used to say, 'Oh, Helen's just so much better in person than she is on television.' So she took the view that if that was true then she'd go out and meet every bloody New Zealander. And she damn near did."

Pressed by friends and advisors, Helen also began to devote more time to her appearance and presentation in the media. It was something she did reluctantly. To her, substance was more important than style and she objected to the idea that how a politician looked or sounded should be of prime importance to the electorate. She was resistant to the idea of being "made over". She was her own person and wished to remain so.

And she was all too aware of the double standard that applied to women and men in politics. Women's looks were constantly commented on. Men's almost never were. No one thought Norman Kirk was unfit to be Prime Minister because he was massively overweight. No one thought Rob Muldoon should be denied the highest office because he was unattractive. No one thought David Lange's girth was an impediment to leadership.

But Helen could also see that the constant talk about her appearance and her voice and how she presented herself on the public platform, on radio and television, was distracting public attention from the enormously talented and capable person she really was. The style was getting in the way of the substance and undermining her career. She was, as ever, pragmatic. Prompted in particular by Cath and Judith Tizard, she began to take advice from Maggie Eyre on make-up, grooming and presentation. And she was introduced to top fashion designer Jane Daniels, who continues to design her clothes today.

The changes were gradual but perceptible and Helen began to accept that she did not have to sacrifice either her true personality or her integrity in order to improve her image. Style and substance could go together.

Brian: "In those days you were opposed to the idea that image is important."

Helen: "I was. And wrongly so."

Brian: "Resistant to the idea that make-up and hair and clothes really mattered."

Helen: "No. I've always had reasonable clothes and by that period I always had good clothes. But it took me a long time to get the haircut right, because I've got extremely difficult hair."

Brian: "Have you formed any conclusions on the importance of image?"

Helen: "Very important. But you can't do it on image alone. It's got to be style and substance. One without the other won't work. I had an abundance of substance, but I didn't have the style. However, it's easier to do something about that than have an abundance of style and not have substance. You'll never plug that gap."

Brian: "The image must be a genuine reflection of the substance."

Helen: "Yes. It can't be disconsonant."

Her presentation skills were put to the test at the Party's annual conference in 1994.

Judith: "She wrote this absolutely breathtaking speech. I think it was over 45 minutes long, and she had the whole of it off by heart. And she practised it three times with a video camera. And Maggie would play it back, or play part of it back. And any number of times she ended up in tears. And she kept saying, 'I can't do it. I'm not a performer.' And

Right **Stylist Maggie Eyre transformed Helen's image in the mid-1990s. A more glamorous Leader of the Opposition emerged.**

we were saying, 'Of course you're a bloody performer! Look at your performance in election campaigns, look at your performance in Parliament. You're a great performer. But you've got to forget it's about performance and just perform.' And she said, 'I don't want to be an actor.' I think she found the whole process quite false. But we told her, 'It's also about projecting energy, it's about sounding confident, looking confident, looking attractive.' It took her a long time. And I had to keep thinking, 'This is the grand-daughter of working-class Highland Scots and Irish peasants and she is really struggling with the idea of showing off.'

"But in the end she stood up and gave this absolutely breathtaking speech about who she was and why she was in the Labour Party and why she was the Leader of the Labour Party. And she got an absolutely fabulous response and was completely buoyed up by it. She was tearful and excited in a way that I've never seen her before, with the huge surge of love and acceptance and support that she got from that conference. And from that moment on, I don't think she ever doubted that she would be Prime Minister."

Colin James was present at the conference and regards Helen's speech as a pivotal point in her career: "The turning point was Helen's decision to deliver a personal statement as her Leader's address. I remember reading it and thinking, 'This is totally different from what she's done before.' And in a sense that was almost an act of desperation because they were in a pretty dreadful place in the

Left **Peter and Helen in the sitting room of their Mount Eden home.** *Opposite Page* **Relaxing at home in the conservatory, October 1996.**

polls. But I think it was also the beginning of her decision that she would be Helen Clark as Leader of the Opposition. And while you can't call that confidence, it's the beginning of her statement that she will be her own person in the job, and not someone else's person, and even though she's a servant of the Party, not the Party's person either. And I think that was the turning point."

There were minor improvements in the polls, but the media remained uninterested or hostile.

Brian: "Your other problem as Leader of the Opposition was getting media attention."

Helen: "Yes. It was very, very hard."

Brian: "How did the media treat you?"

Helen: "Well, it's quite an interesting topic, actually. Because up until the time we were defeated in 1990, I'd had very little to do with the media. You might find this strange, but if you come into Parliament as a back-bencher from Auckland, who gives a stuff about you? No one rings for your opinion. You're a nobody. Then, from 1984 to 1987, I was still a back-bencher, attracting virtually no media attention at all. In 1987 I became Minister of Housing and Conservation. But from the time I went into Government I always felt on the back foot. My job in Housing was to save the Housing Corporation, but I could never speak frankly, because I was actually at war with Roger Douglas and what he was trying to do. I had a disastrous start in Conservation with the head of the department deliberately overspending his budget. And then, as Minister of Health, I was always on the defensive. So basically I had nine years where I had no positive relations with the media at all. Because I was always either irrelevant or on the defensive.

"After 1990 we had to go out and build new relationships, sell our story, start from the bottom. It wasn't an easy period. And when I became Leader, after the first three months fascination, some of the media really turned on me. Linda Clark went for me with a vengeance. I remember in April in 1994 going down to Mount Cook at Easter and waiting for Peter to turn up. And on the Easter Thursday night I was watching the news. And Clark basically stood up in front of Parliament, on camera, and said, Helen Clark won't last the year as Leader of the Labour Party. I was completely written off, and that was pretty much the norm. Clark was working for TVNZ. So the most powerful medium in the country denounced me within four or five months of my becoming Leader. I was terminal and couldn't last. And that's what I thought."

Brian: "So you can scarcely have enjoyed appearing on radio and television."

Helen: "No, it was very difficult. I remember doing an interview with you around this time, when you were standing in for Kim Hill. And I remember you saying to me, 'You don't sound very happy.' And this was on air. And I went, 'Shit!'"

Brian: "Your ratings at the time were poor."

Helen: "Dreadful."

Brian: "And the media just weren't interested in you."

Helen: "No. Well, I just wasn't regarded as a serious contender. And from the time Linda Clark put her mitts in, the mutterings began: Had the Party made the wrong choice?"

Brian: "And you were aware of this?"

Helen: "Oh yes. Absolutely."

Helen's relations with the media improved over the next two years but the Party's and her personal ratings remained stubbornly in the doldrums. The mutterings increased in volume.

Brian: "During this period there is a process of destabilisation of your leadership."

Helen: "Constant. If you went back through the media reports of the time, there were constant rumours. And constant attacks in the caucus. Basically every caucus has a Leader's Report and then they'd all get up and pick away. The polls are disastrous, everything's disastrous, no one trusts us, no one believes us, people are moaning back home in the electorates, we haven't got a strategy, where's the strategy, can we discuss the strategy… It didn't matter how many strategies you put up, it still wasn't a strategy. It went on and on like that. And there was constant leaking by unnamed people.

"Then, in May 1996, just before caucus, I get this delegation telling me to stand down. From memory there was Michael Cullen, Phil Goff, Annette King, Koro Wetere, Jim Sutton. I had heard that they were intending to come, so I'd mobilised my Deputy, David Caygill, Steve Maharey, Trevor Mallard and Jonathan. I can't remember if I had anyone else there.

"Anyway, these people had rushed around the caucus counting numbers and then decided they'd come and confront me and ask me to stand down, and say there was a majority who wanted that to happen. And the line was, you're a nice person blah, blah, blah, but you can't win the election and we don't want to have to challenge you directly at the caucus, so it would just be better if you resigned. And I said to them, 'Well, if you want a change of leader, you're going to have to go into the caucus and move a motion.'"

Brian: "Did you take that line because you were reasonably sure you had the numbers?"

Helen: "I didn't know at that point. But what I did know was that a leadership change was not the answer to the problem, because there wasn't anyone else. They actually seriously proposed bringing Mike Moore back at that point. So I thought, if the caucus wants to make a ridiculous decision, it's going to be hard for them. First they're going to have to vote to have a motion put. Then they're going to have to vote me out. And then they're going to have to vote him in. So this wasn't going to be made easy for them. So I basically decided to stand. I always said, when Bolger was bluffed out in '97, if he'd called the caucus together straight away when he got off the plane, and gone into that room and said, 'If you want me out of here, you're going to have to move a motion to have a ballot, and then you're going to have to vote me out,' he'd probably still be in the job. Well, he would have lasted the election anyway. So you must stand. And if you stand, people start to slink away."

Brian: "So you said, 'Fine, take it to caucus and we'll see what happens.'"

Helen: "That's right. And they never did it. They walked out into the corridor to the caucus and so did I, and nothing was said."

But inevitably word of the attempted coup leaked out.

Helen: "I remember doing interviews from a hotel room somewhere or other. I certainly commented extensively on the situation. And I remember people saying, 'Well, what are you going to do about it?' So I said, 'I'm getting on with the job, I'm in Rotorua' or wherever the hell it was, 'trying to get support for Labour for the election. We've just had a very successful conference and this is absolutely nutty behaviour.' And I treated it with complete disdain. I took it on, head on."

Brian: "You must have felt a certain sense of satisfaction with the outcome."

Helen: "But we couldn't recover in the polls with this sort of crap going on. And it went on for three years."

Brian: "How do you feel towards those people today?"

Helen: "Relatively benign. Well, it takes a while to feel relatively benign. In the end you've got to work with people, and the only reason I survived in those years was because I never took a winner-takes-all approach. I always kept people who had grossly undermined me on the front bench and in senior positions."

Brian: "Is that inclusiveness an expression of generosity, or because it's best to keep your opponents close to you?"

Helen: "It's just practical. When you're talking of someone like Phil Goff, you're talking of people with very considerable ability. And if you were to take an exclusive approach, you wouldn't last long. Because it would become a source of discontent. And then, as other people fell out with you – and people do fall in and out with leaders – they'd gravitate to another camp."

Brian: "It must require a special quality to be as sanguine at that. You must surely have been annoyed at the time."

Helen: "Oh, furious. Furious!"

Brian: "So in the weeks immediately following this attempted coup, what was your relationship with those people?"

Helen: "Well, funnily enough, quite civil. It's not like having a row with the National Party, where you just would walk past someone in the corridor. No, you just carry on."

Brian: "So it's almost as if it didn't happen?"

Helen: "Yes, life goes on. People keep meeting in their little factions, corners and groups, but it all goes back under the surface."

Helen's approach to the treachery of colleagues displays something akin to the political astuteness of a Machiavelli, a quality, as David Lange notes, not previously seen in Labour leaders:

"She handled it in a way which was most original, quite novel in my experience of the Labour Party. She promoted her enemies and put them on the front bench and that was quite extraordinary."

Bob Chapman sees this willingness to embrace her former enemies as one of the great strengths of Helen's leadership: "The job which she took on in 1993 as Leader of the Opposition is one only a highly intelligent, very equable and strong person-ality could have done. That was to bring together two discrete parties in the caucus and meld them and come up over time with policies which went back to funda-

mental Labour attitudes. And she did it. Instead of exiling people like Goff, she brought them in. Her shadow cabinet was a melding of the different elements. Had she got it wrong, she would have tried to make the Left win to the exclusion of the Right. She did not do that. She brought them in together, because she had to construct the Labour Party whole. And when it is working well, it is a broad church."

Bill Ralston has a more sociological take on the issue: "It's a female thing. Be more collusive. Boys would regard anybody who is a competitor as a threat. She would draw them close. I think a lot of women tend to be more collusive in situations like that. They tend to say, 'How can I neutralise this person, get them on board, get them on side?' Whereas boys tend to be more competitive and say, 'Let's have a fight. Let's have a good slapping.'"

But despite Helen's efforts to reunite the factions in her caucus, the publicity from the abortive coup proved damaging to both the Party's and her personal ratings. Labour continued to languish in the low 20s while the Government polled in the mid to high 30s. In the 'Preferred Prime Minister' stakes, Helen was nowhere in the running. To a degree this is the fate of all Leaders of the Opposition for, as David Lange so tellingly puts it, "You can't exude an aura which inspires trust or commitment if they know you're playing a fake violin."

But Helen had an additional problem. Her television image was dreadful. In news and current affairs interviews she appeared defensive and ill at ease. Despite her reputation for toughness, she allowed herself to be bullied by interviewers, responding to their generally negative questioning with a weak and unnatural smile. Her vocal delivery was more appropriate to the debating chamber than to the intimate atmosphere of the television studio.

At the urging of Party President Michael Hirschfeld, Helen reluctantly agreed to undergo a single session of television training. The session would be exploratory. If either party was unhappy with the outcome, there would be no further meetings.

It was apparent from the moment she arrived that Helen was uneasy. She made it clear that she did not want to be "deconstructed", that she did not intend to be turned into an actress, that she was uninterested in some cosmetic transformation. The session went extremely well and Helen was buoyed by the outcome. Far from being asked to "perform", she had been encouraged to do nothing more than be herself, to let the viewer see the Helen Clark that people met face-to-face.

In the next couple of weeks she had the opportunity to test the effectiveness of the training before two relatively small television audiences. She was interviewed on successive Sunday mornings on *Marae* and *Tagata Pasifika*. Helen proved to be a quick learner. The improvement in her performance was instantaneous. Her delivery was intimate and smooth. She appeared confident, relaxed and warm. She was enjoying the experience.

It was decided that the training sessions would continue. In future all of Helen's major television and radio appearances would be workshopped. The interviews on *Marae* and *Tagata Pasifika* had been relatively gentle. But how would she handle the more abrasive styles of a Paul Holmes or a Kim Hill? As it turnd out, the answer was, with aplomb. Helen was in the process of becoming the best media exponent of any of the Party leaders. Within weeks the improvement in her television performance was producing comment in the media itself. Reviewers and political pundits observed that they were seeing a new Helen Clark – more at ease, more assured, more buoyant.

The effect of all of this was to reverse the downward spiral that had been the consistent pattern since Helen assumed the leadership – negative comment, leading to lack of confidence, leading to poor performance, leading to further negative comment. She was now being praised for her performance, felt better about herself and more confident, and in consequence upped her performance even more. All of this was reflected in her Preferred Prime Minister ratings, which began to improve gradually. She was becoming a serious contender.

But if Helen's personal ratings were improving, her party's remained uninspiring. By the end of August Labour was trailing National by as much as 20 percent and facing demolition at the ballot box. But that was about to change. Labour effectively put all its eggs in one basket by running a presidential-style campaign centred almost entirely around its leader. It was a gamble, but by the end of September the gamble was beginning to pay off. And it was television that made the difference. In *New Zealand Politics in Transition*, Stephen Levine and Nigel Roberts record

LOTTO WIN...
TROPICAL HOLIDAY...
GOLDEN SUNRISE...
NEW CAR FOR EVERYONE...
WARM PUPPY...
BREAKFAST IN BED...

I DON'T KNOW WHAT THE OTHERS ARE MOANING ABOUT. THE WORM IS CHILD'S PLAY..

the extraordinary final events of the 1996 television election:

Above **Tom Scott's view of the infamous 'worm', the device that measured audience response to the leaders' performances in televised debates for the 1996 election campaign.**

For Clark and Bolger alike, the turning point in the campaign came during a TVNZ debate on 26 September. Bolger looked fatigued, was apparently ill, and appeared palpably uncomfortable bracketed between Peters and Anderton. An invited (and at times vocal) studio audience comprised equal groups from the four parties, so that three of four people present were opposed to the National Government. In addition, the programme introduced a polling technique new to New Zealand, whereby the moment-by-moment reactions to each leader of a sample of eighty randomly selected floating voters in Auckland were registered, using a device known as 'the worm'. In general, the sample reacted adversely to comments from the Prime Minister; Clark's performance, by contrast, received a much more favourable rating. Subsequent post-debate media commentary focused on these assessments, which were given a further round of publicity when it became known that Bolger had complained about both 'the worm' and his seating arrangements, several hours after the programme. A second debate, with 'the worm' still being employed (but with Bolger now no longer seated between his opponents), also reached a substantial television audience. While Bolger was better prepared, his more polished performance was still unpopular with the sample, whose response received wide publicity in news coverage after the

programme and the following day. Again, Clark – identified generally by the media as 'the winner' following each debate – emerged strengthened from the televised encounter. Opinion polls during the campaign showed National's support dropping and Labour's rising. Labour also made gains at the expense of the Alliance – Anderton appeared at times shrill and self-righteous – while some National supporters moved to support ACT, at least in part to improve its chances of crossing the 5 percent threshold. So much of an asset had Clark become that by the end of the campaign, the Labour Party was paying for full-page advertisements carrying her photograph (beneath the slogan 'New heart. New hope. New Zealand'), her words and her signature. This was a remarkable turn-around not only for Clark, but for a party that had criticised a former leader, Mike Moore, after the 1993 election, for (among other things) running too personal and self-centred a campaign.

An interesting sidelight on the first television debate is provided by Tom Scott, who was at the Avalon television studios:

"All the seats were the same height. Now Winston's not a tall man. And as soon as he got in his seat you could see that Helen Clark was going to be the tallest person on the panel. And Jim Anderton didn't notice that she was taller than all of them and sat there saying, 'She's just a wee bit taller than Winston.' And Winston reaches down to the pump on his seat. Pump, pump, pump. He must have had his knees crushed up under the table, so that he looked like he was the tallest person in the studio.

"And she was there and she did very, very well that night. Her television performances had improved tremendously. She certainly won that debate out at Avalon. And Bolger was furious and stormed out. I was there when he was screaming and shouting at Paul Holmes in the Green Room afterwards, drinking bloody whisky."

But despite Helen's bravura performances, the result of New Zealand's first MMP election, held on 12 October 1996, was a disaster for Labour which gained only 28.19 percent of the party vote, its smallest share of electoral support since 1928. National got 33.84 percent, New Zealand First 13.35 percent and the Alliance a disappointing 10.10 percent. National won 30 of the electorate seats, Labour 26, New Zealand First six, including the five Maori seats, with the Alliance, ACT and United on one each.

The result gave National 44 seats in the new parliament, Labour 37, New Zealand First 17, the Alliance 13, ACT eight and Peter Dunne's United Party one. On the reasonable assumption that on most matters ACT and United would vote with National, and the Alliance with Labour, the Right could marshal 53 votes and the Left 50 votes. Who governed New Zealand for the next three years was now in the hands of Winston Peters.

The loss of the traditionally Labour Maori seats to New Zealand First was a bitter blow to the Party and to Helen: "We were under a lot of pressure in the Maori electorates in that '93-'96 period. Tau Henare was portrayed by Winston as representing the up-and-coming generation of Maori leadership, so that New Zealand First looked like it was becoming the Maori party. Winston also had this following amongst the superannuitants, so their party conferences were always a bit odd with older people side by side with the Maori component. And thirdly, in that series of quite carefully crafted speeches in Auckland in early 1996, there was an implied anti-immigrant message which was seen as quite divisive."

Brian: "How do you explain Peters' appeal?"

Helen: "I think part of his appeal is that he's kept a bit of a sense of mystery around him. He stays within the shadows, when most of the rest of us are pretty exposed out there. But he holds back a lot, so there's a bit of mystery. And secondly I think he got his prominence in the National Party as a Maori who was prepared to have a whack at Maori for not being get-up-and-go. 'Look, you have all these opportunities staring you in the face. What's wrong with you?' sort of thing. So a Maori who beats up on other Maori will always get a certain following."

Brian: "Which is in tune with the anti-immigration theme."

Helen: "Yes. And that had resonance within the Maori community too because they were concerned at the time about the level of immigration and Maori diminishing as a proportion of a growing population. And Winston really was one of those Muldoon National Party people. Muldoon always appealed to the older people as well, so he took on that mantle. And he attacked the surcharge right through the 80s. His big cause was the superannuitants. And another aspect is that he got himself a reputation as a scam-buster. He was a man who exposed scandal. So all that explains it, I guess."

Peters seemed intent on preserving his sense of mystery. Having spent the day after the election on a boat, he appeared to be eluding the media. The election result might hang in the balance, but the country could wait. He was the king-maker and intended not merely to enjoy his reign but to prolong it as long as possible. The negotiations to determine which of the major parties would govern in coalition with New Zealand First were to last nine weeks.

Helen: "New Zealand First really didn't have a policy. So what they did with both parties was sit down and write a policy, a coalition agreement. And it went on and on and on. And about a month into it we decided that this was all getting a bit silly. So we said, 'Look we've got bottom lines here.' And our bottom lines included going back to income-related State House rentals, new industrial legislation and so on. And we said, 'We can't go into Government with you without these, because this is basic to our policy.' And in doing that we were well aware that we'd given him the out not to go with us. And we realised that we actually didn't want govern-ment on any terms. That if we went into government we had to be able to deliver certain things that had been our cornerstone campaign policies. If we couldn't deliver those, we were better to sit it out."

Brian: "What were the issues that were unacceptable to him?"

Helen: "He would not budge on income-related rentals. He wanted the market rent system. Now if there was one thing we'd gone blue in the face on, it was getting rid of market rents for State Houses. And he had no sympathy at all for unions' and workers' ability to negotiate with employers. And that again was a cornerstone of Labour Party policy. We had to produce the industrial legislation. So those two things stand out in my mind as the two big sticking points. But there were a cluster of things like that where we said, 'We've got to have these things in any agree-ment.'"

Brian: "How were those negotiations conducted?"

Helen: "What happened, as I recall, was that there was a meeting about weekly where Michael Cullen, Mike Moore, Heather Simpson, maybe one or two others and I, would meet with him and his people. And Heather would do a lot of work in between, writing up policy statements and agreements with their equivalent staff person, whoever it was. And there would have been some meetings where their spokespeople and ours got together. So a semi-credible coalition agreement of great detail was produced, but there were sticking points on issues. But the real issue was that I said I had to have Michael Cullen as Minister of Finance. That was the real issue. And Bolger was prepared to give him the Finance job and I wasn't. And I remember the day when they brought their MPs and Party Councillors together to discuss who they'd go with. And Tau Henare, who I think really did want to go with Labour, as I suspect most of their MPs did, rang me from a phone outside their caucus room and said, 'Are you firm on Winston not being Minister of Finance?' And I said, 'I have to be, Tau.' That's what threw them the other way. And the announcement came within the next two or three hours.

"Dick Griffin was working behind the scenes with Peters to get him to go with National. And it was clear from the early days of the talks that Griffin was lubricating Peters and that Peters had every intention of going with Bolger."

The former Radio New Zealand Political Editor had been Bolger's Chief Press Secretary and political advisor since 1994 and was indeed heavily involved in the negotiations between his boss and Winston. According to Griffin, the Labour Leader's gender was a significant issue for Peters:

"Winston didn't really know what he wanted, but he knew he didn't want to work with Helen Clark. By nature this is a conservative politician, a conservative New Zealand male. And I always believed that he would find enormous difficulty having to work with a woman, a woman of her ilk and her background and of virtually similar age. I didn't have to go to a lot of trouble to convince him of that. In a sense his attitude to Helen was a bit like Bolger's attitude to Helen. He found her intimidating. He found her on occasions overweening. He thought that she was dismissive of him. And she probably was.

"And after all those years of paddling his own canoe he was not going to get into another canoe with Helen navigating. He'd worked with Bolger before, and despite the fact that they'd been bitter enemies and said appalling things about each other both privately and publicly, in the end he knew the makings of the man. He did not know the makings of Helen Clark.

"The issue of being Treasurer was also a big factor, but that issue was only raised at half-past 10 on the evening prior to the decision on who he'd go into coalition with being made. Winston happened to be in my office with Paul East. The Prime Minister then came out and said, 'Rich, can I see you for a minute? He wants to be Treasurer. You never told me that.' And I said, 'Well, I told you he didn't want to be Finance Minister. Obviously he has got a different view.'

"Winston wasn't doing the negotiating at that stage; his brother Wayne was. And when Labour refused to do it, at the very 11th hour, Wayne put the acid on Bill Birch. Only Bill Birch and Bolger were in the office with Wayne at this stage.

"Winston was in my office looking like the cat that's got the cream and saying, 'It's either this or we go with the other lot.' And Bolger didn't know what to do. He either had to dump his mate Bill Birch and accept the role of Treasurer as a new reality, or go back to the drawing-board, or face the prospect of being out of government the following day. And I had told him earlier in the piece that Winston had said to me, 'Don't worry, I don't want to be Finance Minister.' And Bolger very reluctantly agreed that night. Birch turned puce and went home. And Bolger looked as though he'd done a Judas."

Helen believes that Peters had broached the Treasurer issue with Bolger much sooner than Griffin suggests. But the point is academic. On 10 December Peters appeared on television to deliver an inordinately long address justifying his decision on a coalition partner. It was an extraordinary piece of theatre, an elongated tease with the actual announcement left to virtually the last sentence. New Zealand First would go with National.

The decision represented an absolute betrayal of every New Zealand First voter who had accepted Peters' clearly expressed intention throughout the campaign to depose the National Government, that is to say the vast majority of those voters. In an NBR-Consultus poll, released on 22 November, 62 percent of New Zealand First voters expressed support for Labour as a coalition partner. Only 22 percent wanted National. Those formerly Labour Maori voters who had now unwittingly given their support to a party they abhorred, must have been particularly embittered, not least because Tau Henare had vowed during the campaign that he would

Opposite Page **The moment of truth: Jonathan Hunt reaches out in sympathy, just after Winston Peters' theatrical announcement that New Zealand First had opted for a coalition with National, December 10 1996. Helen's personal secretary, Jane Leicester, is at right.** *Left* **Helen's staff were instructed that if they cried they had to leave the room. Determinedly cheerful: Dot Kettle, Sian Roberts and Jenny Toogood.**

never serve in any Cabinet with Jim Bolger as Prime Minister, Bill Birch as Minister of Finance or Jenny Shipley in any social policy portfolio.

Winston Peters' rationale for his decision, that the Alliance's non-negotiable demands effectively made a coalition with the Left impossible, and that the National Government had in fact been deposed by a new and different coalition government, was neither ingenuous nor convincing. But the outcome remained the same – Labour had been denied office for a further three years.

This was a body blow for Helen who, on election night, had every reason to believe that the glittering prize was hers, and whose photograph had appeared on the cover of the South Pacific edition of *Time* magazine on October 21 with the caption "Prime Minister In Waiting?" She watched the Peters announcement on television in her office:

"I actually remember everyone coming to my room, and everyone else was in tears, and I was saying, 'For Christ's sake, leave the room, I've got to go and front the media. You'll upset me.'"

Brian: "You didn't cry?"

Helen: "No. It was quite emotional, but it wasn't a surprise."

Brian: "The speech was such a piece of theatre."

Helen: "Totally."

Brian: "And the decision was virtually in the last sentence."

Helen: "That's right, but there were plenty of clues before that. I said, 'It's quite clear what he's going to do.' But I knew from the time of Tau's phone call anyway,

Prime
Minister
In Waiting?

that it was hanging on the Treasurer issue."

Brian: "So how did you feel at that moment?"

Helen: "I certainly felt disappointed, but on the other hand it didn't take me terribly long to realise that it was the best thing that had ever happened."

Brian: "You wouldn't have realised that on that night?"

Helen: "Oh, I wasn't without insight that night. Because when we put the stake in the ground on the Treasurer issue and the other policy issues, we were well aware that that would probably mean he'd go the other way. So we weren't unprepared for it."

Brian: "Nonetheless, the media were referring to you as 'Prime Minister in Waiting'. You were within a hair's breadth of being the New Zealand's first woman Prime Minister."

Helen: "Yes. For all those reasons it was disappointing. But it wasn't unexpected. You just turn around and say, 'What's next?'"

It is Helen's view that Winston Peters never had any intention of going with Labour, that his pledges during the campaign to remove the National Government were little more than a cynical strategy to plunder Labour votes. Had he declared his true intentions, he would, as the polls were showing, have lost massive support.

Peters, as Dick Griffin has suggested, would not have been happy working under a woman Prime Minister, a view shared by Jonathan Hunt: "The real sticking point was that he had worked out that in a Clark-Peters government, Clark would be the focus, the first woman Prime Minister. In a Bolger-Peters government Peters would be the focus. And Peters is an extraordinarily vain and selfish man. And I think he went against the wishes of his own Party, the majority of whom wanted to go with Labour. Certainly the Maori members did, by and large."

Peters, Bob Chapman believes, was simply returning to his natural home: "I frankly didn't believe he would do it and I'm still surprised. But it is a tribute to one thing – he loved that National caucus, he loved being part of it. It suited his true beliefs and he made his decision as much on sentiment as anything. He wanted to be a big wheel in the National caucus. And he was. He was Treasurer and Deputy Prime Minister. He didn't feel that way about the Labour caucus. He didn't want to be a big wheel in Labour."

It's a view which Tom Scott endorses and takes further: "I knew he was going to go with National. Peters had unfinished business. Throughout his time in the

National Party he'd felt that he was patronised, that he was the barefoot Maori boy who'd put on a suit and they hadn't taken him seriously. So he was going to come back and haunt them one way or another. And I think he may almost have thought that if he came back to National, National and New Zealand First might merge. He and Bolger may even have talked about that over whisky. About Winston being his natural successor. He might even return to the National Party and take over and be a National Party Prime Minister. I think that was the grand plan. Articulated over whisky."

But the 'grand plan' was fatally flawed. Peters' duplicity during the election campaign and his betrayal of those who had voted for him could not go unpunished. His credibility was in ruins and, despite his reputation as "the comeback kid", it is doubtful whether it will ever be restored. Nigel Roberts describes Peters' decision to go with National as "the third great betrayal in New Zealand politics":

"You'd had the fourth Labour Government dash people's hopes and betray their promises. Then you'd had the fourth National Government do the same. Hey presto, as a result of those two we get MMP, and then along comes Winston Peters. So that was wonderful in some ways for the Labour Party. I've never seen them so united. They were like a jilted lover. They felt so spurned they were united. And in the process what was overlooked was that Labour only got 28 percent of the votes. Twenty-eight percent is appalling, an even smaller share of the votes than they got in 1990. And if you'd combined that with a Leader of the Opposition who'd been polling around three or four percent, as Helen had right up until the middle of the year, I think it would have been 'goodnight nurse'."

The point is well made. Though Labour polled poorly in the 1996 election, its leader had staged the most remarkable comeback in the second half of the year. Her personal ratings soared and she was the undisputed winner of the televised debates. Had she not risen, like a phoenix from the ashes, it is doubtful whether Labour would have polled even 28 percent and almost certain that she would not have survived to fight another election.

Helen could not yet know that the 1996 result would turn out to be a blessing in disguise for her and her party, but she emerged from the election strengthened in her leadership and more confident in the belief that she would one day be Prime Minister of New Zealand. Joan Caulfield puts it well:

"I think that campaign was a campaign for Helen's survival. And I think that was when her true steeliness and confidence and ability came through. She had to give it everything. She had to draw out everything that she had within herself, because if she didn't do well, she would have been history. And that was actually quite exciting to see. I felt like a very proud older sister. And I can stand back now and say, god she was fantastic! It was an absolutely crucial time in her political life. It was about survival. She was fighting for survival and she proved herself."

chapter thirteen

THE GLITTERING PRIZE

THE National-New Zealand First coalition government was almost certainly doomed from the outset. Supporters of both parties were singularly unenthusiastic about the merger. And there was another significant factor. By 1999 National would have been in office for nine years. Given New Zealanders' historic attitudes to parties retaining power for lengthy periods, it was highly unlikely to win a further term.

Though publicly the Coalition partners managed to maintain an impression of unity for most of 1997, there was considerable disaffection with the new arrangement in National's Cabinet and caucus. Jenny Shipley, according to Dick Griffin, had not even wanted the written coalition agreement to be circulated or printed and had actively tried to stop it. She had no time for Winston Peters and, within a couple of months of the Government's taking office, had begun to undermine its Treasurer and Deputy Prime Minister.

The first of a series of what would prove to be terminal embarrassments struck the Coalition early in the year, when it was reported that the New Zealand First MP for Te Tai Hauauru, Tukuroirangi (Tuku) Morgan, had spent $89 at an expensive menswear store for a pair of underpants while he was a director of the Government-funded Aotearoa Television Network. The underpants were said to be part of a spending spree on clothes, running to thousands of dollars, by Morgan and fellow ATN director Morehu McDonald, between July and September 1996.

Right **Murray Webb depicts Jenny Shipley and Helen Clark "chit-chatting" over the tea cups, for a Griffins biscuit advertisement. An unlikely scenario.**

Morgan was also said to have been paid exhorbitant fees by ATN both while he was a director of the company, and after his resignation in August 1996 in anticipation of his candidacy for New Zealand First. There was talk of an ATN-funded trip to Disneyland for him and his family.

All of this was taxpayers' money and on 8 February, the Serious Fraud Office seized documents from ATN and began an investigation into "specific matters concerning the expenditure of public money".

On 25 February Tuku Morgan made his maiden speech. Referring to what had come to be dubbed "Undiegate", he told the House, "I won't get caught with my pants down again."

In July, ATN lost its licence and went off the air. In the same month, Judge Jamieson, the Acting Director of the Serious Fraud Office, reported: "It is my carefully considered view after weighing all the material available to me, that the evidence here falls short of establishing any serious or complex fraud on the part of any of the persons associated with Aotearoa or its associated company Pumanawa to justify any criminal charges." But he noted: "The level of spending by Mr Morgan and Mr McDonald on personal clothing was clearly disproportionate to that of the other executive producers. However, because there was no obligation to account for expenditure, either to Aotearoa or to Te Mangai Paho, in the most general terms I cannot say it was criminal."

The ATN affair and "Undiegate" nonetheless made a laughing-stock of New Zealand First and, by association, the Coalition. By September 1997 public support for National had dropped to under 30 percent, and for New Zealand First to 5 percent. Support for the Labour Opposition had risen to an unprecedented 50 percent. Helen Clark's Preferred Prime Minister rating was now 30 percent, while the actual Prime Minister languished on 15 percent. The Coalition Government was in disarray and headed for oblivion.

In October Jim Bolger resigned to make way for a new leader of the National Party and New Zealand's first woman Prime Minister, Jenny Shipley. His departure, as Helen tells the story, was not entirely voluntary:

"Poor old Bolger went off to the Commonwealth Heads of Government meeting in Edinburgh. And the moment he got on the plane they all got busy. And when Bolger arrived back, he was met by Doug Graham who told him that Shipley had a lot of support. My public and gratuitous advice to Bolger at the time was to do what I'd done – just stand there and say, 'Well, vote me out.' Chances are he'd have kept his job if he'd done that. There are always plenty of people who'll say they want a change of leadership, but won't be prepared to cast their vote against someone. They want to psych them out. And I think he was tired. He was exhausted. His term when he was in Government hadn't been easy, and he just sat down in his Irish way and said, 'Well bugger it!'"

But there was a consolation prize. After spending four months writing a book, the former Prime Minister packed his bags in March and headed to Washington as New Zealand's Ambassador to the United States.

Helen was contemptuous of the new Prime Minister: "It was farcical, wasn't it? It's one thing to win a mandate in a general election. It's another to get a majority of 44 votes in a party back room. So she suffered from the fact she never had a mandate. And I used to make a joke of it. I'd say, 'You feel like a climber struggling up Mount Everest. And you've got the oxygen tank on your back and you can see the top and you know you're going to get there. And some other beggar comes in by helicopter.' So I just flicked it away like that.

"When I was at school we used to have what was called 'social promotion', where people weren't held back because they weren't performing. You went up with your age group every year. In a way Shipley's succession to the leadership reminded me of that. She happened to be the woman in the right place at the right time. She came in in '87 when they'd lost a second election in a row. There was only her, Ruth Richardson and Kathy O'Regan, as against quite a few Labour women, so she got a certain profile. And she had the physical presence. It was quite imposing. And then she went into Cabinet. She was really inexperienced, but Ruth Richardson was the only other woman Minister, so she always attracted attention. And that tide carried her up the ranks. I don't think there would have been the slightest prospect of her becoming Prime Minister if I hadn't been Leader of the Opposition. They decided to put a woman up against a woman. And I felt that she could never really say what she wanted to do. To be successful as a leader you have to have a clear idea of where you want to lead people to. And I didn't feel that she ever communicated that clear vision. So I think those were her limitations."

Though Helen downplays it, Shipley's accession to the Prime Ministership must have irked her considerably. Elected or not, Shipley was the country's first woman Prime Minister and had pipped the Labour leader at the post for that distinction. Dick Griffin believes that Helen was hugely and adversely affected by the change in leadership:

"I was amazed at how negatively she reacted and how it seemed, from my perspective, to take the wind out of her sails. She suddenly seemed to be carping and disappointed and generally disorientated by the changeover. And for three months that seemed to continue. You were left with the distinct impression that she wasn't just chagrined, she'd somehow lost her way, because this other woman, who had never won an election, had finagled the Prime Ministership."

Neither woman could have known that Jenny Shipley would eventually suffer precisely the same fate as the man she had deposed, Jim Bolger. Returning from an overseas trip in late September 2001, she found that the knives were out. In the face of appalling personal ratings and pressure from her caucus colleagues, she would resign on 8 October as Leader of the Opposition, to be replaced by her deputy, Bill English.

But in October 1997 she had just become New Zealand's first woman Prime Minister. She was a woman whom Helen intensely disliked. That dislike may have been less personal, than because she saw her as the personification of everything she despised in the National Party and as a symbol of the vilification and character assassination which she had endured for so many years at their hands. Certainly Helen was not able to deal with the topic of Jenny Shipley in the same disinterested, phlegmatic or amused way that she handled discussion of other political opponents, and her contempt for her rival was patent when the two appeared together on television.

Barry Gustafson interprets Helen's animosity to Shipley partly as a case of sour grapes:

"But I think it's also that Shipley put her down. Shipley and the front bench did

Left **Helen** and **Peter** on a visit to **China** in May 1997. *Below* **Turkish** children perform for the **New Zealand Prime Minister. Gallipoli, 2000.** *Opposite* **Walking the battlefields of Gallipoli in 2000, Helen examines a bullet from the time of conflict.** *Previous Page* **Portrait taken after 1981 election. It is proudly displayed in the homes of her parents and her Auntie Fay.**

Above **President Bill Clinton visited New Zealand in 1999 for the APEC conference.**
Left **Outside No. 10 Downing Street with British Prime Minister Tony Blair.** *Opposite, Top* **On a state visit to China, April 2001, Helen inspects a guard of honour with Premier Zhu Rongi outside the Great Hall of the People, Beijing.** *Opposite, Lower* **President Jiang Zemin greets Prime Minister Helen Clark at his official residence, Zhougnanhai, Beijing.**

Left **With the Dalai Lama, September 1996.** *Below* **After a filming session at Lower Hutt during the 1999 election campaign.** *Opposite, Top* **New Zealand women in power at swearing-in of the new Governor-General: from left, Hon. Margaret Wilson, Attorney General; Rt. Hon. Helen Clark, Prime Minister; Her Excellency Dame Silvia Cartwright, Governor-General; Dame Sian Elias, Chief Justice.** *Opposite, Lower* **The first meeting of the new Coalition Cabinet, 13 December 1999.** *Overleaf, Top* **Conferring with the Canadian Prime Minister Jean Chretien, Berlin, 2000.** *Overleaf, Lower* **A family gathering in the Prime Minister's office at the opening of Parliament, December 1999: standing, Sandra, Helen and George Clark; seated, Peter Davis, Margaret Clark, Fay Burndred.**

To Prime Minister Helen Clark,
with my best regards,   Jean Chrétien

Left **In 1997 Joan Caulfield and her husband Graham launched a road safety campaign, which Helen was happy to support.**

attack Helen personally. Over a long period of time they put the boot in. And Helen did genuinely believe that they played on her sexuality, her lack of children and, as they tried to paint it, her ambiguous marriage with Peter. They constantly attacked her personally in a scurrilous way. Now that wasn't an accident. It was Shipley and those around her personally indulging in that type of politics. And she hated them for it.

"But that's not necessarily to say that she hated the National Party in the way of, say, Arthur Faulkner or Norman Kirk. I was down at a conference recently and someone – it may have been Bob Tizard – told this story that Labour was having a caucus meeting back in 1968 and somebody said, 'Well, I dislike Holyoake.' And someone else said, 'Well I dislike National's policies.' And Kirk got up and said, 'I'm different from all of you bastards – I hate every member of the National Party and what they stand for.' And Norman Kirk was a good hater, he really was."

Al Morrison sees Helen's dislike of Shipley had deep-seated historical roots: "My explanation, for what it's worth, relates to my own experience. People have always said the Tories are born to rule, and I've always thought it's a rather meaningless cliché. But it isn't. It's really hit me that after nine years in office these people are absolutely bemused as to why they're not in power. And they are carrying on as if they have a right to be there and it really means something. And we face it in the media. Whenever you say anything positive about the Coalition, it's not because that positivity is deserved, it's because you're a lackey of the Government.

"And they refuse to look to themselves to find the reason why they're not there, they look to everybody else. Now that attitude expresses itself in a haughtiness, in a born-to-rule attitude. You see it in Parliament, in their body language, in the way they speak, in the nature of their questions, in the way they behave in opposition as if they were still in power. And Clark can't stand that affected, pompous, rather British Tory attitude. She hates it. It's anathema to a colonial-based society where Jack's as good as his master.

"And it's anathema to a totally un-class-conscious person like Helen who is absolutely unaffected by all the power and the trappings that surround her. And I think that's what she's reacting to. I mean, Shipley has this unfortunate persona in public. But there are lots of times when I've talked to her and she is actually a very down-to-earth person and not at all the image she presents. She is not the person she looks and sounds on television, but you very rarely see the other side. Sometimes in public meetings, when she throws away her notes and gets stuck in, you see it. And sometimes in Parliament. But not very often. And she's got this lecturing, hectoring, holding-the-mouth style that doesn't really sum up her character at all. But that's what Clark saw and she really reacted to it."

Though neither would appreciate the thought, Shipley and Clark did have one thing in common – their public image was at odds with the impression they made in person. Those who know Shipley well both like and respect her. Her staff are unfailingly loyal. In private conversation she betrays none of the dowager artificiality that affects her on television. She is easy and pleasant to talk to. Those who meet her for the first time are surprised by her natural charm and unaffected manner. And though she may not scale the dizzy intellectual heights of Helen Clark, she is certainly intelligent.

For her part, Helen was perceived for years as a bloodless bluestocking, cold, humourless, remote in her thinking and interests from the concerns of ordinary people, a mind without a heart. Her "marriage of convenience" and self-imposed childlessness were advanced as evidence of a lack of womanly feeling and a willingness to sacrifice everything and everyone to political ambition. Her sexuality was called into question, her looks disparaged, her manner of speaking ridiculed.

It was not uncommon to hear people refer to her as "that hard-faced bitch". Yet

Left **Photographer Emma Bass caught Helen in a relaxed mood shortly before the 1999 General Election.**

those who met her in person found her a little shy perhaps, but warm, funny, interesting, attractive, and with a deep understanding of and concern for the lives of ordinary people.

Shipley's misfortune was that her public image resisted improvement. Whereas the 'real' Helen Clark became ever more distinct on the radar screen of public perception, Jenny Shipley, despite every attempt to portray her as a down-home wife and mother, has been unable to shake off a rather plummy, condescending and affected image. In the end it would cost her National's leadership.

The new Prime Minister and her party nonetheless enjoyed a reasonably lengthy honeymoon. National's polling support rose steadily over the next six months from

28 percent to 38 percent, briefly overtaking the Labour Opposition in May. The change of leadership appeared to be working.

On 6 February 1998 the Leader of the Opposition travelled to the Waitangi Marae to celebrate the anniversary of the signing of the Treaty. On arrival, she discovered that the Prime Minister, Jenny Shipley, had already attended an early morning ceremony on the marae, at which she had been allowed to speak. A later attempt by Clark to speak on the marae was noisily interrupted by Maori activist Titewhai Harawira, who shouted that it was an insult to Nga Puhi women for a white woman to speak on the marae when they themselves were denied that right. The Labour leader was reduced to tears.

These are the bare facts of what happened on Waitangi Day 1998. Arguments about marae protocol and about the rights and wrongs of Harawira's actions continue to this day, but are largely irrelevant to this text. What can be said with certainty is that Helen Clark had not merely been asked to speak on the marae by local Maori, she had been implored to do so. If protocol was indeed breached by her standing to speak, then blame for that breach could not be laid at her feet.

Perhaps the more interesting question is how a woman, steeled in the cauldron of party politics for 17 years, could be reduced to tears by the verbal assault of a lone protestor. Helen's answer is in part that Harawira was not a lone protestor; she was supported by her daughter Hinewhare. Both women had violent histories. Both had received jail sentences for assaulting a psychiatric patient at the Carrington Maori Health Unit. The daughter, Hinewhare, was jailed for six months in 1995 for spitting on the Governor-General, Dame Catherine Tizard, during that year's Waitangi Day celebrations and has faced other assault and criminal charges. Helen believed she had reason to be fearful:

"The daughter's behaviour was very menacing. I had no doubt that she was physically threatening me. The whole thing was like a tinder box. If I'd persisted to speak, I think I would have been hit. I was left in no doubt about that. By the daughter. And potentially others."

Brian: "In retrospect, how do you see your own tears?"

Helen: "They were tears of utter frustration. I actually wish I'd got up and walked out. That was what people deserved. The marae was a shambles, there was no effective kaumatua leadership there. You don't invite people into your house as guests and treat them like that. I should have got up and walked out. That would have been an even bigger incident. But they were literally tears of frustration. There they go again! How many times does Waitangi have to be wrecked by idiots? That was what it was about."

Brian: "What was the fallout from all of this?"

Helen: "It was very damaging. I suppose because I had a reputation for being a strong person, and my tears were used to try and suggest that I wasn't strong at all. But I did go back the following year, because people had said I didn't have the guts to return. Shipley also went in 1999. That was the year when she walked hand in hand and had a cry with Harawira. The media portrayed all that very positively. They were very destructive."

There was some evidence of damage in the polls. Helen's rating as Preferred Prime Minister dropped for several months, giving Jenny Shipley an unaccustomed lead. A similar pattern was seen in the party vote. The damage might have been less if Television New Zealand had not continued to use the shot of Helen crying at Waitangi in its nightly news bulletins for some considerable time after the event, regardless of its relevance to the particular story. The Waitangi Day affair thus confirmed what Helen already knew:

"The media are very cruel about women in tears. They will tolerate tears in men as a strength. Bob Hawke crying on television over his daughter's drug addiction seemed to be a great strength. Helen Clark shedding tears for Waitangi seemed to be a terrible weakness. A real double standard."

May was to bring more bad news. Jim Bolger's resignation from Parliament had necessitated a by-election in Taranaki-King Country. Labour did not expect to win the seat, but had hopes of coming a credible second, a PR victory at least over the other losing parties. But it was not to be. Though the Party increased its share of the vote from the 1996 general election, its ranking went in the opposite direction. Helen was unimpressed:

"That was a low point. We were polling very well in '97, then along came that bloody by-election which up and bit us in the backside. The Alliance went feral and ran an election campaign that targeted Labour. And that really revived all the memories of the 1990, 1993 and 1996 elections, where the Left fighting each other ensured that the Right won."

The Taranaki-King Country result gave both major parties a fright. In this traditionally blue-ribbon seat, National's majority was reduced from 8681 to 988. Labour came a poor third behind ACT, and narrowly avoided coming fourth behind the Alliance. But Labour's poor performance was to bring the Left to its senses. It is, Helen says, an ill wind that blows nobody any good:

"Because it was after that, that I approached Sandra Lee, the Deputy Leader of the Alliance, and said, 'I think we've got to talk about how we're going to run the next election, because we're going to wipe each other out again if we carry on like this.' And she agreed. So the low point actually was a circuit-breaker for something to happen, for the two parties to get together."

One of the earliest signs of a possible accommodation between Labour and the Alliance came in June when Jim Anderton, in a speech to the New Labour Party's annual conference, acknowledged the unpopularity of the Alliance's progressive tax policy. As Chris Trotter notes in *New Zealand Government and Politics*:

"The acceptance by the NLP of the need to re-examine the Alliance's fiscal policy was a clear signal to the Labour Party that a genuine rapprochement between the two organisations could now be considered seriously."

The bond between the two parties was finally sealed in August when Helen accepted an invitation to address the Alliance's annual conference at Massey University in Albany. The standing ovation which she received was clear evidence that the Left had taken on board the lessons of the 1996 election and of the Taranaki-King Country by-election, that there was no future in division. Labour and the Alliance would unite to defeat the National Government.

But while they were in the process of getting together, the National-New Zealand First coalition was in the process of falling apart. In August, after a New Zealand First walkout from Cabinet over the sale of Wellington Airport, Jenny Shipley sacked Winston Peters as Deputy Prime Minister and Treasurer for refusing to accept Cabinet collective responsibility and publicly criticising the Government. Reacting to these developments, Helen observed that Winston had been given the martyrdom he desired and that everything now hinged on how many New Zealand First MPs he could keep with him.

The answer to that question was eight. Deborah Morris, who had held a number of portfolios in the Coalition Government, including Minister of Youth Affairs, declared herself an independent and later announced her intention to resign from Parliament at the end of the year. The remaining eight, led by Tau Henare, opted to remain with the Coalition. The Prime Minister now found herself leading a minority government which was dependent for its survival on the support of ACT and a raggle-taggle bunch of independents and one-member parties – the eight disaffected former members of New Zealand First, Deborah Morris, United's Peter Dunne and two former Alliance list members, Christian Heritage's Frank Grover and the tragi-comic leader of Mana Wahine, Alamein Kopu. As Steven Levine and Nigel Roberts observe in *New Zealand Government and Politics*:

"Not surprisingly the collapse of the coalition – and the accompanying dismemberment of New Zealand First – did little to enhance National's image as a coherent governing party. It entered the final year of its stewardship in tatters, its image as a stable, decisive and competent force a dwindling asset, and yet, perhaps, its only one. Nevertheless this too was squandered, surrendered in stages almost right up to election day."

Helen's relationship with the media had by now blossomed from indifference or outright hostility on their part to something bordering on affection. As her personal ratings as Preferred Prime Minister continued to suggest that she would lead Labour to victory in the election, her views were sought on every conceivable issue. She began to be used in effect as an independent political commentator, assessing the performance of the parties and their leaders, analysing the progress of their campaigns, occasionally offering gratuitous advice to her rivals and consulting her crystal ball on the likely outcome in November.

Jenny Shipley's relationship with the media was rather more troubled. She first got into difficulty over a dinner she had had on 31 August 1998 with advertising guru Kevin Roberts, CEO Worldwide of Saatchi and Saatchi. At the time Roberts' company was in line for a major contract to implement the Government's tourism policy. It would therefore have been entirely improper for him to be offering advice to the Leader of the National Party on how to win the election, or indeed to be discussing party politics with her at all.

Shipley's difficulty arose less from the fact that the dinner had taken place, than that she produced several different versions of the event, from indicating that it had never taken place, to claiming that she had not discussed politics with Roberts, to an apologetic admission that she had. Helen was as intrigued by the Prime Minister's mind-set as she was by this drip-feeding of the truth:

"Her first response was, 'I did not discuss politics with him.' And then, 'Well I discussed how to keep Labour out of office.' Think of the arrogance of believing that it's not political to discuss how you keep Labour out of office forever. You're dealing with the 'natural party of government' here. Self-proclaimed. It's really not politics. People made the same comment to me about Kevin Roberts, that he was the sort of man who'd think, 'Well, wouldn't every thinking person vote National?' That's the mind-set. And I think she uttered that contradiction almost unthinkingly. It wasn't political to have a conversation like this with Kevin Roberts. The natural party of government was simply asserting itself here. Weird! She'd have been better to come up front and say, 'Yes I did have dinner with him, and of course we discussed politics."

Brian: "So not telling the truth doesn't work?"

Helen: "No."

Brian: "But is it possible to be totally honest in politics?"

Helen: "It's possible never to tell a lie."

Brian: "What's the difference between being totally honest and never telling a lie?"

Helen: "Some would say that being totally honest required a complete Dorothy

Dix confession of every aspect of an incident, which is generally not called for. But in that situation, given that they did discuss politics, she should have just laughed it off. A number of us have developed a style in Parliament where we say, 'Yeah we talked about it. So what?' And at that point the Opposition's totally deflated. Did anybody seriously think that she went to dinner with Kevin Roberts, who'd addressed the National Party caucus and was well known as a supporter, and they didn't discuss politics? 'Yeah, we discussed it. So what?'"

The Prime Minister's credibility was further eroded in June when, in the course of a *Crossfire* television debate hosted by Linda Clark, she announced that TV newsreader John Hawkesby had been paid a million dollars by TVNZ in compensation for having terminated his $750,000 per annum contract.

Shipley subsequently accepted that no such payment had been made and apologised to Hawkesby. But the matter was not over. IRN Political Editor Barry Soper reported that, in a conversation after the programme, Shipley had responded to a question on where she got the million-dollar figure, "I made it up." The story was initially greeted with disbelief, but was confirmed by Linda Clark herself.

In a personal explanation to Parliament, the Prime Minister said that she had had no intention of misleading the public over the million-dollar payout; she had merely got it wrong. She could not recall making the reported comment to "Helen Clark, sorry Linda Clark, Freudian slip!" There had been a light-hearted conversation and some flippant remarks, but at no time did she remember saying, "I made it up."

The episode was doubly unfortunate for Mrs Shipley, since it not merely eroded her credibility further, but provided the Opposition with the opportunity to accuse her on every possible occasion and every possible topic of having "made it up". It was an opportunity which Helen rarely missed.

The Prime Minister gained some traction later in September when she hosted the annual Asia-Pacific Economic Cooperation (APEC) forum in Auckland. She was widely praised for her handling of the forum, which took place in the midst of an escalating crisis in East Timor. The presence of US President Bill Clinton also provided Mrs Shipley and her husband Burton with numerous photo-opportunities. Indeed many saw Burton as the real star of APEC as he hosted the forum wives and played golf with the President. But none of this was enough to make a lasting dent in Labour's lead in the polls.

The election campaign was again presidential in nature, concentrating heavily on the personalities and styles of the two women leaders. In public opinion polls assessing their respective characters and leadership

Right **Labour's official 1999 campaign photograph of a glamorous Helen Clark caused considerable comment.**

potential, Helen outpointed the Prime Minister in most categories. She was seen as intelligent, in command of the issues and in touch with ordinary people.

The Party campaigned on the traditional Labour platforms of restoring equity in Health, Housing, Education and Welfare. It highlighted the plight of super-annuitants and beneficiaries unable to make ends meet, of State House tenants paying unaffordable market rents, of young people burdened by crippling student loans, of people with debilitating medical conditions denied urgently needed hospital treatment, of ordinary citizens trapped in their homes by fear of violent crime.

To meet the cost of its programmes, Labour undertook to increase the rate of personal taxation to 39 cents in the dollar for those earning over $60,000 a year. This undertaking, extraordinary in an election campaign, was the prime illustration of Labour's expressed intention to be utterly transparent in its dealings with the voting public. Labour would "tell it as it is". And more than that, it would put it in writing.

The 'pledge card' was an idea which Helen had borrowed from Tony Blair. The idea was simple – a card, just like a credit card, with a photograph of the Party's leader, and a series of election promises or "pledges" which the Party undertook to carry out, if it won the election. The card had worked for Blair in the 1997 British General Election, but Helen initially needed to be reassured of its worth:

"We invited John Prescott out to our Party Conference in '97 and had good sessions with him on how the card had been used. Did people just say, That's silly, that's just a gimmick? 'No,' he said. 'You've got to realise that most people aren't that interested in politics. In Britain there's a lot of indifference. Labour had been out of Government for 18 years and people said, Well what are you going to do? – Well, here's what we're going to do. So the core pledges have to be in areas you know voters are

concerned about.' And he said, 'The problem with that is, you've got to front up in four or five years' time and say, This is what we have done.' Which is exactly what they did. They produced a little card which said: This is what we've done. Flip over: This is what we'll do through the next term. So on that basis we adopted the concept."

The Pledge Card contained a photograph of Helen, with her signature and the words "MY COMMITMENT TO YOU. WE WILL DELIVER." There were seven pledges on the back of the card under the words "MY COMMITMENTS ARE":

1. Create jobs through promoting New Zealand industries and better support for exporters and small business.
2. Focus on patients not profit and cut waiting times for surgery.
3. Cut the cost to students of tertiary education, starting with a fairer loan scheme.
4. Reverse the 1999 cuts to superannuation rates. Guarantee superannuation in the future by putting a proportion of all income tax into a separate fund which <u>cannot</u> be used for any other purpose.
5. Restore income-related rents for State Housing so that low income tenants pay no more than 25 percent of their income in rent.
6. Crack down on burglary and youth crime.
7. No rise in income tax for the 95 percent of taxpayers earning under $60,000 a year. No increases in GST or company tax.

Helen believes that the card was a considerable success, that voters, who had seen a succession of governments abandon not only their election promises but their core values, welcomed the idea of a political party that was prepared to put its money where its mouth was.

National's campaign warned of the dire effects on the economy of voting in a

Labour-Alliance Government, predicted industrial chaos if the Employment Contracts Act were repealed, forecast increased costs to workers and employers if accident compensation was returned to state control, offered tax cuts instead of tax increases, and attempted to make capital out of the Prime Minister's status as a wife and mother. The Shipley family were much in evidence.

The five party leaders fought it out on television in a series of debates where they were questioned in a manner more appropriate to game show contestants. In face-to-face confrontation, Jenny Shipley and Helen Clark were deemed by some commentators to be evenly matched on style, but there was little doubt that Helen was the outright winner on substance.

The polls in the last week of the campaign gave Labour, on 34 percent, a five-point lead over National on 29 percent. The Alliance was on 9 percent, ACT on 11 percent, New Zealand First on 5.5 percent and the Greens on 6 percent. Since, under MMP, the party vote was the only one that really counted, it now seemed probable that Labour would win the election.

But National was to suffer one final setback. Three days before the election, Jenny Shipley sacked her Minister of Immigration, Tuariki Delamere. The former New Zealand First MP had approved a scheme granting residency to two groups of Asian immigrants in exchange for investing in the commercial development of Maori land. Instructed to rescind the approvals, Delamere refused. Jenny Shipley had no alternative but to fire him. The move could have been seen as an example of strong leadership on the part of the Prime Minister at a difficult time, but was undermined when she allowed Delamere to keep his other portfolios. It was, as Steven Levine and Nigel Roberts aptly put it in *New Zealand Government and Politics*, "the coup de grâce for an already moribund regime".

On Saturday 27 November 1999, New Zealanders went to the polls in their second MMP election. Labour won 38.7 percent of the party votes, National 30.5 percent, the Alliance 7.7 percent, ACT 7.0 percent, the Greens 5.2 percent and New Zealand First 4.3 percent – below the automatic threshold for representation in Parliament. But the "comeback kid" survived with his Tauranga majority reduced from 8028 to a derisory 63. In the new Parliament Labour would have 49 seats, National 39, the Alliance 10, ACT 9, the Greens 7, New Zealand First 5, and United 1. Labour had won the election.

Helen Clark watched the results come in on television at her Mount Eden home with Peter, George, Margaret and her Chief of Staff Heather Simpson. At around 1:00 am she received a call from Jenny Shipley conceding the election and offering her congratulations. No dances of joy were danced, no champagne corks popped, no fireworks lit, no hip-hip-hoorahs shouted. Helen went off to write some notes

for her speech to her supporters waiting at the Party's election headquarters at the Avondale Racecourse.

Brian: "So now you were New Zealand's first elected woman Prime Minister. And not even a few celebratory thoughts?"

Helen: "No. I've always focused on the next step, which in this case was how I was going to handle the crowds out at the campaign headquarters and handle the media. It was quite workmanlike really. That's it. We've done that, now we'll get on with the next thing. It's probably because I tend to be emotionally even. I'm never depressive, but I don't go off the other end either. I just kept thinking about when I was going to get enough sleep."

There is, in retrospect, no doubt that the Peters betrayal in 1996 was a blessing in disguise for the Labour leader. In a coalition with New Zealand First she might well have inherited the same difficulties, embarrassments and alarms as Jim Bolger and Jenny Shipley did. And while they attempted to deal with the chaotic experience of holding together New Zealand's first coalition government, Helen was able to look and learn and not only continue to rebuild her own party, but to heal the wounds that had divided the Labour movement since 1984.

On 27 November 1999, New Zealand's Prime Minister-Elect had been in Parliament for 18 years. That is how long it had taken to win the glittering prize. In assessing the qualities required to run and win a race of that duration one must surely speak of courage, sacrifice, endurance, discipline, strength of purpose – of

THE GLITTERING PRIZE

NEW ZEALAND HERALD

Above **1999 election night triumph: Helen is now the Prime Minister-Elect of New Zealand.**

mind and heart focused firmly on the goal. But also of a passionate commitment to the idea that it was possible to create a much better society for New Zealanders to live in. Why else would anyone do it?

On 27 November, Joan Caulfield was at the Avondale Racecourse: "The night of the election was absolutely fantastic. And I was so content. After Helen had gone I rang my daughter in Germany. And I said, 'I just want to tell you that your mother works for the Prime Minister and your father's the Deputy Prime Minister.' There are all these ironies in my life."

chapter**fourteen**

REPORT CARD

A S THIS chapter is being written, the fifth Labour Government has been in office for almost two years. Even its most strenuous critic would be hard put to deny that its story to date has been a success story. And even its most devoted fan would be hard put to deny that that success is largely, if not exclusively, due to Helen Clark. There are even those who speak of her as potentially one of the greatest Prime Ministers New Zealand has seen.

The going has not, of course, been entirely smooth.

Police Commissioner Peter Doone provided the Prime Minister with an early test of her management skills when it was revealed that a vehicle in which he was a passenger had been stopped by a squad car in November 1999. The car was being driven without lights by Mr Doone's partner, Robyn Johnstone. The Commissioner got out of the car and spoke to the young constable, and the couple were allowed to drive away without Ms Johnstone being breath-tested. Helen was not impressed, and Mr Doone was forced to resign as Commissioner. He was demoted to the rank of constable, but given a six-month secondment to the Department of the Prime Minister and Cabinet on his previous salary. He resigned from the Force after completing a report into ways of reducing Maori crime.

An infusion of over $80 million of government funds into the Arts pleased that community, but was regarded as élitism by many working-class people, not least those smokers who were penalised at around the same time by a stiff increase in the

R
E
P
O
R
T

C
A
R
D

tax on cigarettes. People on low incomes were seen as subsidising the pastimes of the wealthy middle-class. The fact that the Prime Minister abhorred smoking and held the Arts, Culture and Heritage portfolio was duly noted.

The axing, early in 2000, of the top tier of royal honours, so that there would be no more New Zealand knights or dames, was considered by many New Zealanders to be taking egalitarianism too far and as symptomatic of a somewhat austere and joyless administration, intent on creating a drab and monochrome society. The theme that Labour and its Prime Minister are too politically correct persists to the present day.

The use of the word "holocaust" by the Associate Minister of Maori Affairs, Tariana Turia, to describe the effects of European colonisation on Maori, and her claim that "post-colonial traumatic stress disorder" might be a factor in Maori crime and domestic violence, had the country up in arms in September 2000. Turia was firmly told not to use the word again and made a "voluntary" apology in Parliament to "all people whom I have offended".

There was some potentially damaging publicity for Helen around the same time when, with others in the neighbourhood, she opposed extensions to a down-market boarding house just around the corner from her Mount Eden home. This was characterised by the Opposition and segments of the media as hypocrisy and self-interest on the part of the former Housing Minister, a long-time supporter of cheap accommodation for the poor and the underprivileged. Headlines read "Not in my Backyard", but the story had all the hallmarks of a beat-up.

The *Sunday Star-Times* showed indifference to the Prime Minister's privacy and security when it published a map showing where she lived and the proximity of her home to the boarding house.

Four Cabinet Ministers lost their jobs in relatively short order, two of them to be later reinstated.

Allegations that the Minister of Maori Affairs, Dover Samuels, had had sexual relations with a minor in his care were an embarrassment to the Government, while his sacking by Helen Clark before the allegations had been substantiated – which they never were – called into question the Prime Minister's judgement and her fairness. Though Samuels was rehabilitated, he was not returned to his former job. However, his failure to declare a range of previous, albeit minor criminal convictions to the Labour Party or its Leader made him, in many people's eyes, the author of his own misfortune.

Two other Ministers, Marian Hobbs and Phillida Bunkle, were similarly dis-patched under a cloud of suspicion that they had been double-dipping on their accommodation allowances. An official investigation cleared Hobbs, but left

unanswered questions about Bunkle. Hobbs got her old job back, Bunkle did not.

Above **The election over, Helen and Peter crossed the Ball Pass in the Southern Alps. Seen here with her nephew Ashley Waterworth.**

The fourth Minister, Ruth Dyson, resigned after being arrested for drink-driving. She was returned to Cabinet six months later.

Claims by Wyatt Creech that a $750,000 Health Research Council grant to Peter Davis and a team of researchers to study health sector restructuring between 1988 and 1999 involved a conflict of interest, since Davis's wife had been Minister of Health for part of that period, produced an uncharacteristically intemperate response from the Prime Minister who referred to National's attack as "scumbag behaviour from sleazeballs."

The fracas had been precipitated when it was revealed that Professor Davis had unwisely sent an email via the Prime Minister's office inquiring whether there had been "any genuine movement" on the appointment of Dr Joel Lexchin, a friend and colleague, to review the Government's drug-buying agency, Pharmac. Helen later told the media that she had had "the row of all rows" with her husband.

Peter was not the only one to experience the Prime Minister's public censure. Marian Hobbs, Lianne Dalziel, Annette King, Steve Maharey, Mark Burton and Margaret Wilson were all hung out to dry for failing to perform to her demanding standards, provoking comment that she was too hard on her Ministers.

A group of retired defence chiefs, who chose to publicly question the Government's policies on the armed forces and in particular its decision not to replace the Air Force's aging Skyhawks with the F16s the previous Government had contracted

COURTESY CHRIS SLANE/ALEXANDER TURNBULL LIBRARY

to buy from the Americans, found themselves defenceless against a withering verbal assault from the ninth floor of the Beehive.

The Prime Minister found herself at odds in May with both her Social Services Minister, Steve Maharey, and departmental officials over the handling of proposed changes to entitlements to the Community Services Card. Ministers and Heads of Government Departments were given a stern warning to sharpen up their act and ensure that they provided reliable advice.

A mistaken reference during the Samuels affair to Auckland actor John Yelash as a "convicted murderer" – Yelash had in fact been convicted of manslaughter – led to defamation proceedings against the Prime Minister and an out-of-court settlement of $55,000. Confidentiality clauses in the settlement agreement led to accusations that Helen had attempted to conceal from the public the payment of a substantial sum of taxpayers' money. She, in turn, denied having asked for the confidentiality clauses or indeed knowing very much about the agreement at all:

"The settlement was faxed to me in China when I was preoccupied by rather more weighty matters. It was provided to me as the negotiated settlement and on that basis I did not object to it."

This uncharacteristic example of inattention to detail was a mistake which Helen promised herself not to repeat.

The Government ran into trouble in July with its "closing the gaps" initiatives. The policy, which involved the widespread insertion of Treaty of Waitangi clauses into social legislation, was seen as racist and discriminatory and the Government

Left **Leader of the Alliance Party Jim Anderton became Deputy Prime Minister in the Coalition Government of 1999.** *Opposite* **This Slane cartoon gave a cynical view of the controversial 'Close the Gaps' campaign.**

was forced to rethink the policy and abandon the slogan – an embarrassment for it and the Prime Minister.

The Christine Rankin affair held the country's attention for several months in mid-2001. Though Rankin lost her court case for reinstatement as Head of the Department of Work and Income – an indirect victory for the Government – neither the State Services Commissioner, Michael Wintringham, nor the Head of the Prime Minister's Department, Mark Prebble, nor the Minister of Social Services and Employment, Steve Maharey, emerged from the case entirely smelling of roses. All three were tainted by accusations of sexism and male chauvinism in their dealings with the colourful but controversial Ms Rankin.

Conservation Minister Sandra Lee came under sustained attack from already disgruntled West Coasters in August when she cancelled permission for GRD Macraes to proceed with a gold mine expansion in the Victoria Forest Park near Reefton.

In September 460 Afghans were rescued from a disintegrating Indonesian fishing boat by a Norwegian freighter, the *MV Tampa*, off Australia's Christmas Island. Australian Prime Minister John Howard adamantly refused to allow the refugees to disembark on Australian soil, provoking a humanitarian crisis and incurring worldwide censure for his country. But his hardline approach was popular at home. There was considerable hostility in New Zealand as well to the suggestion that the Government should agree to take some of the refugees. The Prime Minister was nonetheless responsible for brokering an arrangement under which New Zealand would take in 150 of the refugees for processing and possible resettlement in this country, while the rest would be processed in Nauru. Her actions were widely applauded by the international press, but the country remained divided on the issue.

In mid-September, the Government was faced with the prospect of bailing out the financially ailing Air New Zealand. The airline had cut adrift its wholly-owned subsidiary Ansett Australia, creating massive job losses in that country. In retaliation, furious Ansett employees blockaded Air New Zealand planes, preventing them from leaving Australian airports. The Prime Minister, who happened to be returning home from a cancelled European trip following the terrorist attacks on New York and Washington, found herself a virtual hostage at Melbourne's Tullamarine Airport. She was eventually flown out by a New Zealand Air Force Orion and received a savaging from the Australian media and public for what they saw as the New Zealand Government's failure to act sooner to prevent the demise of what had been Australia's leading domestic airline before Air New Zealand bought into the company in 1996.

The Prime Minister found herself in further hot water when she advised Air New Zealand shareholders not to sell their shares. This advice led to warnings of possible insider trading and to the suspension of trading in the company's shares.

Helen had previously warned of the possibility that Air New Zealand might be placed in statutory management. In a *Listener* cartoon, Slane depicts an Air New Zealand plane nose-diving into the sea, next to a picture of the Prime Minister, with the caption "Loose lips sink ships".

Despite these various setbacks, Labour retained the confidence and support of a majority of New Zealanders and Helen Clark continued to dominate the Preferred Prime Minister ratings.

Though it had difficulty convincing the business sector of its friendship and good intent, the Government was widely perceived as stable, transparent, energetic and reforming.

A huge amount of legislation was passed, implementing Labour's policies on a wide variety of issues, including taxation, industrial relations, accident compensation, the provision of hospital services, income-related rents for State House tenants, student loans, bulk-funding and enrolments in schools, energy conservation, shop trading hours, and a raft of others.

The Pardon for Soldiers of the Great War Act, which pardoned five soldiers of the New Zealand Expeditionary Force executed for mutiny or desertion, met with general public approval.

Reaction was mixed to the Property (Relationships) Amendment Act, which extended the provisions of the Matrimonial Property Act 1976 to apply to de facto partners, including same sex partners who had lived together for three years or more.

But the Forests (West Coast Accord) Act, preventing further logging of indigenous timbers by Timberlands, incensed not only the Coasters, but their Labour Member of Parliament, Damien O'Connor.

In much of the Government's legislation the hand of the Prime Minister could be clearly seen. Her critics saw this as evidence that she was autocratic – a one-woman-band, "control freak", the "Minister of Everything". Others approved of her hands-on style and were refreshed by a leader who was personally proactive and got things done. She developed a reputation as a "fixer" – if something was wrong, Helen would fix it.

No one doubted her energy or ability. She worked 19-hour days, travelled extensively at home and abroad, turned up at everything and appeared to be everywhere. She skied, tramped and climbed mountains. There was general agreement that the job suited her, that she had grown into it, blossomed. In her handling of the media she was confident, direct and available. She appeared to be having fun.

Though a week is a long time in politics, Helen Clark seems likely to be returned to office for a second term in 2002. That at least is what her report card from colleagues, political commentators and the media, would seem to suggest. It is, for the most part, glowing, but there are areas where, in their judgement, she "could do better".

On Helen's intellect, there is absolute consensus. The woman is scarily smart.

Mike Williams: "The thing about Helen is her sheer intellectual horsepower. The sheer intellectual grunt. The processing power. She's like a Pentium when everyone else is a 286."

Geoffrey Palmer: "The most interesting thing about her, from my point of view at least, is her very strong intellect. People don't always relate to that, but I do. And I also think she's got very good judgement. She's got good political judgement, which isn't the same thing as having good judgement. Political judgement is about whether you can go this far without getting into hot water over it."

Bill Ralston: "The greatest strength is her mind and her analytical ability, the fact that she's so capable of breaking a problem down to the core issue. A problem may appear complex, but she's capable of stripping away layer after layer after layer around that problem till she gets down to the vital core. And then you can address it. And that's what she does."

Richard Long: "A formidable intellect and a formidable will. Some Prime Ministers have one or the other, she seems to have both. She leaves everyone else

Above **With Dame Kiri Te Kanawa in December 1999. Colleagues and journalists commented that Helen blossomed after she was elected Prime Minister.**

for dead in terms of intellect and willpower too."

Barry Soper: "I think debating for Clark has always been a way to express her intellectual prowess. Because every time Jenny Shipley has a question on the order paper you can just watch Clark's body language. She sighs like a teenager, she looks into the air as Jenny Shipley is directing the question at her, she shifts in her seat, she tut-tuts, and she tries to throw her off her stride. And invariably she does."

Jane Clifton: "I can't remember when I've seen her caught out, in the House or on television. She quite enjoys the House actually, the cut and thrust, and just knowing that across the floor there are so few people who could put her pot on in any way, shape or form. You can be relaxed, you can read the paper, you can get up and have a whack and sit down again, and you're not even breaking into a sweat. She enjoys that."

Colin James: "Over the past three or four years I've been surprised. I'd underestimated her intellect. I thought she was very bright, but I think she's actually super-bright, the more I deal with her."

Tom Scott: "Her focus, her powers of concentration and application are staggering. Her intelligence is obviously bloody remarkable."

Super-intelligence combines with an appetite for work. Mike Williams, who was

Labour's Campaign Manager in 1999, compares his workload with hers: "I did 18 hours a day, six-and-a-half days a week for eight weeks in the campaign – and collapsed. She did exactly the same thing and then went in and formed a Government. The 18-hour days just seem to be water off a duck's back."

Over the last two years a significant part of each of those 18-hour days has been spent dealing with the media. Given the practised cynicism of most political journalists, not to mention their self-interest, one might expect their report on the Prime Minister's performance in their own area to be at least tinged with disapproval. But, for the most part, it is not.

Jane Clifton: "She's amazingly generous in the way she handles the media. She doesn't play favourites. Or she plays favourites, but she doesn't disadvantage anyone. I'm sure most of us journalists are bloody irritating creatures. And she probably finds some of us intolerable. But she never gives herself the luxury of having snitches on people. If she's cross she'll tell you so. She's very approachable and she always rings back. Very quickly. She just about returns your call before you've even rung her. And that's unusual in a Prime Minister and even in most Ministers. She's great."

Al Morrison: "She's hell of a tough at one level, quite ruthless, and yet at another level she's actually quite kind. On the whole, I think that my colleagues respect her. That would be the main word I would use. I respect her, and not just because of her position. I think most people in the Press Gallery respect the office of the Prime Minister and anybody who makes it there, particularly someone who's grafted their way to the top like Clark has and who maintains her hold over the office in such a strong way. So she's earned the right to be there. She is highly respected. She's respected for her intellect, and she's respected for her honesty."

Barry Soper: "Clark has become more assertive and more sure of herself. She sees the media ad nauseum. She sees us on Monday afternoon in the post-Cabinet press conference, which is what Bolger canned. He couldn't stand the bloody questions. And then on Tuesday, on the way to caucus, she always waits for the door-stop. We're all there. And she actually quite enjoys it. You can ask Clark the most difficult of questions that you'd think would get really up her hooter, but she'll turn them round quite well. She never backs away from them. She's quite happy to answer anything. You feel as though you can ask her anything.

"Although she does like to gossip. She's a good gossip. There's a lot of gossip around the place. If you want to find something out, it's not hard. You simply go to a few key people and they'll tell you what's going on. Clark is one of them. If you really want to find something out you can go to Clark, which is most unlike other PMs. You can say, 'What's going on there?' But she'll be calculated. And even if she doesn't tell you, she'll certainly have a good yarn about something else."

Tom Scott understands that his journalist colleagues appreciate the Prime Minister's accessibility and openness, but shares Soper's view that her approach to the media is calculated:

"She'll chat away in a very gossipy way and reveal quite a lot of information. She has quite a cunning way of embroiling people, giving them information and making them feel part of the circle. And then you don't want to lose access to those phone calls, you don't want them to taper off, so what you do is go with the information you've got. So she's almost handling her own publicity. Bolger used to send Dick Griffin round the Press Gallery, but she's doing a lot of the stuff herself and has built up these personal relationships. And all the journalists who take part in that are to a greater or lesser extent compromised, but they also get good information from time to time which they are allowed to use in ways that she proscribes."

But could this strategy, if indeed it is a strategy, backfire? Jane Clifton see Helen's penchant for "chatting away in a very gossipy way" as dangerous in the long term:

"I think the gossip is going to get her. I mean, she does gossip, and we love it. It's great. But it's a very fine line, and she's not always going to get away with it. I think it's almost a form of collegiality. There are people who gossip because they're trusting. And there are others who do it because it's the only form of intimacy they will allow themselves. And I wonder if that's the case with her. What she tells you is often useful in your appreciation of what makes certain personalities tick. But it's dangerous, because there can be a

perception of lack of loyalty. For example, when Marian went down for that period of time, Helen said things like, 'Oh, she's beside herself, she's so upset.' That's the sort of thing you shouldn't say to journalists, because we shorthand it to mean that someone is having a breakdown, which obviously wasn't the case. It's not deliberately disloyal, but it's damaging. In this game, which is very bitchy, just a nuance can do damage."

But it's in her handling of her colleagues that Helen gets the most mixed reviews. While loyalty, it seems, is at best taken for granted, disloyalty appears to be rewarded.

David Lange: "One of the nicest things about Helen is that if you want to know who her enemies are, look at who gets promoted. And it's happened every time. The plotters in various cliques and factions all end up on the front bench. Michael Cullen goes in with a deputation and they say to her, 'It's time to go, lady.' And she announces her continuing support for him and confirms him as Deputy Leader. It's a most amazing capacity and a style which is a total abandonment of the usual instincts of a tribal party politician."

Nigel Roberts: "Lyndon Johnson said it's better to have them inside the tent pissing out, than outside the tent pissing in. I think it's a mark of leadership. And I think she has matured as a politician. That inclusiveness is not something she would have practised hugely in 1984 or 1987. She's learnt that the Labour Party has different factions and the way for the Labour Party to survive is not for one faction to destroy another but for the factions to work for their common beliefs."

Mike Williams: "She convinced herself she could win the 1996 campaign. And that was the first person she had to convince. And then you have these people going to see her and telling her to bugger off. That was very destabilising for her, because

they were up close. They could see just how hard she was working, and they panicked, and they were wrong. And they're now all Ministers. Thank you, Helen."

Rather less fortunate have been a number of Ministers, some close to Helen, whose loyalty has never been in question, but who have failed to meet her dauntingly high performance standards. It is the Prime Minister's treatment of these Ministers that attracts the highest level of disapproval not only from colleagues and commentators but from friends and family as well. It is, many of them say, the one thing that in the long run could bring her down.

Colin James: "This is high on the list of things that could be her undoing. New Zealand voters respect, even admire a whacker, but only within bounds. Muldoon, a vicious whacker, demonstrated that. But after a while too many had been whacked or were members of a whacked group, and respect turned to fear, loathing and contempt. That's what we're starting to get from Helen. And if she doesn't curb it, in the end she'll suffer the same fate."

Al Morrison: "I've had Ministers and their staff talk to me about this. It's hurtful and they can't understand it. It's probably going too far to say that Clark is getting into a position where she rules Cabinet by fear, but there is certainly an element of that. And don't forget that under MMP the leader of a party is in a much stronger position, particularly in the case of MPs who are there by grace and favour of the party list. And so – whether she knows it or not, I'm not sure – patronage has become an unfortunate by-product of that system. And what's developing in the Cabinet is a feeling that this is somebody to be feared rather than somebody to be liked."

Jonathan Hunt: "She must be very careful that she doesn't criticise her Ministers in public. That's a mistake. Behind closed doors, rip shit out of them by all means. But in public she must stand by them, because there'll come a time when someone will talk back and that will be fatal."

Cath Tizard: "I think she's made herself a lot harder than she is by nature. Perhaps she doesn't make enough time to do what I call 'stroking'. She needs to make a little more time available for her colleagues, to give them some encouragement and perhaps a bit of praise. Her own very high and demanding standards for herself are projected on to other people, perhaps rather too much. I mean she is the most remarkable person, and other people on the whole are not remarkable people. And there are a few vultures out there, still circling, waiting for her to slip up."

Barry Gustafson: "And there's another issue. National's publicists will be keeping a checklist of this, and there'll be an ad in the paper one of these days: 'Which Cabinet Ministers have not been publicly done over by the Prime Minister?' To destroy Labour and this Government, they've got to destroy Helen."

But not everyone regards the Prime Minister's public criticism of under-performing Ministers as a fault. Nigel Roberts and Bill Ralston both see it as consistent with her philosophy of transparency in government and as evidence of strength.

Nigel Roberts: "Here you have a Prime Minister who will not only tick off her Ministers but will also tick off her husband as well. And I think that's why Helen Clark is riding high in the credibility stakes. Because if Marian Hobbs or Margaret Wilson or Annette King or Michael Cullen has done something that doesn't meet her standards or lacks commonsense, I think a Prime Minister gains in credibility by saying so. We can all tell when the Emperor's naked. And previous Prime Ministers have gone on pretending the Emperor's wearing all sorts of suits of clothes that didn't exist. That's been the problem with Prime Ministers in the past."

Bill Ralston: "The other thing is that she has kept a very strong hand on Cabinet. When she has seen a weak Minister or someone potentially damaging to her Government, she has moved in and cauterised the wound very quickly. And the casualty rate has been high. But by and large, when someone has appeared to be trailing blood in the shark-infested waters of Parliament, she's cauterised the wound and cut them loose, which is what you have to do. And you compare that with the

Shipley and Bolger Governments that carried the walking wounded for ages and did themselves immeasurable damage because of it."

Helen's perceived abrasiveness in dealing with colleagues and with those, both inside politics and without, who publicly attack or disagree with her, has led to her leadership style being compared to that of Rob Muldoon. Though the comparison my seem fanciful at first, it is remarkably common.

Richard Long: "The downside parallels with Muldoon are obvious. I think she is so enamoured with being popular after all the years as 'Miss Three-Percent' that she will not tolerate anything which threatens her image. The result is that she gets respect rather than personal loyalty. There have also been occasions when she has put short-term damage-control ahead of long-term objectives. On cold nights the Nats no doubt comfort themselves with the thought that she is a tactical rather than a strategic thinker. But then again, like those chess-playing computers, she learns from her bad moves and is unlikely to repeat them."

Barry Soper: "Muldoon remembered everything in minute detail and was an engaging chap to talk to. That's not dissimilar to Clark. I suppose the public persona of both these people is that they are dominant. And they are. But Muldoon used to dominate the media much more than Clark does. Clark is very good at schmoozing with the media and very good, some would say, at manipulating the media. Whereas Muldoon liked to attack the media and it was always a jousting match when you interviewed him. Clark is not as vicious at this stage, although she's early in her Prime Ministership."

Jane Clifton: "Comparisons between her and Muldoon are made all the time. It's sort of unavoidable, really. All the obvious things that people say, that she's a control freak – 'I decide what happens.' But there's also an un-ingratiating thing that she's got going. I get the impression that she really doesn't care whether people like her or not, which is so unusual in a politician. Most of them really want to be liked. They certainly want to be respected. And they want to be thought of as nice people. Muldoon couldn't give a flying, and I don't think she could either."

Barry Gustafson (Rob Muldoon's biographer): "I think their outward abrasiveness does to a certain extent conceal a shyer inner self that can be hurt. But they'd never admit it. Neither of them, I was going to say, tolerate fools gladly, but they probably don't tolerate them at all. They handle them differently. I think Helen is more up-front. You wouldn't find Muldoon tearing his Ministers to pieces in public. But they probably got a much harder mauling from him behind the scenes than Helen would hand out. What you see is what you get with Helen. It wasn't always the case with Muldoon and that's the big difference between them."

Geoffrey Palmer, who describes Helen as "probably the best manager of the

Labour Party we've seen in modern times" – a job he compares to "herding cats" – believes her ability to "ride rough-shod over Ministers" will, in the end, make her unpopular with colleagues:

"While it's justified, it's extremely tough on the people involved, because it's a sort of public and ritual humiliation for them and they don't like it. And that's something you've got to be careful about. But I think she's got very few weaknesses, very few."

But weaknesses nonetheless: Colin James believes that Helen can be rigid in her judgements and policy setting and not open enough to other arguments:

"The most obvious example is the defence issue. She's just blocked off debate there. There's isn't room for debate in her head. Another of her weaknesses is that when she's attacked on something like this, she attacks back ad hominem. And she's doing that more and more."

It's a view partly shared by Judith Tizard: "Helen can be very rigid. I used to say in the early 90s that Helen will be the greatest Prime Minister this country will ever have, if only we can get her there. And part of it will be in spite of her and part of it will be in spite of us. We have never had a model of a woman leader, and Helen can be very stubborn; she can say 'Bugger you all!' and walk away. She will not compromise beyond what she believes is reasonable for her. So she will not go and meet people on their terms; she will offer herself as she is. And if she can make the connection, that's great. But if not, too bad."

Barry Soper thinks she can be insensitive: "One instance was the lighting of the Christmas tree at Premier House. Now that's been a bit of a tradition, that the people of Wellington get to see the Christmas tree, a Norfolk Pine. She decided not to do it for austerity reasons. And that caused a great furore. And the public perception was, 'For god sake, she may not have kids but she should be able to enter into the Christmas spirit, and she doesn't do it.'"

Her mother worries that she may overdo things: "I think she takes on far too much and doesn't get enough time for relaxation or rest or getting away from politics. She makes herself too available. But she said on the phone the other day, she just feels she has to make herself available to a wide range of people. She was going off that night to Dannevirke for some fashion parade, flying down from Auckland. You know, after a long day in Auckland. I think she overworks. I think she does."

Cath Tizard thinks Helen tends to be "a bit quickly judgemental sometimes": "She ain't perfect. I said to her the other day, 'Is this a hagiography that Brian is doing on you?' And she said, 'I hope so.' I said, 'Come on, you've got to have a wart somewhere. If Oliver Cromwell can have a wart, you can have a wart too.'

chapter**fifteen**

A VERY
CONSIDERABLE
PRIME MINISTER

W HEN this book was first mooted, Helen said, "I don't want to be portrayed as a nasty person." An interesting comment, since it implied that she considered there was a possibility, perhaps even a probability, that this was how she would be portrayed. Yet it was surely unlikely that someone who had worked with her as an advisor for five years and considered himself a friend, would paint such a negative portrait. Indeed, when news that I was writing a book about Helen first became public, there was a widespread assumption that it would be a hagiography. I didn't know the word and had to look in the dictionary to discover that it means the biography of a saint.

So while many assumed that this would be an exercise in flattery, the subject of the book was anxious that it might instead show her in a less than flattering light. This is how someone thinks who for the greater part of her career has been variously misrepresented as a hard, unfeeling, unattractive woman, a dry-as-dust academic with little understanding of or empathy with ordinary people, an ambitious political manipulator who lacked even the talent to realise her own ambition. This is how someone thinks who for the greater part of her career has been either ignored or branded "least likely to succeed". This is how someone thinks who for the greater part of her career has had too few reasons to assume that the world will think well of her.

Of course that has all changed now. The world, with the possible exception of

A VERY CONSIDERABLE PRIME MINISTER

some Australians, thinks very well of Helen Clark, and, as she grows more confident and reveals more of her true personality, it has become easier to do so. But history is not easily rewritten. Memory persists. And when Helen says, "I don't want to be portrayed as a nasty person," she is remembering how it was and is not entirely confident that it will not be so again. There is scar tissue here.

As to whether Helen is a nasty person, we show different faces to different people, and I have never experienced any nastiness in her dealings with me or those I know. I have observed her under extreme stress before two elections be more unpleasant to staff than I would have considered acceptable. But these were rare occasions and they are people who will not hear a word against her. The truth is that I do not know her well enough to judge. So I am reliant on the opinions of those who do. On that basis I have to conclude that we are talking about someone who is caring, generous and kind, yet demanding, impatient and judgemental; who is shy, vulnerable and capable of being hurt, yet domineering, determined and tough; who is serious, austere and ascetic, yet passionate, joyful and fun; who is honest, straightforward and forthright, yet wily as a fox. One could go on, concluding only that Helen is a complex personality. But as a summary, "nasty" will certainly not do. "Nice" is not right either. But "good" may be close. My impression from knowing her a little and talking to those who know her more, is that Helen is a good person.

That, certainly, is what her friends and family say. Examples of her kindness and generosity are legion:

Judith: "She's a very kind person. If you're a friend, you're a friend. I remember when Bill Rowling's daughter Kim committed suicide. I was doing a couple of university papers at the time. And Helen came and found me, because she didn't want me hearing about it on the radio. She actually had to spend several hours searching through the library because I was working in the senior common room. I had a part-time job there in the lunchtimes. And she came and said to the woman I worked for, 'Look a friend of Judith's has died, I need to take her away.' But that's typical of Helen. She wasn't going to let me just hear that Kim had died. I'd forgotten how painful it was."

Few people are so acutely aware of Helen's kindness as Joan Caulfield. Helen, as we have seen, was a tower of strength when Joan's marriage to Jim Anderton broke up in 1982. But there would be worse tragedies in her friend's life. In 1993, while Joan was living and working in Canada, her daughter Philippa committed suicide. She returned to New Zealand with her husband Graham for the funeral:

"Graham and I stayed here for quite a while, a couple of months. And Helen and Peter were going away and she said to me, 'Just use the house.' So Graham and I stayed in her house. And I've got the feeling that my daughter Jillian did too. And that's always surprised me about Helen because there's this dichotomy – she's so open about you staying in her house and yet she's such a private person. It doesn't quite match up. But she's always been very generous about people staying in her house. And it's, 'Take me as you find me, but the house is yours.' She's very relaxed about it. She's incredibly relaxed about letting friends stay in her house."

Helen's sisters talk constantly of her generosity, Suzanne describing her as "the most generous person I've ever met":

"When Rosie, our youngest daughter, was born, we had a bit of a bad time. She was a very fussy baby. So when she was six months old Helen shouted Alan, myself and the baby a ten-day trip to Rarotonga, all expenses paid at the Pacific Resort, a really flash resort right on the beach. It was absolutely wonderful and we didn't have to pay for a thing. It came right out of the blue: 'I'm shouting you and Alan a trip to Rarotonga. When do you want to go? When should I book the tickets for?'

"And then there's the way she used to bring gifts home whenever she went overseas. She'd come back with presents for all the kids: little dresses, knick-knacks. She was always thinking of other people. She'd always come back with something."

Helen's nephews and nieces are regular beneficiaries of their aunt's philanthropy, whether in the form of ski trips to Queenstown or visits to Auckland. Suzanne's daughter Elizabeth reports: "She got us tickets to go and see the ballet in Auckland. It was pretty expensive, I think. And the ski trips were fun. We all flew down to Queenstown and she'd pick us up from the airport and drive us to our motel. We'd stay in the motel and get up really early to make lunches and go to the ski fields. We'd get up, have a shower and breakfast. Muesli, it was always muesli. That was her choice. And then we'd make our ham and cheese sandwiches."

Brian: "Who made the ham and cheese sandwiches?"

Elizabeth: "Oh, we all did. She made dinner – rice and tuna or something. It was actually good. Or maybe it was because we were all so hungry. She did the cooking every night… And then we'd all jump in the car and drive up to the ski field, up the really winding road in the snow. Helen and Catherine and Ashley would get out and put the snow chains on."

Brian: "And she was fun to be with?"

Elizabeth: "Yes. She took us to a symphony concert once and I found it a bit boring. But she's definitely fun, yeah. I mean, when we went up to stay with her in Auckland she said to us, 'Oh, you've got to go to Rainbow's End.' And she took us to Kelly Tarlton's and all these things. That was cool. And she told us where to go ice-skating and things like that."

Brian: "Did you tell her you found the symphony concert boring?"

Elizabeth: "No, I wouldn't tell anyone that I found it boring if I'd been out. That would be impolite. I mean, it wasn't like I was, you know, dying of boredom. It's just that I can think of other ways I'd rather spend an evening."

But, as Susanne explains, Helen's involvement with her nephews and nieces is not merely a matter of showing them a good time: "She's paid our oldest daughter's university fees for the last two years. She doesn't have to do that. But my daughter works pretty hard so she's trying to help her. It's extraordinary. The fees are pretty high and these cheques just turn up.

"She takes a great interest in how all the kids are doing academically. She'll want to know how they've done in their School Certificate, how they're doing at university. It's all got to be accounted for. If they're not doing well, they've got to do better. It's just concern for them to do well, I think. And interest. She's really interested in what they're doing."

Brian: "So what does she talk to you about?"

Elizabeth: "School and exams. She concentrates on things I know something about. So I can talk to her. And she'll listen to your arguments even if she doesn't think you're right."

Brian: "Do you have arguments with her?"

Elizabeth: "Discussions. But not too many because she does know so much more than you do. It's very hard to argue with someone who's always got the answer there. We had a big discussion on prison sentencing. I said they should be much harsher and she said no, it won't work. I remember that one quite clearly. I definitely thought they should be longer and she was saying no, that's not going to help the people in prison. They should be rehabilitated."

Brian: "But you disagreed?"

Elizabeth: "Yeah. I definitely think there should be longer prison sentences. Bring back the death penalty. Some people deserve to die."

Brian: "Did she give you a chance to put your viewpoint?"

Elizabeth: "Yes. Sometimes she'd butt in and go over the top with pure facts. But mostly she let me get my point across, even though she thought I was wrong."

Brian: "So she talks about issues."

Elizabeth: "Subjects and grades. Very much so."

Brian: "Pretty serious stuff. But what's this story about *The Simpsons*?"

Elizabeth: "When we were staying in Auckland. Before Auntie Helen came home, Uncle Peter would get home and we'd all sit down and watch *The Simpsons*. Then we'd hear the door unlocking and Peter would go, 'Quick, here she comes, here she comes! Turn on the TV News.' And we'd have to turn on the TV News quick. She came in once and caught him!"

Despite being deprived of *The Simpsons*, Peter has enormous admiration for his wife's concern for her family: "What do I like best about her? I think she has enormous depths of human potential that are constantly developing and emerging, and she has the ability to surprise. But also, despite the face she has to put to the public and in dealing with opponents, she has enormous compassion. She is concerned about her family. She wants to know how her nieces and nephews are doing at school, and it's genuine. And she wants to be sure that I'm happy in my work or how my Dad's getting on. Those are the genuine things which at base are what keeps her in touch with why she's in this whole business. She's grounded in little things that matter, that make life worthwhile, the little family things and domestic things that are crowded out a lot of the time, but are still there."

It's these "little things" that impress Helen's Aunt Fay so much as well:

"I see her through rose-coloured spectacles, of course. I mean, I love Helen. I've always liked her and I think she's intelligent and caring. And she has a goal which is to get better conditions for people in New Zealand. But I tell you what, she'll do little things that you wouldn't expect a busy person to be bothered with. Cyril and I pop round occasionally to tidy up the place and she can take time to leave a little note for me. She writes on her *Listeners* – we get her old *Listeners* – 'Fay and Cyril'. Or she'll leave a magazine for us. She'll ring up to ask me how to look after the silly begonia that they gave her for her birthday. And she'll worry about her little fern in the office, that it needs re-potting. She's got an amazing mind really that she can do all these things. If I was in her position I wouldn't even think about them."

Cath Tizard believes that Helen's generosity and kindness are most evident in her dealings with family and friends: "She made time to come to a dinner I put on for Silvia Cartwright before she was sworn into office, because I said I thought it was important for Silvia and secondly it was important to me. And I said, 'I'll find a night that suits your schedule first and then we'll sort the others out afterwards.' So her people came back to me with a whole list of nights that she'd be willing to come and it was just a private dinner. It was a great fun dinner, but I wanted her, Margaret Wilson, Judith, and some other personal friends and judge associates of Silvia's to be there. But Helen was the key person and she gave up a whole night for that."

Brian: "You know there are some politicians and leaders who care about people en masse, but care less about people individually. Do you think that, aside from friends and family, Helen cares about people individually?"

Cath: "I don't think she's sentimental, I don't think she cares in a sentimental way, but she does, I think, care very much about opportunity and fairness and all of the old catch-cries of seeing that people get a fair go. The things Muldoon used

Scenes from Helen's 50th birthday party. *Clockwise from Top Left* **Cath Tizard** arrives in style with her daughter Anne and friend **Ken Richardson; James Harrison** serenades the Prime Minister; a surprise visit from the **Chapman Tripp Opera Chorus;** with her extended family; flowers for a milestone birthday; **Jonathan Hunt** in one of his more colourful shirts; listening to her favourite music left Helen with tears in her eyes.

to cry about, the ordinary bloke getting a fair go. I don't think she has any sort of bleeding-heart feeling of great compassion for the unwashed masses or even the washed masses. But I think she's very loyal in personal relationships, and I'm sure that she sees what she's given her life to doing as something worthwhile."

Loyalty is a word which crops up in almost every conversation about Helen's personality. Loyalty to family and friends:

Judith: "She is deeply loyal as a friend. If I'm upset or unhappy, Helen is usually one of the first to say, 'What's happening and why and what can I do to help?' You know that she would actually crawl over broken glass for you. So she is fiercely loyal."

Joan: "She's a very loyal friend. She's always been there in my times of need. And maybe because of that and the life she leads, I avoid telling her about things that aren't going quite right in my life, because she worries about them. She worries about things happening with her friends actually. But she was there when Jim left. She was there when Philippa died. She is there for her friends. She has this incredible loyalty."

To kindness, generosity and loyalty, friends and family add a range of other qualities. Helen is bossy, domineering or a natural leader, according to your (and her) perspective. She is rarely frivolous, but has – everyone says – a good sense of humour. She is frugal and a hoarder. She shows disapproval, according to her sisters, by "a very severe tone and her whole body language". She is competitive, but not a bad loser. She is determined (or wilful), cool-headed and shows physical courage. She is honest. She is easily hurt, but less so now than when she first entered politics. She is inclusive.

There are stories to illustrate most of these qualities.

Joan on Helen's sense of humour: "She has a wicked sense of humour, as a matter of fact. I think about the time she and Peter used to come up to Karekare and stay with us for the summer. And I can't recall what year it was, but it was the Year of the Rabbit anyway. And I was born in the Year of the Rabbit. Well, Helen was absolutely hysterical about the fact that I had five kids and had been born in the Year of the Rabbit. And she laughed her head off. She didn't let me forget it for ages. It was very funny. So she has quite a wicked sense of humour. And sometimes she can laugh at some quite… Well, I would never called Helen a prude, put it that way."

And on Helen's hoarding: "She's an unbelievable hoarder. The only tension I ever notice between Helen and Peter is trying to get stuff out of the house, clearing out paper. A few months ago Peter got rid of a whole swag of stuff and Helen noticed a bag of papers he'd put in the wheelie bin. So she took it out, took it back inside and started going through it all again. She said, 'Oh, there's bound to be stuff he's thrown out that I need.' She's an incredible recycler. We take piles of papers away and usually get a volunteer to take out the staples and then take it back to the house. She uses the backs for writing on and in her fax machine."

Peter on Helen's cool-headedness and physical courage: "At times I think it's foolhardiness myself. I don't have a good head for heights. But Helen is trusting. So if Gottlieb [their guide] thinks that she can climb a thing, then she thinks she probably can, even though she's never done it before. And she's not disconcerted by heights, she looks ahead. Frankly I think she should be more circumspect.

"But she has a coolness in decision-making generally, as she has a coolness about going the next step in climbing. There are times when I think it's a lack of sensitivity. I feel this is potentially dangerous. Maybe I veer too much in the other direction, but she's cool under fire generally. In politics she's shown coolness, ability to stand her ground and think things through, when others are losing it.

"I don't think I've ever seen her afraid. We're not put in circumstances where we're likely to be afraid. On neither Aconcagua nor Kilimanjaro were we actually climbing. I've been more afraid climbing in the Southern Alps, because that's real climbing where you're roped up. There have been circumstances where I've genuinely been a little bit concerned, like when Helen and Margaret were in South America at a Socialist International conference. The day after they'd been travelling on a train trip, the train got blown up. You think to yourself, 'Oh my god!'

"There are times when your imagination can get to you. When we were thinking about Kilimanjaro, Helen said, 'What about seeing the gorillas over in Western Uganda?' And the travel agent said, 'I recommend against that.' And I'm glad he did, because not long after that some people were ambushed and killed. So, looking back, there've been times like that when I've realised we've been lucky or perhaps just been thoughtful and had the right advice. But she doesn't like injections. She's more concerned about them."

Buddy Arthur on Helen's inclusiveness: "I remember George and Margaret's Golden Wedding in 1999. Helen wasn't Prime Minister then, but I was beginning to see another side of her – how she spoke about people and how she included everybody. And she had all these little stories, even about Eddie finding the car, and about all the families in Te Pahu. And she more or less acknowledged everybody who was there. It was just amazing really. I'd never noticed it before, but it really made you feel good."

I can tell my own story of a similar occasion – a party held on a hot summer day at Helen's cousin Gillian's property in West Auckland, to mark the new Prime Minister's 50th birthday. Judy and I were among the guests, more than a hundred

friends and family who had been invited to this celebration. Standing on the verandah and working from a few scribbled notes, Helen made an informal and often
light-hearted speech. But the remarkable thing was that virtually everyone present
was mentioned in that speech, included, acknowledged for whatever contribution
they had made to Helen's life, career or happiness. And it really did make you feel
good. And I remember thinking that this was a very special person, that she was
warm and loving and funny, and that these were qualities which I had barely
glimpsed before, and that something had changed. Perhaps it was nothing more
than that Helen also felt good about herself and was prepared to show it.

"I think," says her mother, "that Helen is quite a kind-hearted person and that
really, under her perhaps tough exterior, she's got quite a sensitive heart."

But were we right in asserting that the success of the fifth Labour Government
has been largely, if not exclusively, due to Helen Clark? A week may be a long time
in politics, but at the time of writing, the answer to the question is quite clearly Yes.

Helen's leadership is not without its imperfections. In particular, she is slow to
praise and quick to judge, a significant failing in one who relies on the goodwill and
support of others.

But her strengths as a politician hugely outweigh her weaknesses. She is fiercely
intelligent. She has a command of national and international issues probably
unmatched in the history of New Zealand politics. She is hard-working and
energetic. Her managerial skills, nowhere better illustrated than in her success in
holding together the Coalition, are exceptional. She is a problem-solver and fixer.
In her dealings with the media and the public she has brought a new transparency

Left **With Sandra, Peter and guide in Arusho, Tanzania, 1998. They later climbed Africa's highest peak, Mount Kilimanjaro.** *Opposite Page* **In Argentina, December 2000. Helen and Peter tackled the highest mountain in the Western Hemisphere, Aconcagua. The weather defeated them not far from the summit.**

to New Zealand politics. She is straightforward and honest. She is idealistic, but her idealism is tempered by pragmatism and commonsense. She is a practitioner of the art of the possible. Though she does not lack ambition, she is uninterested in the trappings or privileges of power. She sees herself as a servant leader.

Has she been a good Prime Minister?

David Lange: "She has been an enormously successful Prime Minister. In fact, in a funny way, she's too successful, because you cannot conceive of this Government without her. You cannot explain this Government except by her personality and diligence, by her perception of what's required to be done. So you run the risk of perceiving the show as being Helen Clark."

Bill Ralston: "I've been terribly impressed with her as Prime Minister. I think she's doing incredibly well, far better than I expected. Based on her performance as Leader of the Opposition, I thought, 'Shit, the chances of her being good in this job are pretty poor.' So she's been a revelation. She's done extremely well. She has really flowered in the job. And if you could clone her, you would have a super-Cabinet."

Richard Long: "Eighteen years of doing hard battle within Labour has turned Clark into a formidable political animal – hard as nails and sometimes quite correctly referred to as a control freak, though often in admiration, rather than as a criticism. She is acutely sensitive to shifts in public opinion, hugely influenced by the opinion polls and knows how to use her position to set the political agenda. Intellectually she can outdistance any of her opponents. Someone once said that politics was more a matter of will than intellect. I suspect that Clark has both."

Above **Dawn parade in Crete, May 2001. Helen has visited many sites where New Zealanders fell in battle.**

Geoffrey Palmer: "She's a professional politician to her bootstraps, and she has been for a long time and she's extremely effective because of it. And she's not self-indulgent, not selling her own personality to people. That's what I like about her style. She's not trying to say, 'Here's Helen Clark, and I'm a celebrity because I'm Helen Clark'. She's saying, 'Here I am, I'm the Leader of the Labour Party. These are the things we've done. And these are the things we're going to do.'"

Dick Griffin: "Her strength as Prime Minister is in doing pretty much what she said she'd do, and doing it with élan and style and panache. There's no bullshit with this woman. She doesn't patronise. She speaks her mind and gets straight to the point. She seems to me to be one of the first leaders I can remember whom you can respect as an individual, who can foot it on an intellectual plane with virtually anybody, and look good doing it. What you see in her is an articulate, tough-minded, to-the-point woman who never equivocates. What you see is what you get."

So what next? There is a consensus among the political pundits that Helen wants three terms in office and that this is not a matter of personal vanity. There is work to be finished. Geoffrey Palmer sees that work as the displacement of National as "the natural party in government" and the creation of "a Social Democrat nation in New Zealand, where social justice is important, but the economy is strong."

Barry Gustafson takes a similar view: "I think she will be seen as one of most ideologically motivated Prime Ministers in our history. Perhaps not ideological in the sense of a comprehensive political philosophy like socialism, but certainly a set of ideas and principles which her policies have to conform to. She quite clearly wants a non-sexist, non-racist society. She wants an economy that operates efficiently and productively, so that through an element of redistribution in the taxation system she can attack deprivation, and particularly deprivation that leads to inequality of opportunity. And she clearly has a worldview along traditional Labour lines of a moral foreign policy, intent on peace-making and peace-keeping."

The impediments to a three-term Labour Government under MMP are clear: the uncertainty of retaining a cohesive relationship with the Alliance, assuming that the Alliance survives; the destabilising potential of the increasingly popular Greens; the possibility of resurgent divisions within the Labour Party itself or of Ministerial disaffection provoking a leadership challenge; electorate fatigue; world events beyond her control; and the possibility that Helen herself may tire of the job and look for higher mountains to climb.

David Lange doubts that three terms are likely: "I have this feeling that she's not going to get nine years, but that will not reflect on her at all. No government is a nine-year government in its own right. Helen would have to depend entirely on her Opposition being so pathetic that no one would be tempted to vote for change. That's the way people work these days."

Nigel Roberts sees divisions within the Coalition and the Party on the horizon: "Inevitably there are going to be greater difficulties in the second term. Come the 2002 election, inevitably the tensions will be there. With the coalition partner and within Labour itself. For the good of the Party people will accept the discipline. Michael Cullen will allow himself to be criticised in public, as will Margaret Wilson. There's already a string of Ministers, and it will be a string that gets longer. And some people will have been consigned to the back benches and then brought forward again. But after five years, seven years perhaps, it builds up. And the big danger for the Prime Minister is in outstaying her welcome."

Al Morrison believes that Helen may tire of the job: "In a sense she may bring herself down. She may lose interest. I really believe she is a person who will only keep the job while it continues to interest her. And if the challenge goes out of it, then it would not surprise me if she was one of the few people who would be able to say, 'I've done my bit and I'm going to walk away.' Not because they're pushed or frustrated like David Lange, but because they've simply achieved what they can achieve. I don't believe that Clark will be a maintenance Prime Minister. And if we get to a third term and it's steady-as-you-go, maintain-the-helm kind of thing, she could well lose interest and say, 'I'm going to go and do something else.'"

Speculation on what that might be ranges from a chair at one of the world's great universities to following in the footsteps of Norwegian Prime Minister Gro Harlem Brundtland as Director General of the World Health Organisation or Irish President Mary Robinson as United Nations Commissioner for Human Rights.

Above **Professional advice from legendary athletics endurance coach Arthur Lydiard, to help promote awareness for the Asthma Society. Helen suffered from asthma as a child.**

Her husband thinks it's too soon to say: "Helen's a person of, huge depths and potential and surprises. And she will continue to be Prime Minister as long as the New Zealand public want her to, and as long as she wants to. Or she may decide, let's enjoy life a lot more and travel. Who knows? My own feeling is that she'd be wasted doing that in a sense. It seems to me that she's got tremendous skills and trustworthiness which are great assets. As to the World Health Organisation and the United Nations, it's a possibility. But I think, take first things first. She's got to do this job properly and she may come to the end of it and say, that's enough for that part of my life."

It is probably also too soon to say whether Helen Clark will one day be remembered as one of the great Prime Ministers of New Zealand. But after only two years in office, even those practised cynics in the Press Gallery are prepared to concede that it's on the cards. So too is Parliament's longest serving member, the Speaker of the House of Representatives and Helen's close friend, Jonathan Hunt:

"I look back to all the Prime Ministers I've seen and read about, and my ideal was Peter Fraser. But so far Helen's been the best on two grounds: she's bright and hard working, and she doesn't make many mistakes. And I think that if she stays there, she will go down as a very considerable Prime Minister."

chapter sixteen

HELEN ON HELEN:
AN INTERVIEW

There is a metal security fence now outside the Mount Eden home of the Prime Minister of New Zealand. You press a button on the gate, speak into an intercom and either Helen or Peter answers. The fence is the only clue that someone of importance lives in what is an otherwise unremarkable Auckland villa.

The interior of the house is equally unremarkable, modest, some would say, to the point of austerity. A classic corridor villa with rooms running off the hall – the Prime Minister's office (an organised mess), bedrooms, bathroom, sitting room. At the end of the hall you come to a living room with a dining alcove and, opposite the living room, a long galley kitchen where Peter and Helen make their famous curries. French doors lead out from a conservatory at the back of the living room to a garden with camellias, citrus and other trees.

More than 20 hours of interview for this book are conducted in the sitting room. In Ireland the room where you receive guests is referred to as "the parlour". The word has a Victorian ring to it. It suggests a very tidy room, used only on special occasions, some-what formal, not terribly inviting, a little cold perhaps, everything in its place, the cushions plumped up and neatly arranged in their preordained spots, the best china and ornaments on display with rather stiffly posed family portraits. There is that sort of feel to Helen's sitting room. The upright piano which her grandmother gave her has pride of place.

I sit in an armchair with my notes precariously perched on my knee. Helen sits on a couch in the bay window, her back to the light. I read no significance into this. I am offered tea. "Peter, make us a pot of tea, dear." Peter obliges, abandoning either the sport on the telly or the piles of work scattered on the conservatory floor. A slippers and cardie man, he has a comfortable air. I wonder if he secretly records The Simpsons *and plays it back when Helen's out at the RSA. Unworthy thought.*

We begin. When the subject interests her, Helen sits forward and speaks in an animated and expansive way, often smiling and laughing. When she is bored or unhappy with the topic, she leans back and speaks so softly that the record light on the machine barely flickers. The answers get shorter. It's not hard to read how Helen is feeling.

But she answers everything and shows no sign of irritation as I go well beyond my allocated two hours. Remarkable really, when you consider that all of the interviews are conducted on the weekend, Helen's only free time and often her only real opportunity to be with her husband. But she is warm and gracious and at ease in her own home.

"Make us another pot of tea, love."

Tell me about a week in the life of the Prime Minister. How many appointments would you have in your diary?

I'll answer it another way round. I don't take a lot of appointments anymore. I haven't got time. But on a Monday I'll have the alarm set before 5:30am, because I'm going to Wellington on the 7:30 plane. At 6:30 I pre-record an interview with Paul Holmes. I then get into the car where I do a 7 o'clock pre-record with 3ZB in Christchurch. On the way from the airport to Parliament I talk to Mikey Havoc at BFM. I almost always return a call from the *Evening Post* looking for a story. I get into the office. I immediately ring Radio Dunedin who like a chat on Monday mornings. At 9:30 I have the Head of the Prime Minister's Department, his Deputy and my own Chief of Staff, Heather Simpson, come in. At 10 o'clock all the Labour Party Ministers come in and at 10:30 we go to the Cabinet. We're there right through till lunchtime. I generally have lunch at one o'clock with other Ministers in the Cabinet dining room when it's available. Two o'clock is the Executive Council, which I haven't been in the habit of going to terribly often. But with a new Governor-General I try to go a bit more often. I normally have a press conference around 3:00, 3:30 and that can go for half an hour or 40 minutes. Then I might have time for one or two appointments or catching up with staff. I often get on the plane to Auckland at half-past 6 to come up for a meeting here, but this week, for example, I've got things in Wellington. I've got the Indian Foreign Minister coming in, and then I'm launching a couple of things and going out for dinner. On Tuesday morning I'll often be on the 8:30 back to Wellington, arriving at 10:00. That's the time when the Party President and Party Secretary can come in for 20 minutes before the caucus, if they want to. I head off down the corridor to the caucus room. The media have a stand-up interview in the corridor, which can take five or ten minutes. I go into the caucus from 10:30 to 1:00. I then go back to my room and get ready for Question Time at 2:00. I'm in the House till 3:00. I come back. Now at that point I might have officials come in from a range of Departments. I've got the Department of the Prime Minister and Cabinet, Arts Culture and Heritage, the Security Intelligence Service and the Government Communications Security Bureau. People are in and out. So I'll either see people like that or take appointments possibly between 3:00 and 5:00.

People from interest groups, people wanting things?

That's right. Organisations like the Family Planning Association, for example, that I've been a patron of. Lobbyists, people wanting to come in. And often between 5:00 and half-past 7 I'll be launching something, sometimes a couple of things. And it's usually not until about 8:30 or 9:00 at night that I'll actually sit down to try and clear the backlog of paperwork that's accumulated through the day. And I might not go home till one in the morning. On Wednesday I'll start at 7:50 with a call to a Christchurch radio station. I have another call at either 8:00 or 8:10, depending on the week. I'll go in and chair a Cabinet Committee at 9:00, another one at 9:30, sit in on the 10:30 and go to the 11:45 if I can. But by then I've probably got other people pressing for attention. And then it's one o'clock and I have to prepare for Question Time. I go down the House for Question Time and it starts all over again. Now on Thursday I'm more often than not in Wellington. So I might be on a plane quite early for somewhere else in New Zealand and I'll have a very tight programme. With the Maori visit days we're packing in eight or nine different things, a dinner at night and a forum the next day.

The Maori visit days?

Every month I've been doing a day of Maori visits. So I go into a particular area – Gisborne, Wanganui, North Auckland, whatever – and have a whole day programme where we go from one group to another, seeing what they're engaged in, how the programmes are working. So that's often a Thursday. On Friday I will also be either out of town or in Auckland, spending the day going out and seeing a lot of people, addressing a conference, opening something, launching something, and that goes right through till Friday night. Then I come home on Friday night – well, I'm often out on Friday night anyway – and try to leave the weekend clear to get on with the accumulated paperwork of the week, read the Cabinet papers, prepare the speeches. But if there are important things out of town, I will do them. I've got to judge them to be important. And I always do electorate things – openings and closings of bowling clubs, local ethnic community functions in Auckland. I do a lot of that. So, in answer to your question, you can see there's very little time in the week for appointments. Very little time.

I'm intrigued by what you consider important. Many of the things you've referred to seem to be little more than networking or socialising or just being seen.

But that is important. Launching things, speaking at functions, they're all important. It's important that the Government should be out there, supporting good causes, supporting milestones in the development of a school, the community, whatever. It's a damn sight more important than sitting in the office seeing the great and powerful who want to lobby you. And that, I think, is a large part of the appeal of this Government, that we do get out there to ordinary communities and we're accessible to ordinary people.

Some would say that schedule is excessive.

That's the way it is.

No, it's the way you've made it.

That's right. Because you're fashioning the job.

Do you know how this compares with previous Prime Ministers?

I think many of them had a tendency to sit in their office in Wellington a lot more.

So how do you cope with such a killing schedule. How do you strike a balance in your life?

You've got to get enough sleep.

But you've described coming home at one o'clock and getting up at half-past five.

Oh, no. I don't often do that. I do have 19 hour days, that's true, but then I'm also looking towards the end of the week. When I came home on Friday night this week I slept for 12 hours. I slept for 10 hours again last night. So you build up a bit of a sleep bank.

Even worse than the schedule for me would be the paperwork. Do you deal with all of that or does someone else sort it for you?

No. Everything that comes in for the Prime Minister's attention you've got to deal with.

But you surely don't read every letter to the PM?

No. A lot of the mail is deflected to other Ministers. Say someone writes in and says, 'I don't think I'm getting my full benefit entitlement.' That will probably go straight to the Minister of Social Services.

And unpleasant letters?

They get filed.

In the WPB?

Sometimes.

So why would anyone want a job like this? Who would work for more than 20 years just to end up working even harder? There must be ambition involved, ego.

Well, it's actually very task-focused: 'If I could get to be Prime Minister, here are the things I'd be able to do.' It's not about seeing yourself as the Queen.

So all these twenty years…

Thirty years!

…have been aimed at getting into a position which would allow you…

…to make a difference.

Very noble.

Hey, it's had its good sides. It's had an overwhelmingly good side in that I've seen the world, I've travelled the country, I've been involved in issues I'm really interested in. Sure, there's a helluva lot of drudgery as well, but if there wasn't that huge plus side I wouldn't do it.

You're saying you're not in it primarily for you, you're in it for the country. Very different, I would have thought, from other leaders, Bill Clinton for example.

Well funnily enough I thought Clinton was very task-focused, very issue-focused. He was a policy wonk. He was there to do things. I don't think he was there just to be able to say, 'I'm Bill Clinton. I'm the greatest.' I think he actually did want to make a difference. Blair is also very policy-focused. And in many ways he comes across as quite a humble man. He's actually quite a religious man and he's never singing his own praises. He's actually quite focused on the job to be done.

Again a very noble, very idealistic approach.

Oh no, I think it's quite practical really. Because the more you put yourself up on a pedestal, the harder and further you fall. You've got to think of a life beyond politics as well and how the persona you've established will cope with that too. There are plenty of examples of people who didn't cope well when it was all taken away.

You've spoken of the good side of the job. What of the frustrations?

The frustrations are having to dampen down brush fires that should never have been lit in the first place. Things that just come out of left field, like the Community Services Card. Why wasn't the Cabinet member alerted to the fact that if you raise Super you change the eligibility for benefits, and the consequences of that? And then you discover a paper trail between Ministers that's been going on for months. And the Cabinet never knew about it. And suddenly you're in China and you read about it in the newspapers. And the media got it totally and completely wrong, I might say. And they took such fixed positions that they couldn't get off their hobby-horse, even when it was pointed out that much of what they were saying and writing was complete and utter rubbish. That absorbs an enormous amount of time. So most of the frustrations relate to the flare-up of an issue in the media which could have been handled better if people had kept everyone in the loop in the first place, or hadn't done something particularly silly. And you deal with them as quickly as you can and move on. Don't let it drag on. If you let it drag on, it will. And then it will annoy you even longer.

So you have the capacity to put things behind you.

Oh yes.

Is it harder for a woman to be Prime Minister?

No, I don't think so. I don't think anyone gives a toss about the gender now. I honestly don't think so.

Being PM is the most responsible job in the country. Do you ever wake in the night with anxiety attacks?

No.

You don't have worries or fears that you've got it wrong or that you're going in the wrong direction?

No.

You're very self-confident about the direction you're going in?

Yep.

In the two years you've been in Government there have been few surprises.

No surprises. If there's a difficult thing to be done, like the Defence issue, we do a lot of foreshadowing. Preconditioning. So that nothing ever comes as a surprise. Mind you, nothing about anything we've done in Defence should have been a surprise. It was all in the manifesto, as I keep pointing out.

So the job that you're here to do is what?

To try to bring back a sense of fairness and inclusion for every New Zealander and to focus on changing the economy to give it a greater underlying strength, so that we build greater prosperity, which everybody then gets a share of. In the 90s we started to see some growth in the economy again, but it never seemed to result in spill-offs for people down the bottom of the ladder. So the two sides of the equation are, how do you reshape the economy so that it can deliver a better dividend, and how do you make society more fair and inclusive.

I think it's Colin James who speaks of your wanting to change the language of politics in this country, so that people come to regard the politics of the centre-left as the norm, rather than an occasional aberration.

Labourising the status quo. I think if you're going to change the language, you've also got to change the substance. And I like to think that's what we're doing. And if you look at the last election in Britain, Tory tax-cuts cut no ice against Labour saying, 'Look we can have better public services.' So you're changing the terms of the debate.

So that the Tories or National are no longer regarded as the 'natural party of government'.

See, I hate the term, 'natural party of government'. I'll never use it. What you want is a New Zealand in which centre-left governments construct the norm, the mainstream. Labour didn't have a lot of success in the post-war years. But the New Zealand that the Party built between 1935 and 1949 endured until the 1980s. The problem was that you then had Douglas and Lange's conservative rule, followed by nine years of National government. But there's no doubt that the first Labour Government shaped New Zealand for half a century.

So you want to change people's values.

I don't think you have to shape their values. I think that the basis is already there. You're merely elevating it. You're saying, this is a public value. It's a mainstream value and as a society this is how we want to be.

What did you hope to achieve as Prime Minister?

The big picture? To set the compass for New Zealand in a different direction while being fully aware you can't change the world overnight. I strongly believe that the course we were on meant we were doomed and that we had to turn the country away from that course. We were on a path where the Government was deregulating ever more, privatising ever more, trying to cut taxes ever more. And this had the end result of leaving society very under-provided in terms of public services. People were falling right through a non-existent social safety net and the Government, with its extreme hands-off approach to the economy, appeared indifferent to the outcome. So what we did was say, hang on, we don't have to go down that track. Modern Social Democratic governments can engage in a whole lot of ways. We can start to look for smart, intelligent ways to support economic growth. The collective public interest requires spending on basic infrastructure and public services and we will give this priority over tax cuts. We're aiming to build a society which is inclusive, where everyone's got a stake. Now I saw the first three-year term as putting in markers in that direction. You're never going to change it all in three years, but you can say, 'Well this is going to be different, and here are the first steps towards that.'

That's fine. But the path we were on was originally designed by the fourth Labour Government, of which you were a member.

Some of it was. But the commentary on neo-liberalism in New Zealand tends to overlook the fact that there was an election at the end of 1990 when social policy was thrown to the wolves, and when quite radical changes were made in Health, Housing, Education and the labour market, and that these changes were taken to a ridiculous extent. The Labour Government in the 80s certainly deregulated the economy. But there were a whole lot of things it didn't touch. It didn't touch social policy. The floodgates were opened after the 1990 election.

To what extent has the reality of government conformed to your expectations?

I think we've actually exceeded our own expectations, because we knew there were three parts of damn-all money, and we've made it go as far as we could. The public services have had more, and they probably expect even more again from a Labour Government. But if the money ain't there, the money ain't there. But I'm more than satisfied that we've done what we said we would, and given another three years, we'll do more.

Well, that's not the view of many in the Health and Education areas. You've got lots of complaining doctors and university people.

Yes, but you always will have. It's not that they've been cut, it's that there are a lot of competing demands. And no matter how much you endeavour to dampen expectations, as we did before the election, there will always be higher expectations. I think people are aware that we'll do as much as we can, but the money is finite.

So what do you see as having been your major achievements so far?

I think the major achievement is to have built a Government that people believe is strong, stable, takes decisions, gets on with it, has a direction that's generally found favour and kept its word.

Where do you see New Zealand on the world stage?

We're 3.8 million people. Objectively, you might wonder why the President of China would even bother seeing the New Zealand Prime Minister. But I think New Zealand has quite an interesting international position. We're quite widely respected for being an independent-minded small Western nation. We don't carry other people's agendas. It's quite clear that we stand full square in the Western tradition of open democracy and human rights, but we do have a mind of our own. We don't get on bandwagons with others, and we're known for really sticking up for things we believe in. We've had a very important role in disarmament issues, far greater than our size would ever give us, and that goes back to the fourth Labour Government and the nuclear-free zone. I think I can say that I played a major role in that. People have also been interested in what New Zealand had to say on environmental issues since the 80s when Geoffrey Palmer took the Environment Ministry and did a lot of good work on issues such as the Law of the Sea. Where trade is concerned, New Zealand was rather out on a limb in the past, with the purest of free trade approaches. We're still out there saying we think more open trade is of benefit to us and developing countries, but we've also modulated that by saying there are other issues. The relationship between trade and environment is a legitimate debate, between trade and labour. Globalisation has to be seen to work for everyone, not just for business. So I think we've taken quite an interesting position in that. But what matters to me is that when people hear New Zealand speak they know that's New Zealand speaking, not something someone else just whispered in its ear.

But you're always faced with compromises, aren't you, in your relationships with other major countries. Trade versus human rights. Trade versus military alignments.

I'm not sure that you are. I remember Bolger getting into absolute agony in 1994 when he went up to Bogor in Indonesia for the APEC conference, and we kept hounding him, Was he going to raise Timor? Was he going raise Timor? Well, the last thing he wanted to do was raise Timor. Now, my approach has been much more direct than that, and I've had some quite tricky international visits. You go to Japan, and all the media really want to know about is whaling and nuclear waste. You go to China and all the media want to know is, are you going to raise human rights? My approach is – look, we have a very friendly relationship with Japan, they're our third largest export market, we've got 41 sister cities, Japanese is the most studied foreign language in New Zealand schools and their tourism's of enormous value, we work closely in international organisations. However, there are a small number of issues which we don't agree on. And yes, I will be raising them. We do not agree with their whaling practices, we do not like the nuclear waste shipments through the Tasman Sea, and we're concerned at their attitudes on fisheries. These issues will be raised. And yes, I will tell you, the news media, what I said and what they said in reply. Or take China. It has huge economic potential, it is already our sixth biggest export market, we have a history of relations pioneered by Rewi Alley, the Kirk Government opened up diplomatic relations with China and was one of the first Western states to do so, we receive many Chinese delegations, we work with China in regional organisations. However, there are issues which cause difficulties in the relationship, and they are around the human rights issues. While the Falun Gong may be a somewhat weird cult, we don't believe that weird cults should be banished to labour camps just because they are weird cults. We are concerned about the destruction of Christian churches, we have concerns about the issues of ethnic minorities. And we will raise these issues and we will tell you, the media, that we raised them and what the response was. So I'm very up-front on that, so that no-one is under any illusion that the New Zealand Prime Minister will not raise these issues. But you put it in the context of the whole relationship.

But if you look in the paper today, there is a story that 500 people have been executed since April in China. This is horrendous abuse of human rights.

It is horrendous. But then so is the execution of Timothy McVeigh.

I agree. But then if you go back to your own past, you'd have been out there on the streets demonstrating against this sort of thing, against sporting contacts with South Africa for example.

But you see, I think South Africa was unique. I think that the institutionalised racism of South Africa was unique. Through law and statute they decreed people to be of a lesser status.

But through law and statute the Chinese decree that these huge numbers of people should be executed.

But it's not apartheid, which was recognised as being a unique form of human rights violation, which then justified other nations taking all sorts of measures. It just is in a category of its own.

But we wouldn't consider sanctions against the Chinese or sanctions against the Americans. We're not prepared to go to that level of idealism.

No. But what we will do is persistently raise those issues.

And does that do any good?

Yes, I think it does. China knows that in its relations with other countries it will always have to face those issues. And the reality is that while that report is shocking and while the things that happen are shocking, the level of shockingness is not as great as it was during the reign of the Gang of Four, Mao and the rest. A lot of things have changed in China. It's still far from what we would consider acceptable. But it is changing.

But there's evidence that the sanctions against South Africa, just in the one area of sport, were enormously effective in the long run.

But because you got wide buy-in to them. You can see with Iraq the sanctions have become very divisive.

Well, they're punishing all the wrong people.

That's absolutely right. It's caused a huge amount of child death and other misery. It's horrible.

So when you raise these issues, in Japan, China, wherever it might be, how is that protest worded?

You say, 'Look I come from a country which cares about these issues. I care about these issues. We have to raise our concern. We have to raise our concern which is consistent with our value system and belief that this is not the way.' And then they will quite vigorously defend their point of view and you'll get into quite a debate about it. But the difference from the past is that the Chinese are prepared to debate about it, which in itself is an improvement.

So on the world scene, you see this little country as a voice for what – reason?

No. I see this little country as a voice for a peaceful, sustainable, inclusive planet, I suppose. That you're looking for ways of solving conflict other than by violence, you're trying to get rid of the threat of the weapons of mass destruction, whether they be nuclear, chemical or biological. You work very, very hard on the environmental issues which are the key to sustainability. And you want a future where every citizen of the planet's going to have a stake in it. Not through the marginalisation of whole continents like Africa, or great swathes of poor people across other areas.

Do you find, as the Prime Minister of this small country, that you're taken seriously by world leaders?

Yes. I remember going in to see the Turkish President when I went there last year. And I'd been reading in the paper that he'd just had the Chinese President Jiang Zemin. So I went in and we sat down for our formal talks and I said, 'Well Mr President, this week you've gone from the sublime to the ridiculous. You've had the leader of 1.2 billion people here in Ankara, and today you have the leader of 3.8 million people.' He said, 'Madam, size is of no account. After you, I have in some days the leader of Iceland coming, a country which has a quarter of a million people. What counts, Madam,' he said, 'is that a State is a State.' It's a great story, isn't it? And it's true. At the UN everyone from Tuvalu, with 10,000 people, gets a vote, right through to a nation with 1.2 billion. And never forget, in the legend and mythology of the UN and the Labour Party, that Peter Fraser went up to the San Francisco conference and argued for the rights of small states against the veto of the great powers. So New Zealand, I think actually because of Labour Governments being prepared to stick their neck out, has long had a reputation that's much bigger than its size. You go back to the League of Nations, the New Zealand Labour Government under Michael Joseph Savage spoke out against the Italian invasion of Abyssinia, when others were pussyfooting around the issue. So there's always been a strong independent-minded streak in New Zealand foreign policy, which has been generally developed under Labour Governments.

Can I change tack completely? I was interested on the night of the election that, when you received that call from Jenny Shipley, there was no real sign of elation or celebration. If it had been me, I'd have jumped for joy. I'd have said, 'Yeehaw, I'm the Prime Minister! Numero Uno! The top dog!' But not you. You seemed to gain no ego satisfaction from it at all.

No. Modesty and humility are good traits, I think. It's a different concept of leadership. There's a wonderful man called Bruce Murray, comes from Tawa College. I once read a piece he wrote about servant leadership. You put yourself at the service of others. And I've got this thing about remembering where you came from. Where did I come from? You already know the whole family history – modest farmers, hard-working sort of people. You're not born into any kind of upper class that

INTERVIEW

assumes wealth, money, status. So, always remember where you came from. Remember that you want to walk out of the job still with the respect of people around you, and your family and friends. Don't assume airs or position. Maintain a modest lifestyle. And never take it for granted. And that's a great leveller. That's why I won't live in Premier House, you know, the official residence of the PM, the bells and whistles. I'm not set up there. I'll camp in a corner a couple of nights a week, but I actually like to be in my own home and my own community with my own networks. And the less pomp and ceremony the better. That's my own philosophy.

So you have no real ego in the job at all. You never think, 'Hey, I'm the Prime Minister.'
Of course I have a sense of being the Prime Minister. But you have to keep earning the right to have this job. You can't assume that it entitles you to rule like some sort of semi-potentate.

Are you really saying that you regard yourself as a servant?
Yes, I'm a public servant. Yes.

And that perspective prevents you becoming light-headed?
I think so. Dizzy with power. What power, as she spends the weekends on the phone doing a balancing act!

I recall David Lange once saying to me that in Western democracies no one person, least of all the Prime Minister, had any effective power. Politicians were cogs in the political machine. The machine exercised power, but not the individual cogs.
I don't agree with that. It's a gradual thing. It's quite subtle and is done by force of personality. You have enormous power to influence outcomes. Globalco might be an example. Had there not been very clear policy direction from the top, from both Michael Cullen and myself, that the Government was supportive of Globalco succeeding as a single-desk farmer co-op, if we'd taken the advice of the officials, the thing would have gone off to the Commerce Commission where it would have been slapped down, and the dairy industry would have gone round in circles for the next five years. So we were very clear that we were prepared to back a strong, single-desk, farmer co-op. And the dairy industry could not have gone down the path it now has, with the overwhelming support of its farmers, if that hadn't happened.

And personal power? How much personal power has Helen Clark got?
Enormous power. Because you've got to realise that while most Ministers read their Cabinet papers carefully and then put up their ideas, it's really only at the top level of the Cabinet – the Prime Minister, Deputy Prime Minister, Minister of Finance or the Leader of another coalition party – that people exercise that oversight role. So the steer we give is very, very important.

So if Helen Clark wants something to happen, it will happen?

Well, I won't push something to the point of splitting the Cabinet down the middle. I don't really have a personal agenda. Everything you know about me should tell you that I've been in this Party for 30 years and I've positioned myself as the Leader of a mainstream party. So the things I will go to bat for are the things I think are consistent with that, consistent with the Party's Policy. I don't put on on a solo act that says, 'Helen thinks this and this is what she's got to have.'

But your personal mandate, your consistently high poll ratings and the fact that to many people the Labour Party is Helen Clark, all that must surely give you tremendous personal power.

Yes, but you wouldn't want to push your luck too much.

How difficult is it for Cabinet or individual Ministers to defy you? How daunting would that be?

We do have disagreements.

The commonest criticism I've heard of you when researching the book is that you are too hard on your Ministers. And this is a criticism that comes not only from journalists and political commentators, but from your friends and family. They say that if you continue to take your Ministers to task in public, you will lose their and the electorate's support and that this is one thing which could be your eventual undoing. So why do you do it?

Partly because of this feeling that it's been a god-almighty effort to get this Party back into Government, and you don't want to see people cock it up. It's as simple as that. And that means everyone trying exceptionally hard, because you've got the responsibility of the whole movement behind you, the people who put their faith in you to do your very best. And sometimes people let you down. And they let you down to a point where, if you don't say something, people think, well maybe that's acceptable. And it isn't. So yes, I have flicked people, that's true. But then I've seen that as my job in terms of keeping respect for the Party in Government.

And you think the public like it. They admire it as strong leadership.

If they think it's fair. I mean, if you're unfair to people, that won't work.

But the public may not go on liking it. They may come to regard it as disloyalty to your colleagues, as they themselves may.

I think it very much depends on their judgement of whether it's justified or not. If they don't feel it's justified, if they feel it's degenerated into flicking people for the sake of it, that would be different. I mean, I don't actually like flicking people at all. But sometimes you're in a position where someone has done something incredibly stupid and you can't really defend it. At that point you say, 'It wasn't the brightest, but we'll do better in future.'

Why not make the criticism privately?

That isn't an option for a Prime Minister who every week is constantly exposed to the media. I hold a press conference on Mondays. There's a press stand-up every Tuesday on the way to caucus, which I can't avoid. I have regular media commitments – Holmes every Monday morning, etc, etc. I can't dodge it. And let's say Minister X has done something incredibly stupid and they ask me, 'Well, are you going to speak to them about it?' And I say, 'Yes I will.' The very fact that I was going to speak to them about it would show that I was displeased, even if I didn't say what I thought. So it's partly a function of being as open and transparent as we are.

But under a system of collective Cabinet responsibility, isn't the fault just as much yours as Minister X's? The buck stops with you.

Well, telling people it wasn't done right and it will be done better in the future is part of that, in my opinion. I won't cover for witless things that people have done. And I don't think anyone else should.

Though you may be building up a certain amount of grievance in your Party.

I don't think so. I think that at the moment everyone's aware that while the success of the Government is not entirely due to me, of course, I'm quite a big factor.

I think everyone's aware that it's mostly due to you.

I'm the last person to say that. But while the public's got a lot of faith in your judgement, you've got a lot of leeway. And yes, you do get some bruised feelings out of it, that's absolutely true. Sorry about that, but that's the way it is.

You may not always have that leeway, but, for the moment, this criticism that you're too hard on your colleagues doesn't concern you?

I'm not bothered by it, no. That's just the way it is. Most people shy away from confrontation. And in the end I won't shy away from it. And if you do shy away from it, you're seen as weak anyway. I'd rather have the abuse that comes from being strong than the abuse that comes from being weak.

What about your own mistakes?

What I have reflected on the nonsense over the Yelash case – this fellow who got $55,000 out of the public purse because I mistakenly called him a murderer when in fact he had been found guilty of manslaughter – is that I didn't protect my own interests adequately. I'm so busy protecting everybody else's and the Government's interests that I was very hands-off with it. I didn't talk to a lawyer. I just said, 'Get on and deal with it.' And if I'd paid a bit more attention, it would have been better. But then the truth of the matter is, the issue's so trivial that while I could have done more to protect my own interests, I really don't think it's a major issue either.

But the issue was that you hadn't made the payment public. So you were bitten in the bum by your own insistency on transparency in government.

Yes, but the allegations that were then made are a complete distortion of everything

I've ever said on those subjects. We have never attacked defamation settlements by others. You have to distinguish. One of the reasons why confidentiality is normally asked for by the plaintiff when they are seeking to settle, is so that the defamation isn't repeated. And there's no question that counsel for Yelash asked for confidentiality. And that's the line the lawyer went down. But that's a completely different matter from Murray McCully's to-ing and fro-ing with the members of Tourism Boards, Chief Executives and others, where people who've been appointed to positions were later paid to go away quietly. As a matter of substance, defamation is something different from matters of employment and questions of directors.

So you think that was an error of judgement?

The truth is I was just too busy to be bothered with it.

So how would you rectify a mistake like that in the future?

I'd take a closer interest. I think my view's generally been that you hire a good lawyer and get them to deal with it.

We talked about your relationship with your Ministers. How about with your staff? When you were Minister of Housing, Conservation and later Health, you had a reputation for being difficult to work with. What is your relationship with your staff like now?

Well, I think part of the key to success with this job is that I have brought intact to the ninth floor of the Beehive the staff who worked with me in Opposition, many of whom have worked with me for years. So my Chief of Staff, Heather Simpson, has worked with and for me since 1987. Mike Munro, my Chief Press Secretary, has worked with me from 1996 on. David Lewis, another of the press secretaries, has been with the Labour Party since I think around '95. Mark Watts came in in '96 as well I think. Then there's Dot Kettle, who is responsible for designing the strategy for my engagements outside Wellington. She's been with me since '94. Tony Timms, my Executive Assistant, I've known of course for many years. He came into my office in '95. Diana Okeby, who does the correspondence, has been doing the job for years. Alec McLean, the Senior Private Secretary, worked for me as Senior Private Secretary when I was Deputy PM. My Personal Secretary in Opposition is still working as a private secretary for me. Even the telephonist was the telephonist for me in Opposition. Need I go on? We brought an intact operation.

And you have inherited a number of public servants.

There's the Department of Prime Minister and Cabinet, which has the advisory group. But the idea is that they should not all be public servants. You need a mix of people who can give you contestable policy advice.

You will have heard comparisons made between yourself and Rob Muldoon. I can certainly see one similarity – Muldoon always described himself as a "counterpuncher", meaning that he didn't strike first, but if you hit him, he would hit you back harder. It seems to me that you will do so too.

I definitely will. And I think you run into people who think it's just fine to shout whatever absurdities about the Government they like, but they don't like it when you hit back. A prime example was the retired defence chiefs, who came out and said the most absurd things and who seemed to think that they should be treated with the most enormous respect because they once held these positions. And they had no sooner opened their mouths than they got a blast from me. And they then played hurt and wounded. But no, I will hit back very, very hard if I think the Government has been unfairly criticised.

Wyatt Creech's attack on the Health Research Council for awarding Peter a $750,000 research grant to study health sector restructuring, including a period when you were Minister, would be another example.

Absolutely. His behaviour was quite ridiculous. So what people have got to understand is that if they take you on on highly political or spurious grounds, they'll get it right back.

In spades.

In spades. Bucketsful.

You're a very determined person.

Yes, but I'm also careful about the fights I pick. A good example would be the business of the medals for the old soldiers. Now I've been a patron of RSAs for 20 years, so I'd heard the grievances about medals for a long time. I got involved specifically in the issue in April, when the *Holmes* show did one of their week-long runs on Vietnam vets and one of them had a genuine grievance which no-one was acting on fast enough. So the next night I went on and said, 'Of course this man has a grievance and I'm going to do something about it.' So then I call in the Vietnam vets organisations, and we sit around the table and they lay out all their grievances, of which medals are only one. They want better services for veterans and their families and so on. And I said, 'Right, we're going to try and deal comprehensively with these grievances because they've gone on for too long.' So I then had one of my best officials work with the Office of Veterans Affairs, which reports to Mark Burton, to draw up a paper dealing with all these issues on the basis of a comprehensive settlement. Now that went to the Cabinet on the 23rd of April, immediately on my return from overseas. The Cabinet baulked at the alleged expenditure on dealing with the medals grievances. So we went away and brought it back at a lower sum. And they still baulked at that sum. So we then went away and reworked it and reworked it, and got it to a point where I thought the Cabinet would be ridiculous not to agree with it. And I really believe that it was the right thing to do. And so I pushed it and was able to get the decision the day I went down to the RSA Conference. Now that was one where I went out on a limb, because I didn't feel that the people who were to-ing and fro-ing about it really understood that there were grievances that had simmered for a long time and there was an opportunity to settle them for a very modest sum of money. And my judgement was that there would be enormous goodwill for whoever settled them. So I pushed it. And I remember saying to Cabinet, 'You may think I'm crazy going out on a limb for these medals, but I've got to tell you, I've been around a long time, I've gone through this issue in great detail, and it has to be settled.' You see, the medals issue goes back to the end of World War Two, because since World War Two people deployed overseas have never received a distinctive New Zealand medal for their service, in Korea, Vietnam, Malaya and so on. The World War Two vets were well treated. If you were a bright boy in the city you got helped through a university degree or Teachers Training College qualification. Working-class people got help with a trade. And the farming kids, like my Dad's older brother, were helped onto a farm. Now you can't fault what was done by the first Labour Government for vets after World War Two, but ever since the Second World War, vets have not been particularly well treated. And probably Governments only got away with it because there weren't very many of them.

Then there was Agent Orange.

Which has demonstrable effects on the veteran's kids. What we've done there is bring New Zealand practice into line with Australia by saying, 'Yes, we recognise that these conditions have a linkage and we will pay for any out-of-pocket health expenses faced by veterans' children with these conditions.' We'll pay for counselling of veterans and their families, because the Australian research shows that the children of Vietnam veterans have a higher suicide rate than other children, and the veterans themselves who are suffering from post-traumatic stress disorder need a lot of support through counselling. And my view was that we could not have veterans in New Zealand less well treated than the Australians.

Was this all done on your initiative?

Yes.

So Cabinet can defy you on these sorts of issues?

Oh, they can have a go. But you see, I wouldn't have pushed it as hard as I did if I hadn't believed it was important.

Sorting out the Moutua Gardens dispute – that was another personal initiative of yours?

Yes.

So there's a sort of 'Helen will fix it' feel about the place. The Prime Minister as fixer.

My attitude's always been, we're here to help if we can. And my offices, both in Auckland and Wellington, do an enormous amount of helping at that individual level. But if I see an issue that's falling between the cracks and has to be addressed, I will pick it up.

Can we talk about your Coalition partner for a moment? Junior coalition partners seem to be in a no-win situation. If they are strident in pursuing their own agendas, the stability of the coalition is threatened. If they are quiescent in their support of the senior partner, they lose support and may eventually disappear. We're already seeing that happen with the Alliance.

I think their problem is a bit different. I think they would be more successful if they fully embraced the success of the Government. Or at least if they talked about their glass being half-full rather than half-empty. They tend to focus on what they haven't got, rather than what they are achieving as part of the Government. The whole direction in which New Zealand is moving is one that they approve of. Now isn't that something they should take credit for? It's not a question of saying, 'Well, we got this policy icon and we got that policy icon.' It's a question of saying, 'We came into politics to stop privatisation, to bring back better labour law.' Why not take that approach instead of saying, 'Oh, we didn't manage to get this in the Employment Relations Act.'

Because they can't take credit for those things.

But they should take credit for them.

Why? They aren't responsible for them. You would have done them anyway.

Yes, but they're in the Government. And they're part of the decision-making. So they should take credit for it, instead of always saying, 'We failed to get this or that.'

But there are few, if any areas where they can say, 'This happened because of us.'

They don't have to say that. That's the mistake. What they have to say is, 'We're part of a Government which is changing the face of New Zealand for the better. We're the Alliance. We've helped work for this. We've pushed for it. We're thrilled with the outcome.' Doesn't that sound a lot more positive? Isn't that the sort of outfit you'd want to vote for, rather than an outfit that says, 'Well we didn't get everything we wanted'?

No, because it doesn't provide anyone with a reason to vote for them. You might as well vote for the Labour Party. Isn't that their difficulty – if you want someone to vote for you, you've got to have something distinctive that identifies you.

I'm not sure that you're right. I think Jim's thinking is more along the lines that I've outlined, that their contribution has been that the Government is stable and predictable, and that the Government is going in a direction that they fully endorse. And on top of that they've managed to pull off some amazing things, like the People's Bank, Laila's advocacy for the Youth Wage, her high profile on paid parental leave. So why not celebrate the direction, the stability, and then the extras on top?

Well, they haven't actually got all those things yet. One wonders why they don't simply say, 'There is really no point in our existing. Why don't we just go back and be part of the Labour Party?'

It would be like going back to the Irish Civil War to find out why. The truth is that over time a different party tradition emerges, and it doesn't just roll over and disappear.

But you still need something that identifies you.

But that's not our problem. Our problem is to brand ourselves.

But because they have no identifiable brand, separate from Labour, the Alliance are languishing in the polls. The Greens on the other hand are well and truly branded. They're stroppy and difficult and their vote goes up. The Alliance are being acquiescent and their vote goes down.

They must find the answer to that.

But the answer affects you as well in the sense that you'd presumably rather have the Alliance as a junior coalition partner, than not have them there, and have to deal with the more difficult Greens instead.

Mmm.

Can we talk about the media for a moment? In your first term as Leader of the Opposition you found the media either hostile or uninterested. How do they treat you now that you're the Prime Minister?

There's a vast difference between the treatment I got in those first three years as Leader of the Opposition and now. In the second three years, because I'd run a relatively good election campaign in '96, there started to be a growing appreciation that I could do the job. But the media are very cautious about how they bet. So right up to the '99 election they kept National's hopes alive beyond a point that was really tenable. So there was always scepticism. Maybe there should always be scepticism, but, as Joe Atkinson observed recently, there's a difference between scepticism and cynicism, and the New Zealand media have tipped right from scepticism into cynicism.

But you find it easier to get coverage now.

You don't have to try to get coverage, there is coverage. As much as you want. Whereas in opposition you have to work very hard for media coverage. And I don't think that's dawned on the present Opposition, who are used to the media coming to them. There's a very great difference. The media have to cover the Government, they don't have to cover the Opposition. Oppositions have to work to be noticed.

We had to work to be noticed.

So your relations with the media are better now.

I think by and large the relationship was constructive during that second term as Leader of the Opposition. And by and large it's constructive now.

You seem to have developed a reputation for being very accessible. Is that a deliberate policy on your part?

It's just the way it is. Who ever gained by going into a siege mentality? I think I probably am the most accessible Prime Minister there's ever been, to be honest, because if you go back through the years, the media was different in the pre-television age. Prime Ministers were really on a pedestal. Then came the television era. But, to the best of my knowledge, Rob Muldoon didn't take calls on his home phone from the media. I really don't know, but you don't get that impression. He was quite controlling. And it was before the age of the mobile. Then, really from the 80s on, we entered the age of the spin doctor, which was taken to extremes by Jim Bolger who just stopped holding press conferences. And that was carried on by his successor. Everything was very carefully arranged, whereas I've adopted a much more open style. And it's based on my experience of those six years as Leader of the Opposition, when you had to really work to get coverage. So you just had to be accessible. And what I didn't want, when the tables were turned, was the media saying, 'Oh well, she was accessible when she was in Opposition, now she's pulled up the drawbridge.' So I just carried on as before. That was a great surprise to the media. They didn't really expect it. They expected that I'd then take on the role of the controlling Prime Minister who doesn't front press conferences, doesn't return calls and speaks through her spin doctors.

So journalists have your home number?

Home number and mobile.

And if they leave a message, do you always ring back?

Mostly I do. Sometimes if they've said, 'I want to talk about X' and X is clearly something I'm just not engaged with, I will ring the Minister whose job it is to talk about X and say, 'Would you ring so-and-so directly?' Sometimes I get a press secretary to ring back and say that. At other times, like today, I've returned a call and said, 'No, I'm not commenting on that, but ring so-and-so.' So I talk about what I want to talk about. But you won't normally face a non-response unless I'm genuinely out of contact.

Is this part of the servant leader philosophy, that in a democracy even the Prime Minister should be available?

Yes. We are accountable.

Of course the journalists love the access, but they say, 'Sure, we love it, but it could be dangerous. Helen gossips a lot. She rings up and she gossips. And she's trusting us not to spread this gossip.'

I wouldn't describe it as gossip. But sometimes they'll ring up and say, 'Look, could you tell us what's going on?' And I say, 'Do you want to talk about this off the record? OK.' But I wouldn't tell them things I didn't want them to know. And there are things that I don't want attributed. There are grades of people you speak to. Some you know a lot better than others.

But you like to chat on the phone.

The conversations are more structured than that.

So you'll only release what you want them to know?

Correct. I don't know if you saw the Joe Bennett piece on television the other night. Mike Munro had that marvellous phrase – 'We manage the issue of information.' Well that actually sums it up quite well. We do 'manage the issue of information.'

So the media are treating you better since you've been PM. How about the general public? How are they treating you?

Very well. People are pleased to see you, want to meet you. A lot of kids ask for autographs.

And you give kids autographs?

Always. I usually ask what their name is – 'To so-and-so, best wishes for the future, Helen Clark.'

So what are the greatest satisfactions of the job?

Making decisions you think should be made. All the things we've done really in fulfilling the key campaign pledges, and a lot of other things we said we'd do, which we've got on with. I take a great deal of pleasure in that.

The satisfaction of delivering what you said you'd deliver?

Yes, and delivering a good programme. That's the satisfaction.

We began this conversation by talking about your week and the punishing schedule which the job requires. How do you manage to keep a balance in your life?

I go to a lot of things that I really enjoy. I am of course the Minister of Arts, Culture and Heritage. There's obviously a work dimension to it, but you won't find me missing out on many opening nights of the ballet or the orchestra or the opera. I probably go to about half the opening nights of the Auckland Theatre Company every year. So those are things that I really like. And then we do programme in time for a break. We might go down to Wanaka for a few days skiing or go to a hut up the back of the Southern Alps, which is right away from it. We get a good break at Christmas and go to my parents' place at Waihi Beach maybe four times a year for a couple of days off. So I think we have a good balance.

I gather from your family that holidays are enormously important to you.

Yes. We tend to work seven days a week here. So at the start of the weekend you think, will I ever get through all of it? It's quite relentless. So sometimes you just have to stop and go and do something else. And in all honesty I've found in public life you cannot have a holiday in New Zealand. I mean, I was away for four days skiing at the start of this last week, but because you're in the country you're picking up the answerphone messages in the morning and responding to them. And you pick them up again when you come in at half-past 4 and respond to them. You're never really off the case. So to have a decent holiday you have to head for Africa or South America or somewhere remote like that. For many years we've gone to Europe. But you just have to get out of it and completely cut off. I don't have any difficulty doing that. If I've gone, I've gone. That's it. With the work travel that you do – and I've done quite a bit this year – you're never off the case. You always have the New Zealand media with you and you have to be completely on top of what's happening at home, because you get asked about it. So you're actually trying to run a full official programme with heavy appointments and speeches, and at the same time somebody wants to know what you think of something Tariana Turia's said at home.

You often take friends with you on holiday.

Yes. Cath and Jonathan. Judith to Fiji. My parents and Sandra came to Latin America with us once. And I took my parents to Seville as well. Took Suzanne on that trip. Sandra, as I say, has come with us to Europe and to Africa and Latin America. She's good company. She's just good company.

So what are you looking for in a holiday? You're not lying on beaches?

No. I'd get bored. Increasingly I've looked to having exercise on holiday. I don't like just sitting around and eating. And if you go to Europe it's cold, so a skiing holiday there is ideal because you get plenty of exercise. We're into the excessively physical holidays at the moment, from Kilimanjaro to the Ball Pass in the South Island. Or we might go to London, pop into the odd exhibition, theatre, the bookshops. Go skiing in Switzerland for a week. We have friends there. And for many years we've spent a week or two in Mexico or Guatemala and some parts of Latin America as well.

But on these holidays you're doing things all the time.

Yes. Studying the architecture in Mexican towns, going to all the museums and galleries, trying the food, reading books at night.

It all sounds terribly strenuous. Most of us think a holiday should be a time to have a rest.

No. A holiday is for doing something different.

Do the friends you take with you share that view?

Left **Helen enjoys active holidays, climbing in the Southern Alps, Africa or Argentina and exploring the countries of Latin America.**

They wouldn't come if they didn't. They know what they're in for.

So you never just veg out on holidays?

I have had some holidays in the South Pacific, but we're constantly looking for how we can keep fit. And the frustration of going to little islands like Naviti and Treasure Island – it only takes about 10 minutes to walk around them. And we walk round and round and round and round and round, trying to burn off the calories from the food. So that is a bit of an obsession. I hate sitting round and putting on weight. That just drives me nuts.

So you go to the gym as well. How often do you do that?

At least twice a week. Normally at weekends. I don't have time in Wellington. I'd like to go three or four times if I could, but that's a bit difficult.

Anyway, you haven't put on any weight.

No, because I'm not sitting round. I'm very focused on that. I have to get enough exercise. Output has to equal input.

A touch of Presbyterianism coming out there.

I prefer to think it's zest for life. It is. Every day is a privilege, as people get bored hearing me say. In this job, and the sort of journalistic work you've done, you're constantly meeting people whose lives are tragic for one reason or another. They've got a debilitating illness, they've had terrible things happen to them. And you can only reflect on how lucky you are. Think of someone like Sue Carty [former Editor of the *Evening Post*] who in the prime of her career can't carry on with her job because of multiple sclerosis. What a blow. So we're privileged.

So not Presbyterian. But there is a view of you as a rather austere person. One or two people have even used the term 'puritan'.

What is a puritan? I'm quite a disciplined person. I don't smoke. I drink very little. I'm a very focused person. If I'm interested in something I'm very focused on that, almost ascetic about it, really. The trouble with the word 'puritanism' is that it implies a sort of narrowness. I'm actually a very liberal person about other people's beliefs, personal behaviour and so on. I really don't care. You know, we're all adults, do what you like. It's of no interest to me at all. But where personal behaviour impacts on public life, then there's a problem.

Don't smoke, don't drink much, don't gamble. But you still think the word 'puritan' isn't the word for you?

No. 'Puritan' implies a closed mind, intolerance. But I often reflect on this branch of things because I am a very self-contained person. I think it goes back to childhood. You were living in a cocoon. The outside world had no impact. You hardly ever went to the city. Your life was around going to country schools. The only kids you ever knew were kids like you, and you actually never saw them outside school either because it required a great effort for your mother to drive you somewhere in the car. So it was really a life around the farm.

And by 'self-contained' you mean?

Well, in the sense of being very self-reliant, not expecting anyone to do anything for you. You're focused on standing on your own two feet. You look after yourself.

And there's nothing frivolous about you.

That's absolutely true.

So you're never just silly?

No.

So you're a pretty serious person. What do you do for laughs?

I get plenty of laughs. I get a lot of pleasure out of cartoons. I subscribe every week to the *New Statesman* which has the funniest cartoons. I like that sort of humour.

And it doesn't have to be political humour, it's just the situation.

Humour with an edge, though.

No, it can be just plain funny. I love cartoons. I get a good laugh out of newspaper cartoons. Quite a lot of them at my expense, but I find them quite funny. There was a marvellous one the other day that had Peter standing just in behind my shoulder with arrows through his head. And I think Wyatt Creech's feet could be seen through a doorway. And I'm saying [BAWLS] 'You pick on someone your own size!' I found that immensely funny.

You also used the word 'ascetic'. You don't see yourself as being almost nun-like in your dedication to hard work?

No. I actually have a relatively enjoyable life in the sense that I get to do a lot of things that I like doing. I get real pleasure out of going to the orchestra, as I did the other night, with the most brilliant young Russian pianist playing Rachmaninov. I get genuine pleasure out of going to the opera, genuine pleasure out of dance and ballet, genuine pleasure out of theatre. Those are things I like doing. I get genuine pleasure out of reading, exercising, skiing, trekking.

Some of those things are quite hard work.

You do them for enjoyment. The first ski instructor I had in cross-country skiing said to Peter and me, 'If you're getting hot, you're going too fast.' And I've always taken that to heart. You're there to enjoy yourself, not to have an endurance test.

What are you like to travel with?

I think pretty good, actually.

Who does all the travel arrangements?

I do.

I know Peter doesn't, because he says he doesn't.

No, he doesn't do a thing. And then he says, 'You never told me about this.' No, he leaves it all to me. I do everything. I research it. I organise it.

Now what is behind all this tramping and the mountaineering? You don't need to go up mountains to keep your weight in balance, so what's the pleasure of that?

It's a physical challenge. This has become an interest over more recent years, over the last five or six years, I suppose. Again, I guess, these places are out there and you haven't experienced it, so get on with it. And particularly, as you get somewhere near 50, you start to think that half your life is gone.

So the only slothful thing you do is lie in bed late.

I hate getting up in the morning. Because I do burn the candle at the other end. But you can combine the two with a skiing holiday where you don't have breakfast until about 10, because we're staying at a lodge in the mountains. So we get out on the skis about 11 o'clock. We then cover 23-24 kilometres and stay out till about half-past four when it gets a bit cold. Come back in, lie on the bed, return the phone calls, pick up a book or a magazine. Have dinner, get back into bed, read the book, read the magazine. And I find that quite relaxing. And even when you're out in say the back of the Southern Alps in a hut, you're going out about 10 and coming back about half-past 4. Apart from it being absolutely freezing, you can get into your sleeping bag and again read. So I find that quite relaxing.

So you like excitement. You like zooming down a hill on skis.

Oh yes, it's fantastic. You get a real buzz from that. But we've got into heavier duty alpine ski-touring now. In cross-country and Nordic skiing you've got groomed trails, but we probably spend more time now out on the back of the Alps where there's nobody, in a freezing mountain hut.

Would you go bungy jumping?

There are some things I'm not attracted to, including scuba diving, parachute jumping and bungy jumping. Cath does scuba diving and she has done a dual parachute jump. I've had an offer from the SAS to do this. But there are things that don't particularly interest me. I do like to be in control of what I do.

Well, commentators sometimes refer to you as a control freak. Are they right?

I do like to know what's going on. And I feel I've got a duty as the Leader of the Labour Party to make sure the Government doesn't do things which it's always said it would never do. Which is perfectly reasonable, I would have thought. But in terms of things I do in my own spare time, yes, I do like to be in control. I mean, if I'm skiing I like to be in control of it. And I feel with scuba diving and bungy jumping and parachute jumping, there's just that element of risk that it might get out of control. I do take calculated risks.

So you'd probably prefer to make the holiday arrangements.

Absolutely. If I left it up to Peter, I wouldn't know what the hell he'd organised. Sometimes I have to go out and stop the gardener from creating mayhem, because Peter's told him to hack something down, so the instructions are countermanded.

What have been your favourite holidays?

We've had wonderful holidays in Latin America. Patagonia, the fiords and little islands off the coast of Chile. The lake district in Argentina. We've travelled extensively in Mexico. The major archaeological sites, the Mayan ruins, the civilisations around Mexico city itself, Tula, Huaxyacao, Chichen-Itza. We've done a lot of travelling there. And Guatemala.

What is the special appeal of Latin America?

I love the colour of it. The Mexican square, the zocalo. You've always got the balloon seller, the kids and their families, the Mariachi band playing. It's just very colourful, very lively. The fantastic architecture, going back to Spanish times. The food is wonderful. You've got this fantastic archaeological heritage, which I personally find very interesting. And then in Guatemala you've got these wonderful ruins in the jungle. And the south of Chile and Argentina, they're just beautiful, remote places. And I love Africa. I could go and hang around the Serengeti or Ngorongoro crater or the parks round the Kruger for weeks. I love it. Love seeing the animals. You're up at half-past 4 in the morning and on the dawn drive. Back out again at dusk, walk during the day. Fantastic. And one of the most wonderful places we went to was Zanzibar, which we'd always read about. And again it was very colourful. It's an island where everything grows. The Spice Islands, you've got the old stone towns from the time of the Arab traders, an appalling slave history. I mean, Livingstone mounted his expeditions from Zanzibar, and the museum there has got a lot on the history of Livingstone and his campaign against slavery. That's very interesting. And we've travelled a lot in Asia, although it's been more work travel. But we've actually seen a lot. We had quite a bit of time in Vietnam, Laos, quite a lot of time in China. Penang. Fantastic!

Do you like to be comfortable when you travel? Do you travel first class?

On official travel I travel first class. That's so I can sleep. And also so that I don't get badgered too much.

But you have travelled down the back with your sisters.

I think more commonly Sandra's been in economy, and Peter and I have been up the front.

Do you like to sit and talk to people?

Well yes, if I'm engaged by what they have to say.

How about dinner parties?

Well, for me it's often work. I always ask who's going to be there, and can I be bothered? I have a lot to do. So we're very light on dinner parties.

Tell me about your interest in music and the arts. I know that you learned piano at Te Pahu and then at Epsom.

Yes. And always classical music. I never learned modern, contemporary music. So you learned the minor classics and went on from there. And it was the age of the wireless, which was reserved for Dad to listen to the news and the football and Parliament. And I can't actually recall us ever listening to music at home on the gramophone. We made our own music. We played the piano, and right through my grandmother's life I used to go down and play the piano for her.

The 1960s, when you were 10, saw the upsurge of rock – the Beatles, the Stones and Dylan. But you weren't aware of that at all?

Well, we weren't really in touch with it, because in 1963 I went to boarding school. I got my first transistor radio then, but the opportunities for listening to it were a bit limited. You were supposed to be doing your homework in the evenings. You couldn't have the radio on because it could be heard by anyone else down the dormitory. Maybe on Saturday morning. But then you were busy cleaning up your room for inspection. So I think really Chubby Checker, Elvis, the Beatles and the rest kind of passed us by, living in a boarding school in the 1960s. You'd heard of them but it wasn't an interest. And besides I had the weekly piano lessons and daily practice with the classical piano, so I wasn't very interested. When I was at Epsom there was a lot of interest in music and a lot of girls were involved with orchestral music. The most prestigious thing for a schoolgirl with an orchestral instrument skill at the time was to make the Junior Symphony Orchestra, or the Junior Training Orchestra, which was the jumping-off point for the Junior Symphony Orchestra. So orchestral music was very much part of the school, so that by the time I was boarding privately in the 7th Form and then at university, I was lining up down the side of the Town Hall for tickets to the proms and that sort of thing. But as students we were as poor as church mice. You didn't really have money to indulge yourself with concerts, and I probably sat out most of the 70s actually. And then when I went to Parliament I started picking up those interests again, going to a lot more things. Peter and I always kept up pretty regular attendance at the theatre. At Theatre Corporate and the Mercury until they both closed, actually.

Can you remember the first time you went to an opera?

No, I can't remember the first time. I've been to a number of opera productions that Raymond Hawthorne did at the Mercury. He was very, very talented. But certainly from the 80s I would have been going to the opera semi-regularly. I first went to opera overseas in Moscow in 1982, and saw *Aida*. I was with a group of Australian MPs attending a conference in Vienna, and we detoured through Moscow for about three days and saw Lenin's tomb and the Kremlin and so on. It was wonderful. It was fantastic. The Soviet Union lavished money on the arts – the Bolshoi, the opera, the traditional orchestra. In New Zealand opera companies came and went. But in the 90s I started going to opera very regularly. I've hardly missed an Auckland Opera Company production in the last 11 years. There've been some magnificent productions. *The Pearl Fishers* was magnificent. Their *Flying Dutchman* with Sir Donald McIntyre was magnificent. Their *Rigoletto* was pretty good. And I thought the *Manon* they did this year was one of the best opening nights I've been to. But I've been to virtually all of them through the 90s.

Does Peter share your taste for opera?

When people ask Peter, 'Do you like cross-country skiing? Do you like opera?' he has this way of saying, 'Oh well, Helen likes it, so I go'. But I actually suspect he does quite like it. Otherwise he *wouldn't* go. I certainly don't go to things he likes but I don't. I wouldn't be seen dead in a jazz concert.

I'm sure Bob Chapman said you loved jazz.

I hate jazz. I hate all of it. Maybe I was never rude enough about it.

To the average punter opera's a bizarre thing.

But that's because the average punter knows nothing about it. The stories are actually quite everyday stories of human emotion – love, hate, envy, remorse, guilt, revenge. It's life.

Is that its appeal for you?

I think so. Because they always take the emotions to the extreme. So revenge ends with someone killing someone, or remorse ends with suicide. And Grand Opera by definition is tragic. Deeply tragic. I actually feel quite let down if I go to an opera that isn't tragic. It's supposed to end in tragedy. With some of these light, fluff-and-bubble operas like *Die Fledermaus*, you just don't feel satisfied at the end. They're not supposed to have a happy ending. They're supposed to leave you contemplating the human condition.

What about the music?

Well, the music reflects the plot, because the music's got all the passion. The music reflects these strong human emotions. It's passionate music. What do we love about the great arias, duets, choruses? People are passionate in them. And they're either passionate with joy or passionate with sorrow. I mean the Slaves Chorus in *Nabucco* is the greatest choral chorus ever, period. It's just so magnificent. Set in the context of the slaves' revolt.

This is somewhat at odds with your own personality, isn't it?

Which is much more even-tempered. Take it out at the opera. It's an outlet, isn't it? I suppose it is an outlet. There are things you'd never do yourself, but it's wonderful to see them on stage.

Though politics is also opera.

Politics is a soap opera. It's not Grand Opera. It's a soap opera.

Do you enjoy the occasion, the dressing up, as well as the opera itself?

You mean on opening night? I go principally for the music, because I enjoy it and because I've gone for so many years in an official capacity. It's definitely a dress-up occasion, which you accept as part of being there. It's also a networking occasion and it's given me access to people in corporate networks which I wouldn't have had otherwise."

You don't mean networking on the night?

Yes, it is networking. Because you're normally there with the sponsors, the corporates, their clients.

My problem with opera is that you have to sit through two or three hours of mind-

numbing tedium, to hear one good tune. The Pearl Fishers *is a classic example.*

The interesting thing about *The Pearl Fishers* is that the same theme or leitmotif runs through everything. That's what's so attractive about *The Pearl Fishers.* It has a very strong theme. A lot of opera is like that. It takes the same background tune, if you like, and runs it right through.

Do you have a favourite opera?

I have a number of favourites. I've seen *La Traviata* too often for it to be a favourite, but I think *Lucia di Lammermoor* never fails to interest, and I think *Rigoletto* is absolutely fantastic."

How skilled are you in the libretto and the music?

I've never 'studied' it. But what I'm looking for is whether it's well-choreographed and whether it's well-sung, because sometimes voices can disappoint. Does the music rise to the occasion? You can get some quite scrappy playing which doesn't do the opera credit. Do you like the set? Personally I prefer a more abstract set, I think it's more intellectually challenging. I don't particularly like fussy sets. With *La Traviata* so often you see it as a drawing room drama, almost Victoriana, which I don't particularly like. The production of *The Magic Flute* I most enjoyed was in Sydney many years ago, where it was done on an entirely bare stage. And I've also seen *The Magic Flute* done like a pantomime, which I didn't particularly enjoy.

I can't understand why you would you want an opera to be intellectually challenging.

It's more interesting to have something to think about. If it's all done for you, it's not quite as interesting.

Then there is your interest in the theatre. I know you enjoy that because I often see you at opening nights for the Auckland Theatre Company.

I love theatre, though I never did anything much in theatre myself as a kid. I remember being the Virgin Mary in the nativity play at Te Pahu Primary in December 1962.

Didn't you play Queen Elizabeth in something?

I can't remember, but I remember doing a dance routine to *Puppet on a String* in the 7th Form with another girl called Jillian Nobbs. But I've never done much on stage myself.

So that would be the closest you ever got to pop music.

That's right. But Mum was very keen on amateur dramatics, and she used to perform in the Country Women's Institute productions. And I always loved watching theatre.

So you're presumably looking for the same sort of thing in a play as in an opera.

No. Not exactly. I've got much wider tastes in theatre. In fact I love a really successful comedy. I can't stand anything corny. But I thought Greg McGee's *Foreskin's Lament* was one of the most tragic plays I've ever seen. Genuinely tragic. I felt quite shattered at the end of it. And then on the humorous side, Roger Hall's plays. Plays like *Market Forces* and that marvellous one about the women camping – *Social Climbers* – I think they're very insightful. I loved them. And then I've seen a lot of Shakespeare, as we all have. Personally I find with Shakespeare that the actors often have a tendency to swallow their words. I often have enormous difficulty following the Elizabethan language, which is quite difficult anyway. If the lines are delivered too quickly or the diction is poor, I find that quite frustrating. I'll tell you what I don't like. I don't like some of the 20th Century American plays that are occasionally recycled out here. Arthur Miller's *Death of a Salesman*. I just can't relate to that at all. I feel like leaving. It's heavy going. But I did really love Miller's adaptation of Ibsen's *Enemy of the People* which I saw in Britain. I thought that was just absolutely amazing. I've seen a lot of theatre in Britain. Some of it good, some I've enjoyed. I never liked *Three Tall Women*.

So what are you looking for in a play?

Well, I am looking for something intellectually challenging. Some comment on the human condition. *Arcadia*, which the ATC ran four or five years ago – I thought that was fantastic. *Twelve Angry Men* – magnificent production. It was just so fantastic.

So it's that intellectual challenge again.

And the same with film. I love films. The tragedy now is that I have so little time to go to any. The film festival's on now and I've got the programme and I haven't got time to go. But when I was a student and a university lecturer, I used to go to 22 films in two weeks. But I still love film.

You realise that the culture you are interested in is not the culture of the average Kiwi?
Well, it's a reflection on the culture of the average Kiwi. You think of *Foreskin's Lament*. That was an exposé of an aspect of New Zealand culture, as were *Gliding On* and *Market Forces*. It may not be the way most people want to look at it, but it's certainly picking up aspects of the culture and analysing it.

Well, most people know Gliding On *from the telly. But 95 percent of New Zealanders would never have heard of Greg McGee or of* Foreskin's Lament. *They would never have been to the serious theatre, never have gone go to an opera. Your cultural interests are remote from the everyday experience of ordinary New Zealanders.*

That is what I'm on a mission to change, you see. I think of bringing arts and culture to a wider audience, because I think the symbolism of the Prime Minister saying this is important and taking on the portfolio, is huge. And there are a lot of very interesting things happening across all art forms in New Zealand, and we are already seeing more people taking an interest. For example, take the New Zealand Symphony Orchestra which gets a work commissioned by Gareth Farr, involving Tainui and kapahaka. Suddenly you've brought two audiences together, you've given them an insight into each other's worlds. The Royal New Zealand Ballet has a touring production at the moment, one half of which is kapahaka, the other half ballet, set to Split Enz music. Now it seems to me that that production reaches out to Maori, but also has Pakeha watching a developing Maori art form. And the Ballet's also endeavouring to attract a younger audience with the Split Enz music, so those young people get to see the ballet form. There is a lot of impetus in Maori theatre, and I think the work being done by young playwrights like Briar Grace Smith is really very challenging. A lot of it still presents as work in progress. It needs a lot of polishing, but it's interesting. And then you have people like Mika, who've trained in traditional dance, adapted it to cabaret, done very well, and is now back here trying to create a New Zealand equivalent of *Riverdance*, working with a group of mainly young Maori and Pacific Islanders to create an authentic New Zealand Polynesian-Maori dance theatre experience. And I think he'll succeed. So I think the country is alive with a lot of initiative. And while I don't personally like contemporary music much, there's no doubt that we've unleashed a lot of energy there. The Music Commission's doing good work, there's a ferment of activity. So the whole idea is to make the point that Arts and Culture isn't just about people going to highbrow things, that Arts and Culture are accessible and have many forms and many different points of entry.

But the Ballet still struggles.

But you see, my sister went to see this *Ihi FrENZy* in Rotorua, and she said it was a hit there because the kapahaka group's from Rotorua, so it attracted both crowds. It attracted the Maori and it attracted the middle class Pakeha. Fantastic!

But the average person doesn't go to the opera or the theatre or the ballet. They come home and watch the telly.

Which is why the quality of telly is so important.

Or they go to the movies. Your areas of interest really are quite refined.

That's not a sin. I'm not pretending to be 'the average person'. But I do think we can open up access to arts and culture to a much broader group than has traditionally seen it as part of their lives. Although interestingly, the surveys that are done show a much higher level of participation in arts, culture, crafts and heritage activities than anyone ever imagined.

And what about the visual arts? Are you a collector?

Not really. My interest in the performing arts has been much stronger than my interest in the visual arts. But if you look around, our neighbour Claudia Pond-Eyley has contributed to our house. That's a Nigel Brown up there. The other room has one of Brenda Hartill's pieces from the white towers of Spain. But we tend to go rather more for art from the Third World countries, I suppose. Batik over there. I've got the most beautiful piece of Balinese calligraphy in my bedroom. So I do open a lot of art exhibitions and I am interested, but I haven't got a lot of time myself to engage in it.

Can I ask you finally what effect being Prime Minister has had on your relationships with friends and family?

I ring my parents every weekend. And I ring my sister Sandra every weekend. The other two sisters are a bit busier. I don't ring them every weekend, but I certainly ring them a couple of times a month.

Can we just talk about your relationship with Peter for a moment. Ruth Butterworth says that from the start it was very close and mutually supportive.

True.

And that Peter needed as much support as you did.

Yes. That's probably true. But in those early days Peter was probably cutting something of a lonely figure in the medical school. He was very professionally isolated as the only social scientist in the medical school. It wasn't very easy.

Ruth also suggests that Peter's colonial background and his boarding school experiences have meant that he's not very easy in social situations.

I don't know. I mean, Peter's always very polite. He's always been a good conversationalist, but he's very easily bored in social situations. On the rare occasions when we go to dinner with people, you can't keep Peter at the dinner table or making smalltalk. He'll go and look at people's bookshelves. He can't be bothered with smalltalk.

Do people take offence at that?

I don't know. They just have to accept that that's the way Peter is.

Are you easily bored as well?

I'm reasonably easily bored as well, but I have a greater tolerance. You see, I don't like parties. I really don't like them. I can't be bothered. I don't like the noise. My spare time is so scarce that I'd rather be at home getting on with things I have to get done or having a bit of sleep or something. You have to be quite organised. You dispense with things that are a bit peripheral.

So Peter needs your support. Do you need his?

It's hard to say. I've always been a very independent person. I mean, I don't want to come home to be argued with, put it that way. But in terms of backup support for the practical arrangements of living, that's been quite important. Peter's always been able to keep the house running. Mind you, that changed when he went to Christchurch. That was the most difficult thing about him going to Christchurch because Peter was always here running the house. He ran the house. And he's not here.

You don't have a cleaner?

Only family help. Peter was very pragmatically supportive. But he's never been an uncritical supporter of everything I did. Peter has his own views.

Can you think of something you've done that he's not approved of?

It's not that he doesn't approve of things, but he does tend to analyse things. For example, he would look at my period as Minister of Health analytically.

That's interesting in terms of recent events – the Creech criticisms.

That's right. That's partly what made me so angry about the whole thing. Peter's never been a sycophantic supporter.

He did say somewhere that you hadn't overcome your rural conservative background. What did he mean by that?

Peter was always struck by the fact that my parents got the *Herald* delivered on Mondays, Wednesdays and Saturdays, which related to the time when the post came on those days. And even when the rural delivery was six days a week, they still only got the *Herald* on Monday, Wednesday and Saturday. My mother used to say that they only had time to read it that frequently, but Peter saw that as a post facto rationalisation. Peter thinks I am quite conservative. I don't know what he means really. I have certain ways I like doing things. I don't like a lot of change.

You have patterns and rituals.

That's right. I don't like shifting. I don't like change much. Change is very stressful. I've had a life of enormous stability – one primary school, one high school, one university, lived in the same house for almost 20 years. My family lived on the same farm for four generations. I don't like change.

Do you and Peter discuss politics?

Oh yes, we've always discussed politics. But we've had a lot of other interests. We're more likely to discuss what George Bush is doing in North Korea than what happened last week in Parliament. Peter doesn't actually buy the papers and he doesn't have television in his flat. He sometimes hears the radio, so he's not particularly focused on the day-to-day events of politics at all. He looks at the big picture. He comes home at the weekend and reads the *Guardian Weekly* and bones up on international affairs. We're more likely to talk about that.

It's quite an atypical sort of marriage, isn't it?

I don't know. I don't know other marriages. Other marriages are very focused around organising kids, and we don't have that.

But in other marriages the man doesn't generally organise the household.

No, but then MP's lives are atypical anyway, because the person who isn't the MP has to really pick up running the home, whether they're male or female.

Who's the boss in this household?

There's no boss. It's a co-op.

So what do you do to have enjoyment together?

Holidays are obviously important. Trips away. We watch something we've recorded on the TV together.

How much time do you get together?

Well, Peter comes home every Thursday night. And I'm usually here on Thursday night. And he goes when I go on Monday morning. So really not a lot has changed.

So you do get to see each other on the weekend.

Yes. And that's how it's been for 20 years.

Most people would think this was very little time for a husband and wife to spend together. You could scarcely be described as co-dependent.

No.

So the two of you can go off quite separately for quite long periods?

Well Peter's gone off for months at a time on sabbatical leave. On one occasion he was away for a year.

You'd actually have to have a very strong relationship to be confident that it would survive that sort of separation. And it's been going on for a very long time.

For a very long time. For 20 years.

Taking this story right back to the beginning again, your birth date, 26 February 1950, makes you a Pisces.

Yes. And the Year of the Tiger.

Do you put any store by astrology?

None at all. However, all the characteristics that describe people born in the Year of the Tiger apply to me.

Namely?

Oh well, the tiger is a very intelligent and smart animal!

And fierce!

{Helen laughs.]